DIRECTORY
OF LITERARY
MAGAZINES
1990–91

DIRECTORY
OF LITERARY
MAGAZINES
1990–91

Prepared in Cooperation with the
Council of Literary Magazines and Presses

Moyer Bell Limited : Mount Kisco, New York

Published by Moyer Bell Limited

LIBRARY OF CONGRESS
CATALOGING-IN-PUBLICATION DATA

Directory of literary magazines / prepared with the Council of Literary Magazines and Presses*—1984—New York: The Council c1984-

v.;22cm

Annual.
Continues:CLMP literary magazine directory
ISSN 0884-6006 = Directory of literary magazines

1. Literature—Periodicals—Bibliography. 2. American periodicals—Directories. 3. Little magazines—United States—Directories. I. Council of Literary Magazines and Presses (U.S.)

Z6513.C37   85-648720
PN2   AACR 2 MARC-S

ISBN 1-55921-026-5 Pb

Printed in the United States of America

---

* Council of Literary Magazines and Presses (CLMP) was until this year known as the Coordinating Council of Literary Magazines (CCLM)

> The little magazine is something I have always
> fostered, for without it, I myself would have been
> early silenced. To me it is one magazine, not
> several. . . . When it is in any way successful it is
> because it fills a need in someone's mind to keep
> going. When it dies, someone else takes it up in some
> other part of the country—quite by accident—out of a
> desire to get the writing down on paper.
>
> —William Carlos Williams*

The *Directory of Literary Magazines* has been compiled as a guide to the changing world of literary magazines of which Williams speaks. The literary magazine is a particularly American tradition that has provided early publishing opportunities for most of our important writers—including T.S. Eliot, E.L. Doctorow, Elizabeth Bishop, Ernest Hemingway, Ralph Ellison, Robert Lowell, Katherine Anne Porter, Raymond Carver, Richard Wright, Ezra Pound, Maxine Hong Kingston and Amiri Baraka. Through the medium of literary magazines, writers see their art in print, are given a place in our culture and find a readership.

This year's *Directory* includes almost 500 magazines from 49 states, the Virgin Islands and the District of Columbia. Entries are designed to include information asked for by **readers, writers, librarians, publishers**, and others.

Entries include:

- descriptions of each magazine in the editor's own words in order to clarify for prospective **writers** the magazine's editorial directions and interests. Writers are strongly urged to research magazines before submitting work, by using these entries, visiting the CLMP Library, and most importantly, by purchasing and supporting the magazines that interest them.

---

* *The Autobiography of William Carlos Williams*, © 1951 William Carlos Williams. Reprinted by permission of New Directions Publishing Corporation.

- listings of types of material published by each magazine, subscription rates, ISSN numbers for use by **librarians** in selecting additions to their collections, and distributors for use by **bookstores** interested in increasing their magazine sections. For more information on package sales of magazines to libraries, please contact CLMP directly.

- advertising information for **publishers'** use, including ad rates and sizes as a complement to the activities of CLMP's Ad Program, which offers advertising space in specially designed packages of literary magazines to interested publishers. For more information on ad rates and CLMP's advertising services to publishers, please contact CLMP.

For the past 23 years, the Coordinating Council of Literary Magazines (CCLM) has been the primary organization serving America's literary magazines. Over the years, its programs have grown and changed as the field of literary magazines changed. This year, 1990, will see many major changes at the organization. In fact, as this edition of the directory goes to press, we are preparing the first press release announcing that the organization's name will be changed to Council of Literary Magazines and Presses to reflect the addition of small literary presses. The board, staff, mission, goals, programs and fundraising of CLMP will all grow and change this year and continue to move in new directions in the following 2 or 3 years, as it responds to new needs and trends in noncommercial literary publishing in America.

CLMP's newly refined mission is to preserve, promote, and support literary magazines and presses. Historically, literary magazines and presses have been an important open door to freedom of expression in America. In addition to economic, technological and demographic trends, the great vitality of today's writers contributes to the great changes occurring in the publishing of serious literature in America. Experimental literature, work by emerging writers and writing by minority groups, are primarily presented by the independent literary magazines and presses of our country. Publishers of periodicals and books that are primarily literary exist in all regions, all populations, cultures and nationalities of our country. The number, size, goals, and needs of literary publishers are changing, CLMP is changing to become the primary service organization and advocate for this dynamic field. If you would like further information about CLMP, please write to us at CLMP, 666 Broadway, New York, NY 10012-2317.

This **Directory** will continue to change and improve in the coming years in several ways. We hope you are well-served by this edition and will be even more pleased in the future. CLMP would like to thank the staff of Moyer Bell Limited for the commitment, patience, good-cheer and dedication to this project. CLMP would also like to thank the National Endowment for the Arts, the New York State Arts Council and *Harper's Magazine* for their general support.

CLMP Library

This special collection contains over 16,000 volumes of more than 1,600 literary magazines in a non-circulating collection that dates back to 1967, with individual magazines dating back to the 1940s. It is recommended that writers use the library in conjunction with the *Directory*, in order to see and select those magazines best suited for an individual writer's work. Open to the public and free, from 9 a.m. to 5 p.m. at 666 Broadway, 11th Floor, New York, NY. Calling (212) 614–6551 in advance to confirm availability is advised.

Ordering Information for Literary Magazines

Magazines may be ordered directly from the addresses listed in this **Directory**. Librarians may order through their subscription agencies or may contact CLMP to order packages of literary magazines.

KEY

NAME OF MAGAZINE
Editor(s)
Address
Telephone number

Material published
Magazine description
Recent contributors
Payment to contributors
Reporting time
Copyright
First year of publication; frequency; circulation
Subscription rate; single copy price; discount for resale
Number of pages; size of magazine
Advertising rates and sizes
International Standard Serial Number
Distributors

Abbreviations

ea—each
ind—individual
inst—institutional
irreg—irregular
pp—pages
var—varies
v—volume
yr—year

All entries contain the fullest information available at date of *Directory* publication.

Index by State (see p. xxx)

ABACUS

Peter Ganick
181 Edgemont Avenue
Elmwood, CT 06110
(203) 233-2023
Poetry
A 12 to 18 page, newsletter format, single-author-per-issue periodical devoted to experimental and language poetry.
Clark Collidge, Jackson MacLow, Carla Harryman, Laura Moriarty, Joan Retallack, Leslie Scalapino.
Payment: 12 copies.
Reporting time: variable.
Copyright: author.
No ads
ISSN: 0886-4047
Small Press Distribution, Small Press Traffic

ABRAXAS

Ingrid Swanberg, Warren Woessner, David Hilton
2518 Gregory Street
Madison, WI 53711
(608) 238-0175
Poetry, criticism, essays, reviews, translations, photographs, graphics/artwork, "found" cultural artifacts.

Contemporary poetry: (non-academic). Some emphasis on narrative and lyric forms. Unusual graphics and "found" poems. Interested in poetry (in translation) from Eastern Europe. Criticism and essays on the contemporary scene.
Ivan Arguelles, Gerald Locklin, Kent Taylor, Andrei Codrescu, Denise Levertov.
Payment: in copies.
Reporting time: 3 weeks–5 months.
Copyright held by Abraxas Press, Inc; reverts to author upon publication.
1968; 4/year; 500
$12/4 issues; $3/ea; 40%
80 pp; 6 x 9
Ad rates: $60/page/5 x 8; $35/½ page/5 x 3½
ISSN: 0361-1663
Bookslinger

ACM (Another Chicago Magazine)

Barry Silesky, Lee Webster
P.O. Box 11223
Chicago, IL 60611
(708) 848-6333
Poetry, fiction, reviews, essays, interviews.
Literary, contemporary, non-regional, socio-political outlook. We look for "successful" writ-

ing whether it be traditional,
experimental, genre.
S.L. Wisenberg, Tom McGrath,
Pablo Antonio Cuadra, Ariel
Dorfman, Maxine Chernoff,
Lore Segal, Sterling Plumpp.
Payment: $5–$25.
Reporting time: 6 weeks.
Copyright held by **ACM**; reverts
to author upon publication.
1977; 2/yr; 750
$15/ind; $15/inst; $8/ea; 40%
220 pp; 5½ x 8½
Ad rates: $150/page/5 x 8; $75/½
page/5 x 3⅞
ISSN: 0272-4359
Ingram, Total, ILPA

ACTS: A Journal of New Writing

David Levi Strauss, Benjamin
Hollander
514 Guerrero St.
San Francisco, CA 94110
(415) 431-8297
Poetry, criticism, essays, reviews,
translation, interviews, graphics/
artwork, photographs, word/
image work.
Contemporary radical poetry, "an-
alytic lyric," word/image work
and photography.
Also book issues on selected
writers (Jack Spicer, Paul Ce-
lan, Robert Duncan) and subjects.

Nate Mackey, Susan Howe, Aaron
Shurin, Norma Cole, Michael
Palmer.
Payment: in copies.
Reporting time: 2–4 months.
Copyright held by Acts; reverts to
author upon publication.
1982; 2/yr; 600–1,500
$12/yr ind; $16/yr inst; $10/ea;
40%
120 pp; 8½ x 11
Ad rates: $100/page/7½ x 10¼;
$60/½ page/3 x 9
ISSN: 0749-3908
Small Press Distribution, Seque,
Inland Book Co., Bookpeople,
Sun & Moon, Ubiquity

AEGEAN REVIEW

Dino Siotis
220 West 19th Street/2A
New York, NY 10011
Modern Greek literature in transla-
tion. Works inspired by Greece
by American authors.
Fiction, essays, interviews, poetry,
art and photography.
Jorge Luis Borges, Lawrence Dur-
rell, Truman Capote, Yannis
Ritsos, Alice Bloom.
Payment: $25–$100.
Circulation: 5,000.
$10/yr ind; $18/yr inst; $5/ea;
40%
Ad rates: $265 per page

AERIAL

Rod Smith
P.O. Box 25642
Washington, D.C. 20007
(202) 333-1544, 965-5200

Poetry, fiction, criticism, essays, reviews, translations, photos, graphics.

AERIAL is interested in what writing is, might be. Many of our contributors are familiar with the works of writers such as Pound, Stein, Bunting, Oppen, Zukofsky, the Black Mountain Community, "structuralist linguistics from Saussure to Derrida," the Beats, $L=A=N=G=U=A=G=E$, Ashbery, O'Hara, Poetics Journal, Temblor, etc.

Hannah Weiner, Gretchen Johnsen, Andrew Levy, Carla Harryman, Joan Retallack.

Payment: copies.

Copyright: held by Rod Smith; reverts to author upon publication.

1985; 1–2/yr; 500

$15/yr ind; $15/yr inst; $6/ea; 40%

100–160 pp; 6 x 9

Ad rates available. Contact CLMP for information.

Sun & Moon (issue #4 only), Paul Green (U.K.), Ubiquity, and S.P.D.

THE AFRO-HISPANIC REVIEW

Marvin Lewis & Edward Mullen
Department of Romance Languages
U Missouri: 143 Arts & Science Building
Columbia, MO 65211
(314) 882-2030

Scholarly articles, translations of Afro-Hispanic texts.

A bilingual journal of Afro-Hispanic literature and culture, publishing literary criticism, book reviews, translations, creative writing, and relevant developments in the field. Jointly published by the Department of Romance Languages and the Black Studies Program of the University of Missouri-Columbia.

William W. Megenney, E. Valerie Smith, Jerry Williams, Guillermo Bowie, Miriam DeCosta-Willis.

Payment: none.

Reporting time: 3 months.

Copyright held by University of Missouri.

1982; 3/yr; 500

$15/yr inst; $5/ea; $1 off inst. rate

8½ x 11

No ads

ISSN: 0278-8969

Faxon, Ebsco

AGADA

Reuven Goldfarb
2020 Essex Street
Berkeley, CA 94703
(415) 848-0965

Poetry, fiction, midrash, memoir, essay, translation, graphics, artwork.

AGADA has a specifically Jewish orientation and emphasis in a universalist perspective, and publishes work touching on traditional Jewish themes and contemporary concerns. Seeks to share insights, memories, and vision of creative Jewish people with people everywhere.

Lou Barrett, Barry Brown, Shlomo Carlebach, Charles Fishman, Lyn Lifshin.

Payment: in copies.
Reporting time: 2–3 months.
Copyright reverts to author.
1981; 2/yr; 750
$12/yr; $6/ea; 40%
56 pp; 7 x 10
ISSN: 0740-2392

AGNI

Boston University Creative Writing Program
Askold Melnyczuk, Editor
236 Bay State Road
Boston, MA 02215

Poetry, fiction, artwork, essays.
AGNI publishes poetry and fic-tion, and the occasional commissioned essay. Our special interests are new and underappreciated writers. Every issue features the work of a poet who has not yet published a full-length collection.

Thom Gunn, Marilynne Robinson, Rita Dove, John Updike, Frank BiVart, Ha Jin, Martin Espada, Sharon Olds, Robert Pinsky, Seamus Heaney, Tom Sleigh, Derek Walcott.

Payment: varies.
Reporting time: 2–10 weeks.
Copyright held by The Agni Review, Inc.; reverts to author upon publication.
1972; 2/yr; 1,400
$12/yr; $6/ea; 40%
250–300 pp; 5½ x 8½
Ad rates: $100/page/4½ x 7; $50/½ page/4½ x 3½
ISSN: 0191-3352
DeBoer, Inc.

ALASKA QUARTERLY REVIEW

Ronald Spatz, James Liszka, Thomas Sexton
University of Alaska Anchorage
Department of English
3221 Providence Drive
Anchorage, AK 99508
(907) 786-4775

Poetry, fiction, criticism, philosophy.

A journal devoted to contemporary literature and philosophy of literature.

Stuart Dybek, Jerome Charyn, Maura Stanton, Sam Hamill, Bill Van Wert, Grace Paley, Amy Hempel.

Payment: in copies; other payment depends on grants.

Reporting time: 3–12 weeks.

Copyright held by University of Alaska Anchorage.

1981; 2/yr; 1,000

$8/yr ind; $10/yr inst; $4/ea; 50%

140 pp; 6 x 9

ISSN: 0737-268X

B. DeBoer

ALBATROSS

Richard Smyth, Richard Brobst
13498 Darnell Avenue
Port Charlotte, FL 33981

Poetry, interviews, graphics/artwork.

Since we see the albatross as a metaphor for an environment that must survive, we are primarily interested in ecological/environmental/nature themes, written in a narrative style; however, this is not to say that we do not consider other themes and forms.

Walter Griffin, Daniel Comiskey, Stephen Meats, Duane Locke, Peter Meinke.

Payment: in contributor's copies.

1986; 2/yr; 500

$5/yr ind/inst; $3/ea; 40%

32–44 pp; 5½ x 8

ISSN: 0887-4239

ALTERNATIVE FICTION & POETRY

Philip Athans
7783 Kensington Lane
Hanover Park, IL 60103

Fiction, poetry, interviews, experimental forms, prose, plays, etc. . . .

AF&P is an internationally distributed, reader-oriented journal of experimental/avant-garde writing and art.

William S. Burroughs, Lyn Lifshin, Jello Biafra, Charles Bukowski, Elissa Rashkin, Roque Dalton.

Payment: 2 copies.

Reporting time: 1–6 months.

Copyright held by author.

1986; irreg.; 1,000

$10/4 issues; $3/ea; 50

46 + pp; 8½ x 11

Ad rates: $80/page; $55/½ page; $30/¼ page

ISSN: 0893-2581

Ingram, Flatland

AMELIA

Frederick A. Raborg, Jr.
329 "E" Street
Bakersfield, CA 93304
(805) 323-4064

Fiction, poetry, plays, graphics/ artwork, criticism, reviews, essays, photographs, translation.

AMELIA is a reader's magazine, intended to be enjoyed over a period of time, offering a unique blend of the traditional with the contemporary in virtually every printed artform by both "name" and unknown writers and artists of superior talents. Contributors from its pages have been included in Pushcart Prizes, The Artist Market and other prestigious reprint anthologies.

Pattiann Rogers, David Ray, Lawrence P. Spingarn, Larry Rubin, Stuart Friebert, Merrill Joan Gerber.

Payment: poetry/$2–$25; fiction/$10–$35; non-fiction/$10/1,000 words; artwork/$5–$50.

Reporting time: 2 weeks–3 months.

Copyright held by magazine; reverts to author upon publication.

1984; 4/yr; 1,250

$20/yr ind; $20/yr inst; $6.50/ea; 40%

124 pp; 5½ x 8½

Ad rates: $250/page/4½ x 7½; $140/½ page/4½ x 3¾; $80/¼ page/4½ x 1¾

ISSN: 0743-2755

AMERICAN BOOK REVIEW

Ronald Sukenick, Rochelle Ratner, John Tytell, Don Laing (Managing Editor)
English Department Publications Center
Campus Box 494
University of Colorado
Boulder, CO 80309-0494
(303) 492-8947

Criticism, essays, reviews.

AMERICAN BOOK REVIEW is offered as a guide to current books of literary interest published by the small, large, university, regional, third world, women's and other presses. It is edited and produced by writers for writers and the general public.

Hayden Carruth, Robert Creeley, Diane Wakoski, Marge Piercy, Daniel Berrigan.

Payment: $50 per review.

Reporting time: 2 weeks to 2 months.

Copyright held by ABR; reverts to author upon publication.

1977; 6/yr; 12,000

$18/yr ind; $23/yr inst; $3/ea; 40%

32 pp; 10 x 14

Ad rates: $425/page/10 x 14;
$260/½ page/5 x 14; $150/¼
page/5 x 7; $100/½ col/ 2¼ x
6¾; $60/¼ col/2¼ x 3¾; dis-
counts available.
Trade distribution by Ingram Periodicals, Interstate Distributors,
Lichtman's News Agency Inc.
(Canada), Armadillo, and LS
Distributors

AMERICAN DANE
Pamela K. Dorau
3717 Harney St.
Omaha, NE 68131
(402) 341-5049
Fiction, historical, essays.
The **AMERICAN DANE** Magazine is the official publication
of the Danish Brotherhood in
America—whose purpose is "to
promote and perpetuate Danish
culture and traditions and to
provide fraternal benefits and
family protection."
Payment: appx. $50.
Reporting time: 2 weeks.
Copyright returns to contributor
after publication.
1916; 12/yr; 8,000
$6 domestic, $8 foreign; $1/ea;
No resale disc.
8¼ x 11
Query for ad rates
ISSN: 0739-9170
Danish Brotherhood in America

**THE AMERICAN POETRY
REVIEW**
Stephen Berg, David Bonanno,
Arthur Vogelsang
1704 Walnut Street
Philadelphia, PA 19103
(215) 732-6770
Poetry, translation, criticism, re-
views, interviews, essays.
Lucille Clifton, Sam Hamill,
W.S. Merwin, Jane Miller,
Howard Nemerov.
Payment: $1.25/line for poetry;
$75/page for prose.
Reporting time: 10 weeks.
Copyright held by World Poetry,
Inc.; reverts to author upon
publication.
1972; 6/yr; 20,000
$12/yr ind; $12/yr inst; $2.50/ea;
50%
48 pp; 9¾ x 13¾
Ad rates: $600/page/9¾ x 13¾;
$360/½ page/9¾ x 6¾;
$200/¼ page/4¾ x 6¾
ISSN: 0360-3709
Eastern News Distributors

THE AMERICAN VOICE
Frederick Smock, Sallie Bingham
332 W. Broadway, Suite 1215
Louisville, KY 40202
(502) 562-0045
Fiction, poetry, essays, criticism,
photographs.

THE AMERICAN VOICE publishes daring new writers and the more radical work of established writers. Feminist, Pan-American.

Susan Griffin, Kay Boyle, Marjorie Agosin, Brian Swann, Eduardo Galeano, Michelle Cliff, Linda Hogan, Doris Grumbach, Brenda Marie Osbey, Dennis Silk.

Payment: $400/prose; $150/poem; $75–150/translator fee.

Copyright: first North American serial rights held by magazine; reverts to author upon publication.

1985; 4/yr; 2,000

$12/yr ind; $20/2 yr; $5/ea; 40%

100 pp

ISSN: 0884-4536

Bernhard DeBoer, Ingram Periodicals and Spectacular Diseases (U.K.)

THE AMERICAS REVIEW (formerly **REVISTA CHICANO-RIQUENA**)

Julian Olivares, Evangelina Vigil-Pinon

Arte Publico Press

University of Houston

Houston, TX 77204-2090

(713) 749-4768

Poetry, fiction, criticism, review, interviews, photographs, graphics/artwork.

THE AMERICAS REVIEW, A Review of Hispanic Literature and Art of the USA, is the oldest (16 years) and most prestigious U.S. Hispanic literary magazine. It publishes works by outstanding Hispanic writers and artists of the USA, as well as works by new and emerging writers and artists. Analysis, interviews, commentary and reviews of U.S. Hispanic works and writers.

Sandra Cisneros, Denise Chavez, Tato Laviera, Ed Vega, Gary Soto.

Payment: varies.

Reporting time: 3–4 months.

Copyright held by Arte Publico Press.

1972; triquarter (2 + double issue); 3,000

$15/yr ind; $20/yr inst; $5/$10 (double issue) ea; 40%

128 pp; 224 pp double issue; 5½ x 8½

Ad rates: $200/page/5 x 8; $125/½ page/4 x 5; $75/¼ page/2½ x 4

ISSN: 0360-7860

EBSCO, Ubiquity Distributors, Homing Pigeon, Armadillo & Co.

ANEMONE

Nanette Morin, Editor; George
  Angell, Mid-West Editor
Box 369
Chester, VT 05143
(802) 885-3985

Poetry, reviews, interviews, translations, photographs, graphics/
  artwork, paintings.
ANEMONE is a quarterly literary
  arts journal publishing the expressive voice of the people.
  Our purpose is to help bring the
  spirit of man closer to his true
  self through art. We look for
  work that is different, always
  looking for the new voice.
  ANEMONE encourages "political" and "social" poetry.
Robert Chute, Arthur Winfield
  Knight, Sandy Rankin, Elizabeth Stone O'Neill, John No-
  land.
Payment: one year's plus subscription and five gifts.
Reporting time: 8 weeks.
Copyright held by Anemone Press;
  permission given to publish
  with mention.
1984; 4/yr; 3,000
$10/yr ind; $10/yr inst; $2.50/ea;
  40%
24 pp; 10 x 15
Ad rates: $200/page/10 x 15;
  $100/½ page/10 x 7 or 5 x 15;
  $50/¼ page/5 x 7
ISSN: 8756-7709

ANERCA/COMPOST

Adeena Karasick, Kedrick James,
  Wreford Miller
3989 Arbutus St.
Vancouver, BC V6J 4T2
604-253-5755

Poetry, criticism, graphics, word/
  text/image games/speculation.
A low-budget erratic mocking
  magazine devoted to experimen-
  tal writing (although we also
  publish more traditional work if
  it shows great vision and might
  not get attention elsewhere).
  Mainly 'young' authors, testing
  the constraints of language.
Bill Bissett, Bruce Andrews, B.P.
  Nichol, Christopher Dewdney,
  Jerome Rothenberg, Roy
  Kiyooka.
Payment: 2 copies.
Reporting time: 1 to 4 months.
Copyright held by author.
1986; irregular; 400
$12/4 copies; $3 each; 60
40 pp; 8½ x 11
No ads
Direct Mail Dist., Faxon

ANTAEUS

Daniel Halpern
26 West 17th Street
New York, NY 10011
(212) 645-2214

Poetry, fiction, essays, criticism,
  translation, interviews.
ANTAEUS features a broad spec-

trum of current, previously unpublished fiction and poetry by
both new and established authors, as well as essays and
documents. Frequently publishes special issues offering
essays on particular subjects
(nature, autobiography, art,
etc.).
Czeslaw Milosz, Robert Hass,
Jorie Graham, Gail Godwin,
Paul Bowles.
Payment: $10/page.
Reporting time: 10 weeks.
Copyright held by Antaeus; reverts
to the author upon publication.
1970; 2/yr; 7,500
$30/2 yr ind; $30/2 yr inst; $10/
ea; 20%
280 pp; 6 ½ x 9
Ad rates: $500/page/5½ x 8;
$300/½ page/2¾ x 8; $200/¼
page/2¾ x 4
ISSN: 0003-5319
W.W. Norton & Co., Ingram Periodicals, B. DeBoer & Co.

ANTIETAM REVIEW

Ann B. Knox, Crystal Brown
82 West Washington Street
Hagerstown, MD 21740
(301) 791-3132
Poetry, fiction, photographs.
The **ANTIETAM REVIEW** is a
regional literary magazine for
fiction writers, poets and photographers from Maryland,
Pennsylvania, Virginia, West
Virginia, and the District of
Columbia; however, we look
for strong literary and artistic
quality rather than local interest.
Randall Silvis, David McKain,
Geraldine Connolly, Linda Pas-
ten, Ann Darr, Myra Sklarew.
Payment: $100 for fiction; $20 for
poems.
Reporting time: 6 weeks to 4
months depending on pub. date.
Copyright held by Washington
County Arts Council; reverts to
author upon publication.
1984; 1 or 2/yr; 1,000
$5/yr; $5/ea; 20%
44 pp; 8½ x 11
No ads

ANTIOCH REVIEW

Robert S. Fogarty
P.O. Box 148
Yellow Springs, OH 45387
Poetry, fiction, criticism, essays,
reviews.
ANTIOCH REVIEW is an independent quarterly of critical and
creative thought which prints
articles of interest to both the
liberal scholar and the educated
layman. Authors of articles on
the arts, politics, social and cultural problems as well as short
fiction and poetry find a

friendly reception regardless of formal reputation.

Emile Capouya, Raymond Carver, Perri Klass, Gordon Lish, Joyce Carol Oates.

Payment: $10 per published page.

Reporting time: 3–6 weeks.

Copyright held by **Antioch Review**.

1941; 4/yr; 4,500

$20/yr ind; $30/yr inst; $5.00/ea

128 pp; 6 x 9

Ad rates: $250/page/4½ x 7⅞; $150/½ page; $100/¼ page

ISSN: 0003-5769

Eastern News Distributors, Inc.

ANTIPHONY

Patrick Pritchett

4422 Whitsett Ave., #8

Studio City, CA 91604

(818) 763-2355

Poetry, essays, criticism, reviews, fiction, translation.

ANTIPHONY is a quarterly publication devoted primarily to poetry and essays about poetry. Fiction, book and film reviews, and socio-political articles are also welcome. Humor, whimsical or trenchant, is not to be despised. Essays on feminism and the emergent Gaian politique are encouraged. The only axe we have to grind is the grassblade of eleutheria.

Herman J. Fong, Elena Phleger, Arwo F. Kuus, Eve E.M. Wood, Steven Tracey, Fuschia.

Payment: in copies.

Reporting time: 3–8 weeks.

Copyright held by Crow's Mouth Press; reverts to author.

1989; 4/yr; 1,000

$9/yr ind; $12/yr inst.; $3.50/ea; 40%

60–75 pp.; 5½ x 8½.

Ad rates: $100/page; $50/½ page

Pending ISSN

ANTIPODES

Marian Arkin, Robert Ross

190 Sixth Avenue

Brooklyn, NY 11217

(718) 482-5680 or (718) 789-5826

Fiction, Reviews, Criticism, Essays, Poetry, Interviews, Photographs, Graphics/Artwork

Focus is on Australian literature.

Thomas Keneally, A.D. Hope, Judith Wright, Thea Astley, Olga Masters

Payment: in copies.

1987; 2/yr; 600

$16/yr ind; $20/yr inst; $10/ea (Domestic)

$21/yr ind; $24/yr inst; $12/ea (Overseas)

60–75 pp; 8½ x 11

Ad rates: $300/page/7½ x 10; $175/½ page/7½ x 5 or 3½ x

10; $90/¼ page/7½ x 2½ or
3½ x 5

APALACHEE QUARTERLY

Barbara Hamby, Pam Ball, Clau-
dia Johnson, Bruce Boehrer,
Paul McCall

P.O. Box 20106
Tallahassee, FL 32316
(904) 385-6859

Poetry, fiction, reviews, translation, photographs, graphics/art-
work.

We are interested in well-crafted,
modern fiction and poetry. Stylistic innovation is encouraged
except when it interferes with
narrative intent.

Peter Meinke, G.S. Sharat Chan-
dra, Janet Burroway, Michael
Shaara, David Kirby.

Payment: in copies and money
when grants permit.

Reporting time: 12 weeks.

Copyright reverts to author upon
publication.

1971; 4/yr; 500
$12/yr; $3.50/ea
75–150 pp; 6 x 9
Ad rates: $50/page

APPEARANCES

Robert Witz, Joe Lewis, Bill Mut-
ter

165 West 26th Street

New York, NY 10001
(212) 675-3026

Poetry, fiction, interviews, photographs, graphics/artwork.

APPEARANCES. Literature, art,
civilization. New talent. The
works. Why wait.

Hal Sirowitz, j-poet, Nathaniel
Burkins, Michael LaBombarda,
Jack Wark, Rodolpho Torres.

Payment: is occasional.

Copyright held by magazine; reverts to author upon publication.

1976; 2/yr; 900
$15/3 issues; $5/ea; 40%
76 pp; 8½ x 11
Ad rates: $180/page/7½ x 10;
$110/½ page/7 x 5½; $80/¼
page/3½ x 5

ARACHNE

Susan L. Leach, Kathleen M.
Tenpas

162 Sturges Street
Jamestown, NY 14701
(716) 355-4176 or 488-0417

Poetry, fiction.

ARACHNE is a small press dedicated to publishing well written
poetry with a largely, but not
exclusively, rural theme. We are
interested in new poets and in
poets who have been writing
but have not been largely pub-

lished. We publish four contributors' issues yearly.

Gary Fincke, Penny Kemp, Norbert Krapf, Walt Franklin, Wallace Whatley.

Payment: in copies.

Reporting time: 1 week to 2 months.

1980; 4/yr; 250

$18/yr ind; $20/yr inst; $5/ea; 40%

28 pp; 5¼ x 8¼

ARARAT

Leo Hamalian

530 East 90th Street

New York, NY 10028

(212) 831-6857

Poetry, fiction, criticism, essays, reviews, translation, interviews, photographs.

Although all writing of merit is considered for publication, the magazine strongly prefers material pertaining to subjects of Armenian interest.

Joel Oppenheimer, Peter Balakian, David Kherdian, Elizabeth Young-Bruehl, Laura Kalpakian, Odysseas Elytis.

Payment: arranged with editor.

Reporting time: 6–8 weeks.

Copyright held by author.

1958; 4/yr; 2,500

$14/yr ind; $4/ea

72 pp; 8 x 11

Ads accepted by inquiry

ARTFUL DODGE

Daniel Bourne, Karen Kovacik, Lee Harlin Bahan

Department of English

The College of Wooster

Wooster, OH 44691

(216) 262-8353

Poetry, fiction, translation, graphics, reviews.

ARTFUL DODGE is open not just to American work combining the human and the aesthetic, but also to translation, especially from Eastern Europe and the Third World. We also have an ongoing section on American poets who translate, featuring the poet's own work and his or her adaptations of work going on in landscapes other than English.

Stuart Dybek, Naomi Shihab Nye, William S. Burroughs, Katharyn Machan Aal, William Stafford, Stuart Friebert, Nicholas Kolumban.

Payment: in copies, plus $5 honorarium, as funding allows.

Reporting time: 1–3 months.

Copyright reverts to author.

1979; 2/yr; 750

$10/2 issues; $5/ea

120 pp; 6 x 9

ISSN: 0196-691X

ASCENT
Audrey Curley
208 W. Pennsylvania
Urbana, IL 61801
Fiction, poetry.
Eclectic.
Barbara Phillips, Barbara Nodine,
Pamela Yenser, Brad Hooper,
Sue Normolle.
Payment: $10/page for fiction,
$25/page for poetry when we
are able.
Reporting time: 1 week to 2
months.
Copyright held by Ascent; reverts
to author upon publication.
1975; 3/yr; 600
$3/yr; $1.50/ea; 40%
64 pp; 6 x 9
ISSN: 0098-9363

ASYLUM
Greg Boyd
P.O. Box 6203
Santa Maria, CA 93456
(805) 934-4570
Fiction, poetry, prose poems,
essays, criticism, reviews,
translation, photographs,
graphics/artwork.
Contemporary literature: some
emphasis on short prose forms,
experimental writing, dream
works and surrealism.
Kenneth Bernard, Stephen Dixon,
Richard Kostelanetz, Stephen-

Paul Martin, Edward Roditi, T.
Wiloch.
Payment: in copies.
Reporting time: 2 weeks–3
months.
Copyright held by Asylum; reverts
to author upon publication.
1985; 4/yr; 500
$10/yr; $3/ea; 40%
48 pp; 5½ x 8½
$40/page; $20/½ page
ISSN: 0896-1344

THE ATAVIST
Robert Dorsett, Loretta Ko
Box 5643
Berkeley, CA 94705
Poetry, translation.
We are a magazine devoted to
poetry and translations of poetry
and publish only the most intense and beautiful. We offer an
excellent opportunity to good
poets who have not made their
reputation yet.
William Leo Coakley, R. T.
Smith.
Payment: 2 copies.
Reporting time: 1 month.
Copyright held by The Atavist;
reverts to author upon written
request.
1982; 2/yr; 400
$5/yr; $2.50/ea; 40%
40 pp; 6 x 9

No ads
ISSN: 0731-8987

ATHENA INCOGNITO MAGAZINE

Ronn Rosen, Chris Custer, Greg
    Wallace
1442 Judah Street
San Francisco, CA 94122
(415) 665-0219
Poetry, xeroxable artwork, prose,
    essay, review etc. . . . (1 page
    maximum).
Experimental magazine with
    DADA/SURREALIST and/or
    AVANT/GARDE emphasis.
John Taggert, Diana Saenz, Kurt
    Cline, Barbara Carr.
Payment: 1 copy.
Reporting time: 1–2 months.
Copyright held by author/artist.
1980; Annual; 500
$4/yr + $1 post; same; no dis-
    count for resale.
35 pp
Ad rates: $30/page; $15/½ page
S.F. State Bookstore, Small Press
    Traffic

ATTICUS REVIEW

Harry Polkinhorn
720 Heber Avenue
Calexico, CA 92231
Verbal/visual, poetry, short fic-
    tion.

Payment: 1 copy.
Reporting time: 1 month.
Copyright reverts to author.
1983; 2/yr; 150
$6/yr; $3/ea + $1 transportation
40 pp; 8½ x 11

AURA LITERARY/ARTS REVIEW

Adam Pierce, Stefanie Truelove
P.O. Box 76
University Center UAB
Birmingham, AL 35294
(205) 934-3216
Poetry, fiction, interviews, essay
Contemporary poetry and prose.
    Experimental, traditional or
    genre. Looking for work that
    distinguishes itself from the
    crowd yet remains successful.
    Interested in documentary pho-
    tography.
Payment: 2 copies.
Reporting time: 3 months.
Copyright reverts to author.
1974; 2/yr; 500
$6/yr; $2.50
20 pp; 6 x 9
ISSN: 0889-7433

A/B: AUTO/BIOGRAPHY STUDIES

Rebecca Hogan
English Department
University of Wisconsin
Whitewater, WI 53190

Timothy Dow Adams
English Department
University of West Virginia
Morgantown, WV 26506

Criticism, Reviews, Bibliographical and Newsletter information.

Purpose of magazine is to publish essays—literary and critical—about autobiography and biography. Emphasis of recent issues has been on special topics: women's autobiography, Mexican, therapeutic (forthcoming), European, etc. The journal serves also as a clearinghouse for information about convention panels, members' interests, etc.

Lynn Bloom, Janet Verner Gunn, Richard D. Woods, G. Thomas Couser, Silonie Smith.

Payment: none.

Copyright held by author.

198🛆; 4/yr; 200

$15/yr ind; $45/yr inst

70 pp; 7 x 8½

Ad rates: $150/page/7 x 8½; $75/½ page/7 x 4¼; $40/¼ page/3½ x 4¼

AVEC
Cydney Chadwick
P.O. Box 1059
Penngrove, CA 94951
(707) 762-2370

Poetry, fiction, translation, line art, photographs.

AVEC magazine is interested in innovative work that approaches language and/or form in an unusual way. We are also interested in writing in translation from other countries. Issue #1 included work by Soviet poet Arkaadi Dragomoschchenko and Issue #2 contained previously untranslated work from Tristian Tzara's vingt-cinq poems.

David Bromige, Lydia Davis, Michael Davidson, Steve McCaffery, Jackson MacLow, Leslie Scalapino.

Payment: 2 copies.

Reporting time: 2–4 months.

Copyright reverts to author upon publication.

1988; 1 or 2; 1,000

2 issue/$10; $6.50/ea.; 40% (bookstores)

128–136 pp

Ad Rates: inquire

ISSN: 0899-3750

Inland, Book People; Small Press Dist., Segue Foundation

B

B-CITY
Connie Deanovich
619 West Surf Street #2

Chicago, IL 60657
(312) 871-6175
Poetry, fiction, interviews.
Paul Hoover, Anne Waldman,
Clark Coolidge, Jim McManus,
Bernadette Mayer, Maxine
Chernoff, Jerome Sala.
Small honorarium when available.
$5/yr ind; $6/yr inst; $5/ea; 40%
Illinois Literary Publishers Association

BAMBOO RIDGE: The Hawaii Writers' Quarterly
Eric Chock and Darrell Lum
P.O. Box 61781
Honolulu, HI 96839-1781
Poetry, fiction.
BAMBOO RIDGE has special
interest in literature reflecting
the multi-ethnic cultures and
peoples of the Hawaiian
Islands.
Juliet Kono, Wing Tek Lum, Garrett Hongo, Sylvia Watanabe,
Rodney Morales, Cathy Song.
Payment: $10/poem; $20/short
story.
Reporting time: 3–6 months.
Copyright held by Bamboo Ridge
Press; reverts to author upon
publication.
1978; 4/yr; 1,000
$12/yr; varies; 40%
120 pp, 6 x 9
Ad rates: $100/page/5¼ x 8¼

ISSN: 0733-0308
Small Press Distribution

BELLES LETTRES: A Review of Books by Women
Janet Mullaney
11151 Captain's Walk Ct.
Gaithersburg, MD 20878
(301) 294-0278
Reviews, criticism, essays, interviews, photographs, graphics/
artwork.
BELLES LETTRES reviews literature by women in all genres.
Our purpose is to promote and
celebrate writing by women and
to inform and entertain. Interviews, rediscoveries, retrospectives, theme reviews, and
publishing news are regularly
featured. Queries from writers
are welcome.
Jewelle Gomez, Cheryl Clarke,
Margaret Randall, Evelyn Beck,
Merrill Joan Gerber, Faye
Moskowitz.
Payment: in subscriptions, copies
& $25 per column, depending
on grant funding.
Copyright held by magazine; reverts to author upon publication.
1985; 4/yr; 5,000
$15/yr ind; $30/yr inst; $3.75/ea;
40%
24 pp; 11 x 17

Ad rates: $800/page/10 x 16;
$450/½ page/9¾ x 7½; $250/¼
page/4¾ x 7½
ISSN: 0084-2957
Ubiquity, Small Changes, Inland

THE BELLINGHAM REVIEW

Susan Hilton, Editor; Knute Skin-
ner, Advisory Editor
The Signpost Press, Inc.
1007 Queen St.
Bellingham, WA 98226
(206) 734-9781

Poetry, fiction, reviews, plays,
photographs, graphics/artwork.
The focus is primarily on poetry,
fiction and drama.
Jim Daniels, Joseph Green, Nancy
King, Sibyl James, Maria Win-
ston.
Payment: 1 year's subscription.
Reporting time: 2–3 months.
Copyright reverts to author upon
publication.
1977; 2/yr; 800
$4/yr; $4.50 if agencied; $2/ea;
40% on 5 or more
60 pp; 5½ x 8½
Exchange ads only
ISSN: 0734-2934

BELLOWING ARK

Robert R. Ward
P.O. Box 45637
Seattle, WA 98145
(206) 545-8302

Poetry, fiction, essays, graphics/
artwork, novel serializations,
short autobiography.
We feature work in the American
Romantic tradition, i.e. editorial
content is concerned with universal truths and the idea of
transcending individual limita-
tion. Content of a work is the
primary consideration; form is a
distant second, leading to a
wryly eclectic mix (we are just
concluding the serialization of a
14,000 line epic, for instance).
Nelson Bentley, Susan McCaslin,
John Elrod, Harold Witt, Jane
Greer.
Payment: 2 copies, upon publication.
Copyright held by Bellowing Ark;
reverts to author upon request.
1984; 6/yr; 650
$12/yr ind; $12/yr inst; $2/ea;
40%; comp to libraries on request
20 pp; 11 x 16
Ad rates: only in special circum-
stances
ISSN: 0887-4115
Ubiquity, Faxon, Popular Subscription Service

THE BELOIT POETRY JOURNAL

Marion K. Stocking
Box 154, R.F.D. 2
Ellsworth, ME 04605
(207) 667-5598
Poetry, reviews.
We publish the best poems we receive without bias as to length, form, subject, or tradition. We especially hope to discover new voices. Occasional chapbooks; recently Afro-American, American Indian, and new Chinese poetry.
Susan Tichy, Bruce Cutler, Hillel Schwartz, Brooks Haxton, Lola Haskins.
Payment: 3 copies.
Reporting time: immediately to four months.
Copyright held by magazine; reverts to author upon publication.
1950; 4/yr; 1,200
$8/yr ind; $12/yr inst; $2/ea; 20%
40 pp; 5½ x 8½
No ads
ISSN: 0005-8661
B. DeBoer, Inc.; Maine Writer's and Publisher's Alliance

THE BERKELEY POETRY REVIEW

Natalia Apostolos & Jonathan Brennan

700 Eshleman Hall
University of California at Berkeley
Berkeley, CA 94720
Poetry, fiction, translation, interviews, photographs, graphics/artwork
THE BERKELEY POETRY REVIEW is a small but long-standing literary journal that publishes primarily poetry. We accept submission year-round (4 poems maximum). We are always on the lookout for emerging writers.
Victor Hernandez Cruz, Thom Gunn, Heather McHugh, Opal Palmer-Adisa, Ishmael Reed.
Payment: in 1 copy, upon publication.
Copyright held by author.
1973; 1–2/yr; 500–1,000
$12/yr ind; $14/yr inst; $6/ea; 40%
170 pp; 5 x 8
Ad rates: $50/page/4 x 7; $30/½ page/2½ x 3½

BETWEEN C & D

Joel Rose and Catherine Texier
255 East 7th Street
New York, NY 10009
Fiction.
Sex, drugs, violence, danger, computers. Writers on the edge.
David Foster Wallace, Reinaldo

Povod, Patrick McGrath, Dennis Cooper, Kathy Acker.
Payment: in copies.
Reporting time: 3 months.
Copyright reverts to author.
1984; 3/yr; 600
$15/yr issues post. included; $4/ea
50 pp: 9½ x 11
New York Newpapers

BIG ALLIS

Melanie Meilson, Jessica Grim
M. Neilson: 140 Page St. #1
San Francisco, CA 94102
(212) 777-2079
Prose, poetry; primarily experimental in nature.
Contemporary writing by a wide variety of writers, including those whose work has not been published widely. Focus mainly on writing by women. Publishing new prose and poetry primarily experimental in nature.
Lyn Hejinian, Carla Harryman, Laura Moriarty, Leslie Scalapino, Diane Ward, Bruce Andrews.
Payment: copies.
Reporting time: 2–4 months.
Copyright reverts to author upon publication.
1989; 2/yr; 500–1,000
$10/yr; $5/ea; 40%
80 pp: 9 x 7
Ad rates not available

ISSN: 1043-9978
Segue, Small Press Distribution

BIG CIGARS

José Padua, Michael Randall, Stephen Ciacciarelli
1625 Hobart St., NW
Washington, DC 20009
Poetry, fiction, graphics/artwork.
BIG CIGARS is hand-assembled, limited editions, the purpose of which is to publish new writing from mostly non-established writers, reaching as wide an audience as possible. We are interested in short, lucid poetry and fiction, the more daring the better. While we do not print great quantities, we reach both coasts and several countries.
Ron Kolm, Hal Sirowitz, Lyn Lifshin, Todd Moore, Rollo Whitehead.
Payment: in copies.
Reporting time: 2 to 3 months.
Copyright held by The P.O.N. Press; reverts to author upon publication.
1986; 2/yr; 350
$3.00/ea
40 pp; 8½ x 11
No ads
St. Marks Books, Sohazat, Spring St. Books, City Lights

THE BILINGUAL REVIEW/LA REVISTA BILINGÜE

Gary D. Keller
Hispanic Research Center
Arizona State University
Tempe, AZ 85287
(602) 965-3867

Poetry, fiction, criticism, reviews, scholarly articles.

Devoted to the linguistics and literature of bilingualism, primarily Spanish/English, in the United States. We publish creative literature by and/or about United States Hispanics, literary criticism and reviews of United States Hispanic literature. We do not publish translations.

Rolando Hinojosa, Carlos Morton, Rosaura Sanchez, Alma Villanueva, Alberto Rios.

Payment: in copies.
Reporting time: 30 days.
Copyright held by magazine.
1974; 3/yr; 1,000
$16/yr ind; $26/yr inst; sample copies: $6 ind/$9 inst
96 pp; 7 x 10
Ad rates: $150/page/5½ x 8½; $90/½ page/5½ x 4
ISSN: 0094-5366

BLACK AMERICAN LITERATURE FORUM

Joe Weixlmann
Department of English
Indiana State University
Terre Haute, IN 47809
(812) 237-2968

Poetry, criticism, reviews, interviews, photographs, graphics/artwork, bibliographies.

Critical and pedagogical essays on black American literature, interviews, bibliographies, book reviews, poems, and graphics on black themes.

Amiri Baraka, Gwendolyn Brooks, Ishmael Reed, Houston A. Baker, Jr., Rita Dove, Henry Louis Gates, Jr.

Payment: depends on grants.
Reporting time: 3 months.
Copyright held by author.
1967; 4/yr; 1,200
$19/yr ind; $30/yr inst; $7.50/ea; 40%
192 pp; 6 x 9
$150/page/4⅜ x 7½; $90/½ page/4⅜ x 3¾.
ISSN: 0148-6179

BLACK BEAR REVIEW

Ave Jeanne & Ron Zettlemoyer
1916 Lincoln St.
Croydon, PA 19020-8026
(215) 788-3543

Poetry, reviews, graphics, market listings, current poetry news.

BLACK BEAR REVIEW is an international literary/fine arts magazine published twice a year. We welcome poetry that shows knowledge of / the craft, the world around us / human nature. We attempt to get into print as much poetry as possible and chapbooks. Both the established and new writer are welcome.

Arthur Winfield Knight, A. D. Winans, James Humphrey, Tony Moffeit, Alan Catlin, Harry Calhoun

Payment: in copies.

Copyright: held by magazine; reverts to author upon publication.

1984; 2/yr; 400

$8/yr ind; $10/yr inst; $4/ea; 40%

64 pp; 5½ x 8

ISSN: 8756-0666

BLACK ICE

Editor: Ron Sukenick; Associate Editor: Dallas Wiebe; Assistant Editor: Mark Amerika

English Dept. Publications Center

Campus Box 494

Boulder, CO 80309-0494

(303) 492-8947

Fiction.

BLACK ICE publishes only fiction, with emphasis on non-traditional fiction. The Margaret Jones Fiction Award is given for the best story in each issue. We intend to take risks with the fiction we publish and encourage writers to do the same.

Steve Katz, Erik Belgum, Thomas Glynn, Harold Jaffe, Cris Mazza.

Payment: in 2 contributors copies.

Copyright held by BLACK ICE; reverts to author upon publication.

1984; 3/yr; 500

$7/ea; 40%

100 pp; 5½ x 8½

Ad rates: $150/page/5 x 8

ISSN: 0-918411-01-7

BLACK JACK/VALLEY GRAPEVINE

Art Cuelho

P.O. Box 249

Big Timber, MT 59011

Poetry, fiction, photographs, graphics/artwork.

BLACK JACK's focus is on rural America; regional writing; and interests are on the the Dustbowl; Okie migration; southern Appalachia; Hoboes; American Indians; the West. VALLEY GRAPEVINE focuses on anything in the San Joaquin Valey in Central California.

Bill Rintoul, Gerry Haslam, Wilma McDaniel, Dorothy Rose, Frank Cross.

Payment: in copies.

Reporting time: 1 week.

Copyright held by Seven Buffa-

loes Press; reverts to author upon publication.
1973; 1/yr; 750
$10/yr; $6/ea; 20%–40%
85 pp; 5¼ x 8¼

BLACK MOUNTAIN II REVIEW

Mark Spall
451 Porter Quad, Elicott
Buffalo, NY 14261
(716) 636-2137

Poetry, fiction, interviews, photographs, graphics/artwork, critical essays.

Theme of the 1986 issue is so-called language-oriented writing. Significant practitioners of this writing include Bruce Andrews, Charles Bernstein and Robert Creeley. Antecedants of these writers were the Dadaists, John Cage, William S. Burroughs.

Payment: none.
Reporting time: 30 days.
Copyright reverts to author.
1981; 1/yr; 750
$4/ea
52 pp; 11 x 8½

BLACK RIVER REVIEW

Kaye Collier
855 Mildred Ave
Lorain, OH 44052
(216) 244-9654

Poetry, fiction, critical essay, book review.

BRR presents contemporary writing of diverse styles and genres aimed toward a broad audience. We print work that exhibits originality, craftsmanship, vivid style, by writers both well-known and as-yet-to-be-discovered.

John M. Bennett, Diane Glancy, Prescott Foster, Bayla Winters, Robert Cooperman, Li Mia Hua.

Payment: in copies.
Reporting time: 2 weeks–6 months.
Copyright reverts to author upon publication.
1985; 1/yr; 400
$3.50 per issue
60 pp; 8½ x 11
Query for ad rates

THE BLACK SCHOLAR

Robert Chrisman, Editor: JoNina Abron, Managing Editor
P.O. Box 2869
Oakland, CA 94606
(415) 547-6633

Poetry, fiction, sociology, politics, economy, education, book reviews.

A journal of black studies and research, addressing such issues as black culture, black politics, black education, economics,

Southern Africa, etc. . . . A journal on the cutting edge of contemporary black thought.
Jesse Jackson, Jayne Cortez, Johnnotta B. Cole, Gwendolyn Brooks, Haki R. Madhubuti, P.P. Sarduy
Payment: subscription plus 10 copies.
Reporting time: 2 months.
Copyright held by Black World Foundation.
1969; 6/yr; 10,000
$30/ind; $50/inst; $5/ea; 20%–40%
64 pp; 7 x 10
$1,000/page; $600/½ page; query
ISSN: 0006-4246
L-S Dist., B. DeBoer

BLACK WARRIOR REVIEW

Mark Dawson
P.O. Box 2936
Tuscaloosa, AL 35486-2936
(205) 348-4518
Poetry, fiction, essays, reviews, translations, interviews, photographs, graphics/artwork.
The **BLACK WARRIOR REVIEW** publishes the best of contemporary writing by the best of contemporary writers.
Andre Dubus, Michael S. Harper, Howard Nemerov, John Irving, Jorie Graham, Jane Miller, David St. John.

Payment: $5–10/page.
Reporting time: 1–3 months.
Copyright held by magazine; reverts to author upon publication.
1974; 2/yr; 1,800
$7.50/yr ind; $11.00/yr inst; $4/ea
144 pp; 6 x 9
Ad rates: $150/page/5 x 8; $75/½ page/5 x 3½; $37.50/¼ page/ 5 x 1¾
ISSN: 0193-6301

BLATANT ARTIFICE

Edmund Cardoni
Hallwalls Contemporary Arts Center
700 Main Street
Buffalo, NY 14202
(716) 854-5828
Fiction, graphics/artwork.
An annual anthology of short fiction and performance texts by visitors to Hallwalls, dedicated to innovative prose writing.
Ariel Dorfman, Karen Finley, Holly Hughes, Oscar Hijuelos, Manuel Ramos Otero.
Payment: $35.
Copyright reverts to author upon publication.
1986; annual; 1,000
$10; 40%
168 pp; 7 x 9
Printed Matter (New York), Con-

temporary Arts Press (San Francisco), Marginal Distribution (Toronto), Central Books Warehouse (London)

BLIND ALLEYS

Michael S. Weaver

P.O. Box 13224

Baltimore, MD

Poetry, fiction, criticism, essays, reviews, graphics/artwork.

BLIND ALLEYS is a semi-annual magazine which has a primary focus on the third world, but only because of the identity of the contributor. It does not limit itself to a specific literary approach or political bent, as much as it is possible not to.

Lucille Clifton, Andrei Codrescu, Jerry Ward, Ethelbert Miller, Eric Abrahamson.

Payment: in copies.

Reporting time: 3 to 4 months.

Copyright reverts to author.

1982; 2/yr; 300

$11/yr ind; $13/yr inst; $5/ea

45 pp; 5¼ x 8⅜

Ad rates: $100/page; $50/½ page; $25/¼ page

THE BLOOMSBURY REVIEW

Tom Auer, Publisher; Marilyn Auer, Assoc. Publisher

1028 Bannock Street

Denver, CO 80204

(303) 892-0620

Reviews, graphics/artwork, poetry, interviews, photographs, essays.

THE BLOOMSBURY REVIEW is a "Book Magazine" that includes reviews, interviews, essays, poetry, profiles, and previews of new titles, with an emphasis on new titles from small, medium-sized, and university presses.

Edward Abbey, Leslie Woolf Hedley, John Nichols, Linda Hogan, Peter Wild.

Payment: $15/review; $10/poetry; $20/interviews.

Reporting time: 6–8 weeks.

Copyright reverts to author.

1980; 6/yr; 10,000

$14/yr; $3.00/ea; 40%; less discount through distributors.

32 pp; 10 x 12

Ad rates: $1,550/page/9¾ x 11⅞; $850/½ page/4¾ x 11⅞; $465/ ¼ page/4¾ x 5⅞

ISSN: 0276-1564

BLUE BUILDINGS

Tom Urban, Ruth Doty, Guillaume Williams

1215 25th Street, Apt. E

Des Moines, IA 50311

(515) 277-2709

Poetry, translations, and art.

Michael Benedikt, Marge Piercy,
William Stafford, Richard Shel-
ton, George Garrett, Alberto
Rios, Gary Fincke.
Payment: none.
Reporting time: 6–8 weeks, some-
times longer.
Copyright reverts to author.
1979; 2/yr; 750
$8/ea
50 pp; 8½ x 11

BLUE LIGHT RED LIGHT

Alma Rodriguez, Joy Parker
496A Hudson Street, Suite F-42
New York, NY 10014
(212) 432-3245

Fusion of contemporary writing,
magic surrealism, and mainstream writing together with
speculative fiction.

BLUE LIGHT RED LIGHT, a
periodical of speculative fiction
and the arts, welcomes all international writers, poets and
storytellers inspired by the literature of personal myth, dream
images and folklore.

Gloria Naylor, Harlan Ellison,
Peter Wortsman, E. S.
Creamer.
Payment: small honorarium, plus
issues.
Reporting time: 6 weeks.
Copyright held by BLRL; reverts
to author.

1988; 1–3/yr
$15/yr; $5.50/ea; 40%
176 pp; 9 x 6
$250/page; $150/½ page
ISSN: 10456-0012

BLUE UNICORN

Ruth G. Iodice, Harold Witt,
Daniel J. Langton; Art Editor:
Robert L. Bradley; Contest
Chairperson: Dorothy Burri
22 Avon Road
Kensington, CA 94707
(415) 526-8439

Poetry, translation, artwork.

We are looking for excellence of
the individual poetic voice,
whether that voice comes
through in form or freer verse,
rhyme or not. We want originality of image, thought and music, poems which are
memorable and communicative.
We publish both well-known
poets and unknowns who de-
serve to be known better.

John Ciardi, Charles Edward
Eaton, Emilie Glen, Diana
O'Hehir, William Stafford.
Payment: in copies.
Reporting time: 3–4 months.
Copyright held by magazine; re-
verts to author upon publica-
tion.
1977; 3/yr; 500
$12/yr; $4/ea; $18 foreign.

56 pp; 5½ x 8½
ISSN: 0197-7016

BLUELINE
Anthony Tyler
English Dept.
SUNY
Potsdam, NY 13676
Poetry, fiction, essays, reviews,
graphics/artwork, oral history,
journals.
BLUELINE is dedicated to prose
and poetry about the Adiron-
dacks and other regions similar
in geography and spirit. We are
interested in historic and contemporary writing, from new
and established writers, that
interprets the region as well as
describes it.
Joseph Bruchac, Paul Corrigan,
Roger Mitchell, Noelle Oxen-
handler, Lloyd Van Brunt.
Payment: in copies.
Reporting time: 2–10 weeks.
Copyright held by magazine; reverts to author upon publication.
1989; 1/yr double issue; 700
$6/yr; $6/ea; $4 per copy to dis-
tributors
112 pp; 6 x 9
ISSN: 0198-9901

BOGG
John Elsberg, George Cairncross
422 North Cleveland
Arlington, VA 22201

Poetry, prose poems, criticism,
essays, reviews, interviews,
graphics/artwork.
Editing is a subjective affair, and
we print what takes our fancy.
BOGG is an Anglo-American
literary journal, with contribu-
tions from the U.S., Canada,
England, and Australia/New
Zealand.
Ann Menebroker, Ron Androla,
Harold Witt, Robert Peters,
John Millett, Tina Fulker, Rich-
ard Peabody, Jon Silkin.
Payment: in copies.
Reporting time: immediately.
Copyright held by author.
1968; 2–3/yr; 750
$10/3 issues; $4/ea; $3/sample;
40%
64 pp; 6 x 9
ISSN: 0882-648X

BOMB MAGAZINE
Betsy Sussler
P.O. Box 2003
Canal Station
New York, NY 10013
(212) 431-3943
Interviews, poetry, fiction, photo-
graphs, art.
BOMB MAGAZINE is a spokes-
piece for new art, fiction, the-
atre and film in New York.

Named after Wyndham Lewis's
"Blast," it promotes and en-
courages conversations through-
out the arts.
Kathy Acker, Gary Indiana,
Patrick McGram, Lynn Tillman.
Payment: $100.
Copyright reverts to author.
1981; 4/yr; 8,500
$18/yr; $5/ea; 40%
100 pp; 10 x 14½
Ad rates: on request

BONE & FLESH

Frederick Moe/Lester Hirsch
c/o Hirsch P.O. Box 349
Concord, NH 03302-0349
(603) 228-5723
Poetry, short fiction, essays, reviews, artwork.
BONE & FLESH is an eclectic
blend of styles and voices. We
are oriented towards spiritual
and interpersonal growth. We
look for work that has emotional impact.
Joel Oppenheimer, Jean Battlo,
Arthur Winfield Knight,
Chelsea Adams, Alan Catlin.
Payment: in copies.
Reporting time: usually within 6
weeks.
Copyright reverts to author.
1988; 2/yr; 250+
$7/yr; $5/ea

pp varies; 8½ x 11
ISSN: 9130-1040

BOSTON LITERARY REVIEW (BLUR)

Gloria Mindock-Duehr
Box 357
W. Somerville, MA 02144
(617) 625-6087
Poetry, short fiction (under 3,000
words).
We seek work that pushes form or
content, and that has a unique,
even idiosyncratic voice. 5–10
poems are welcome, as we prefer to publish several poems by
each author.
Eric Panfor, David Ray, Stuart
Freibert, Richard Kostelanetz.
Payment: 2 copies.
Reporting time: 1–3 months.
Copyright reverts to author upon
publication.
1984; 2/yr; 500
$6/yr; $4/ea
24 pp; 5½ x 12½

BOSTON REVIEW

Margaret Ann Roth, Editor
33 Harrison Avenue
Boston, MA 02111
(617) 350-5353
THE BOSTON REVIEW is an
award-winning national magazine with the distinctive voice
of Boston—unconventional

coverage of culture and all the arts. Meet the next generation of gifted young writers alongside with established authors saying what's really on their minds. People like Helen Vendler, David Leavitt, Rosellen Brown, Seamus Heaney.
Payment: $40–$250/depending on length and author.
Copyright held by Boston Critic, Inc.; reverts to author upon publication.
1975; 6/yr; 10,000
$15/yr ind; $18/yr inst
28–44 pp; 11⅜ x 14½
Ad rates: $800/page/10 x 14; $550/½ page/10 x 6¾; $250/¼ page/4¾ x 6¾
ISSN: 0734-2306
Interstate, Ingram, Total

BOTTOMFISH
Robert Scott
DeAnza College
21250 Stevens Creek Blvd.
Cupertino, CA 95014
(408) 996-4545 or 996-4547
Poetry, fiction.
BOTTOMFISH accepts lyric poems and short fiction of 5,000 words or less, including portions of novels. We publish some experimental fiction. We are interested only in carefully crafted work.

Naomi Clark, Janice Dabney, William Dickey, Edward Kleinschmidt, Martin Nakell.
Payment: in copies.
Copyright held by magazine; reverts to author upon publication.
1986; 1/yr; 500
$3.50/ea; 40%
70–80 pp; 17.5 x 21 cm.
No ads

BOULEVARD
Richard Burgin, Editor
2400 Chestnut St., #3301
Philadelphia, PA 19103
(215) 561-1723
Poetry, fiction, criticism, essays, translations, interviews, photos, graphics.
BOULEVARD publishes exceptional fiction and poetry by impressive new talent as well as established literary voices. The editors believe a critical dimension is essential to an outstanding literary publication; thus, each issue publishes essays on literature and the other arts.
BOULEVARD believes in the school of talent.
John Ashbery, Isaac Bashevis Singer, Joyce Carol Oates, Alice Adams, Kenneth Kocho.
Payment: $25–150/poetry; $50–150/fiction & other prose.

Copyright held by Opojaz Inc. for First North American Serial Rights; reverts to author upon publication.

1986; 3/yr; 2,500

$12/yr ind; $9/yr inst; $5/ea. 40%

200 pp

Ad rates available. Contact CLMP for information.

ISSN: 0885-9337

Bernhard DeBoer Inc.

BOUNDARY 2

William V. Spanos

SUNY/Binghamton

Binghamton, NY 13901

(607) 798-2743

Poetry, fiction, criticism, essays, plays, translation, interviews, photographs, graphics/artwork.

BOUNDARY 2 publishes poetry, fiction and literary criticism that try to break out of the impasse that traditional, including modernist, literature and literary criticism have become stalled in. We are especially interested in providing a forum for experiments in open forms that ultimately interrogate the literary tradition and the dominant culture this tradition supports.

Armand Schwerner, Jerome Rothenberg, John Taggart, Charles Bernstein and the l=a=n=g=u=a=g=e poets.

Payment: none.

Reporting time: 4–6 months.

1972; 3/yr; 1,000

$15/yr ind; $13/yr students; $25/yr inst; $8/ea; 40%

300 pp; 9 x 5¾

Ad rates: $100/page; $50/½ page; $25/¼ page

BRIEF

Jim Hydock

P.O. Box 33

Canyon, CA 94516

(415) 376-5509

Poetry, fiction, post-modern fiction/poetry.

Primarily mailed free to "interested" readers and writers (approximately 200 copies mailed quarterly). Sold in select bookstores.

Larry Eigner, Fielding Dawson, August Kleinzahler, Anselm Hollo, Martha King.

Payment: none.

Reporting time: 2–4 weeks.

Copyright held by magazine; reverts to author upon publication.

1988; 4/yr; 250

$10/yr ind; $12/yr inst.; $2.50/ea; 40%

25 pp; 5½ x 8½

No ads

BROOKLYN REVIEW

English Dept., Brooklyn College
Brooklyn, NY 11210
(718) 780-5195

Poetry, fiction, playwriting.

A magazine of contemporary poetry, fiction and playwriting. No specifications as to style, length, form or content.

James Schuyler, Alice Notley, Joan Larkin, Eileen Myles, Elaine Equi, David Trinidad, Ronna Levy.

Payment: 2 copies.

Reporting time: 2 weeks–2 months.

Copyright reverts to author upon publication.

1984; 1/yr; 500

$5/yr; $5/ea

50–80 pp; 4¼ x 5½

BRUSSELS SPROUT

Francine Porad
P.O. Box 1551
Mercer Island, WA 98040
(206) 232-3239

Haiku Poetry, senryu, essays, book reviews dealing with haiku, graphics/artwork.

A journal of contemporary English language haiku and art, with international contributors and subscribers. Seeking haiku and senryu in a variety of styles and forms, from one to four lines. Subject matter is open. **BRUSSELS SPROUT** looks for haiku that capture "the haiku moment" in a fresh way.

Alexis Rotella, Marlene Mountain, Anne McKay, George Swede, Paul O. Williams, Robert Spiess.

Payment: none, 3–$10 editor's awards.

Reporting time: 3 weeks.

Copyright reverts to author upon publication.

1980; 3/yr; 300

$12 domestic/Canada, $15 elsewhere; $4.50/$6.00

40 pp; 8½ x 5½

ISSN: 0897-7356

U. Book Store, Elliot Bay Book Co., Uwajimaya

C

CAFE SOLO

Glenna Luschei
Box 2814
Atascadero, CA 93422
(805) 466-0947

Poetry, fiction, criticism, essays, reviews, translation, photographs, graphics/artwork.

We seek excellence and the avant-garde: Subconscious navigation

in strange waters and Columbus
sighting land. We print new
writers next to known ones. We
emphasize poetry, but encourage imaginative essays and new
literary art forms.
Robert Bly, Denise Levertov,
Gene Frumkin, Gary Snyder,
Lawrence Ferlinghetti, Thomas
McGrath, and prisoners from
the California Men's Colony.
Payment: in copies.
Reporting time: 8 weeks.
Copyright held by Solo Press.
1969; 3/yr; 500
$20/yr; $5/ea; 40%
44 pp; 6 x 9
ISSN: 0773-1796

Berssenbrugge, Bly, Creeley,
Kingston, Wakoski.
Payment: $15–$20, plus 2 copies.
Reporting time: 2 weeks to 1
month.
Copyright held by **CALIBAN**;
reverts to author upon publication.
1986; 2/yr; 1,700
$8/yr; $15/2 yrs ind; $15/yr inst;
$5/ea; 40%, 25% textbook
orders
192 pp; 6 x 9
Ad rates: $100/page/5 x 8; $50/½
page/3½ x 5
ISSN: 0890-7269
DeBoer, Ingram, Bookpeople,
SPD

CALIBAN
Lawrence R. Smith
P.O. Box 4321
Ann Arbor, MI 48106
(313) 662-5427
Poetry, fiction, translation, interviews, graphics/artwork.
CALIBAN has redefined the literary and artistic avant-garde by
cutting across partisan lines,
making different writers and
artists in serious pursuit of the
new aware of each other. **CAL-
IBAN** also insists that the
avant-garde is not the exclusive
domain of white, middle-class
males, bohemian or otherwise.

**CQ (CALIFORNIA STATE
POETRY QUARTERLY)**
John M. Brander
1200 E. Ocean Blvd., #64
Long Beach, CA 90802
(213) 495-0925
Poetry, translation, graphics/art-
work.
Poems may come from anywhere
in the country. We like everything we've published in **CQ**,
some of it a lot, but from now
on we would like to receive not
only poems like those we've
printed but also those which are
unlike anything we've ever
printed.

Suzanne Lummis, William James
Kovanda, Sylvia Rosen, Blair
Allen, Aaron Kramer.
Payment: none.
Reporting time: 2–3 months.
Copyright held by California State
Poetry Society and English De-
partment, Chapman College,
Orange, CA; reverts to author
upon publicaton.
1972; 3 or 4/yr; 500
$5/ea; 20%
84 pp
No ads
Small Press Traffic (San Fran-
cisco), Midnight Special (Santa
Monica), Dutton's (Brentwood,
Los Angeles), CSULB Book-
store, Long Beach

wide and black writers in the
Caribbean and Africa.
Rita Dove, Jay Wright, Edward
Brathwaite, Alice Walker, Aimé
Césaire.
Payment: none.
Copyright held by Johns Hopkins
University Press; reversion to
author depends upon situation.
1976; quarterly; 800
$16/yr ind; $34/yr inst (plus for-
eign postage); $6/ea ind; $9/ea
inst; 40%
180 pp; 7 x 10
Ad rates: $150/page/5½ x 8;
$90/½ page/5½ x 4; cover
2/$200; cover 3/$175
ISSN: 0161-2492

CALLALOO

Charles H. Rowell
Department of English
Wilson Hall
University of Virginia
Charlottesville, VA 22903
(804) 924-6616

Bibliography, poetry, fiction, criticism, essays, reviews, plays,
translation, photographs, graph-
ics/artwork.
CALLALOO is a quarterly magazine which gives special attention to Black South arts and
literature. CALLALOO also
publishes black writers nation-

CALLIOPE

Martha Christina
Creative Writing Program
Roger Williams College
Bristol, RI 02809
(401) 253-1040, ext. 2217

Poetry, fiction.
Interested in both established and
emerging writers, but need not
have published elsewhere. Prefer concrete to abstract images,
work that appeals to the emotions through the senses.
Thomas Lux, Mark Doty, Mark
Cox, Lynne deCourcy, Lynda
Sexson.

Payment: 2 copies and subscription.
Copyright held by magazine; reverts to author upon publication.
1977; 2/yr; 300
$5.00/yr; $3/ea; 40%
5½ x 8½

CALYX: A Journal of Art and Literature by Women
Margarita Donnelly, Catherine Holdorf, Bev McFarland
P.O. Box B
Corvalis, OR 97339
(503) 753-9384
Poetry, fiction, essays, translations, reviews, photographs, visual art, interviews.
Considered one of the finest literary magazines in the U.S., **CALYX** publishes work by women artists and presents a wide spectrum of women's experience. **CALYX** is committed to publishing the finest work by women of color, working class women, lesbians, politically active women, and older women. Winner of 1988 OILA award for literary achievement in Oregon.
Ursula LeGuin, Betty La Juke, Kathleen Alcalá, Ruthann Robson, Eleanor Wilner, Tee Corinne.

Payment: in copies.
Reporting time: 3–6 months.
Copyright held by magazine.
1976; 3/volume; 3,000
$18/yr ind; $22.50/yr inst;
$8.00/ea + postage; 30%–40%
100–128 pp single; 200+ double.
Ad rates: $550/page/5¾ x 7;
$285/½ page/5¾ x 3⅜
ISSN: 0147-1627
Small Changes, Inland, Bookpeople, Ingram, Small Press Dist., Ingram Periodicals, Airlift, Armadillo, Homing Pigeon

THE CAPE ROCK
Harvey Hecht
English Department
Southeast Missouri State University
Cape Girardeau, MO 63701
(314) 651-2636
Poetry, photographs.
We have no restrictions on subjects or forms. Our criterion for selection is the quality of the work rather than the bibliography of the authors. We prefer poems under 70 lines. We feature a single photographer each issue.
Laurel Speer, Laurie Taylor, Martin Robbins, Charles A. Waugaman.
Payment: each issue we award $200 for the best poem and

$100 for the photography. All contributors are paid in copies. Reporting time: 1–4 months. We do not read poetry in May, June or July.

Copyright held by magazine; reprint rights granted upon request provided reprint credit is given The Cape Rock.

1964; 2/yr; 700

$2/ea; 40%

64pp; 5½ x 8½

ISSN: 0146-2199

CAPRICE

James Mechem, Lynne Savitt

229 North Fountain

Wichita, KS 67208

(316) 683-8728

Fiction, poetry.

Cheryl Clarke, Diane Wakoski, Ellen Tifft, George Chambers, Janice Eidus, Joan Aleshire, Joanne Braxton, Kay Murphy, Lyn Lifshin, Mardy Murphy, Roberta Swann, Ursule Molinaro.

$50/yr

THE CARIBBEAN WRITER

Erika J. Smilowitz

Caribbean Research Institute

University of the Virgin Islands

RR 02, Box 10,000 Kingshill

St. Croix, VI 00850

(809) 778-0246

Poetry, fiction, reviews, graphics/ artwork.

THE CARIBBEAN WRITER is an international magazine with a Caribbean focus. The Caribbean should be central to the work, or the work should reflect a Caribbean heritage, experience, or perspective.

Derek Walcott, Laurence Lieberman, Julia Alvarez, Judson Jerome, Toi Derricotte.

Payment: 1 copy.

Copyright held by Caribbean Research Institute; reverts to author upon publication.

1987; 1/yr; 950

$7/ea; 12–24 = 30%, 25+ = 40%

100 pp; 7 x 10

Ad rates: $200/page/7 x 10; $150/½ page/3½ x 10; $100/¼ page/3½ x 5

ISSN: 0893-1550

A CAROLINA LITERARY COMPANION

Nellvena Duncan Eutsler, Managing Editor; Michael Parker, Fiction; Patrick Bizzaro, Poetry

Community Council for the Arts

P.O. Box 3554

Kinston, NC 28502-3554

(919) 527-2517

Poetry, fiction.

A CAROLINA LITERARY COMPANION is published twice yearly, and is intended primarily as a vehicle for emerging Southern writers of poetry and short fiction. Primary consideration is given to writers who live in the South or are natives of that region. All selections are made on the basis of artistic merit.

Ron Rash, Becke Roughton, Marion Hodge, R. T. Smith, Ruth Moose.

Payment: in 2 copies of the volume in which contributors are published.

Reporting time: 2–3 weeks after each deadline (10/15 and 2/15 each year).

Copyright held by Community Council for the Arts; reverts to author upon publication.

1985; 2/yr; 400

$8.50/yr; $5/ea; 40% on 5 or more; 33% on 3 or 4 copies

67 pp; 5½ x 8½

No ads

CAROLINA QUARTERLY

Rebecca Barnhouse

Greenlaw Hall CB #3520

University of North Carolina at Chapel Hill

Chapel Hill, NC 27599-3520

(919) 962-0244

Poetry, fiction, interviews, photographs.

A literary journal published three times yearly. Interested in fiction and poetry by both new and established writers— excellence is our only restriction.

R. T. Smith, Martha Collins, Ian MacMillan.

Payment: $15 per author, fiction and poetry.

Reporting time: 4–6 months.

Copyright held by magazine.

1944; 3/yr; 800

$10/yr ind; $12/yr inst; $5/ea

100 pp; 6 x 9

Ad rates; $95/page; $60/½ page; $40/¼ page

ISSN: 000-8-6797

CATALYST, a Magazine of Heart and Mind

Pearl Cleage

The Fulton County Arts Council

34 Peachtree St., Suite 2330

Atlanta, GA 30303

(404) 730-5785

Poetry, fiction, criticism, essays, reviews, plays, interviews, photographs, graphics/artwork.

CATALYST is a literary publication which focuses primarily on southern writers, but welcomes all submissions in fiction, poetry, drama and criticism. Each issue includes a focus section, and a section for general submissions. The magazine presents writers in a format designed to stimulate discussion and encourage the exchange of ideas.

Nikky Finney, June Jordan, Lamar Alford, John O'Neal, Nikki Giovanni.

Payment: $20–$200; upon publication.

Copyright held by writer or contributor.

1986; 2/yr; 5,000

$10/2 yr ind; $10/2 yr inst; $2.50/ea; 30%

95 pp; 7¾ x 10¾

Ads accepted.

ISSN: 0896-7423

Marcus Books, San Francisco; Common Concerns, Washington D.C.; The Shrine of the Black Madonna, Atlanta; Lammas Book Store, D.C.

THE CATHARTIC

Patrick M. Ellingham

P.O. Box 1391

Fort Lauderdale, FL 33302

(305) 474-7120

Poetry, reviews, photographs, artwork.

THE CATHARTIC is devoted to the unknown poet, with the understanding that most poets are unknown in America. All types of poetry except those that are racist or sexist. Avoid poems over 50 lines or rhyme for the sake of rhyme. Experiment with language and form. Poems that deal with or come from the dark side; intense poems that use words sparingly and forget the poet; peoms that jar the reader's sensibilities.

Eileen Eliot, Joy Walsh, Stefan Anders.

Payment: 1 copy.

Copyright reverts to author upon publication.

1974; 2/yr; 200

$3.75/yr; $7/2 yrs; $2/ea

28 pp; 5½ x 8½

No ads

ISSN: 0145-8310

CEILIDH: AN INFORMAL GATHERING FOR STORY & SONG

P.O. Box 6367

San Mateo, CA 94403

(415) 378-2350 or (415) 591-9902

Fiction, poetry, plays, translation, photographs, graphics/artwork

Patrick Smith, John Moffitt, Traise Yamamoto, Richard Soos, Sarah Bliumis

$7.50/yr; $2.50/ea; 40%

CENTRAL PARK

Stephen-Paul Martin; Richard
  Royal: Prose and Visuals; Eve
  Ensler: Poetry
P.O. Box 1446
New York, NY 10023
(212) 496-7671

Experimental fiction, narrative
  fiction, theory, graphics/
  artwork, poetry, photo-
  graphs, translation, interviews,
  reviews.

CENTRAL PARK is moving in
  three main directions: poetry
  and fiction of an either experimental or aggressively political
  nature, essays in social or es-
  thetic theory, and visual work
  that moves the eye to think
  about how it sees. Prospective
  contributors are advised to order
  a sample copy ($5.00) before
  submitting.

Marc Kaminsky, Rosmarie Wal-
  drop, Rae Armantrout, Ron
  Silliman, Jackson MacLow.
Payment: one copy.
Reporting time: 8 weeks.
Copyright held by magazine.
1981; 2/yr; 1,000
$8/yr; $5/ea; 40%
100 pp; 7½ x 10
Ad rates: $100/page; $50/½ page;
  $25/¼ page
Ubiquity, Segue, Edge

CHAMINADE LITERARY REVIEW

Loretta Petrie
Chaminade University of Honolulu
3140 Waialae Avenue
Honolulu, HI 96816-1578
(808) 735-4826

Poetry, fiction, criticism, reviews.

**CHAMINADE LITERARY
REVIEW** intends to bring together work from both artists
  and writers, talented new ones
  along with those nationally or
  internationally recognized. We
  want writing from Hawaii side
  by side with writing from the
  mainland to demonstrate how
  well our local writers compare.
  We want a magazine at once
  regional and cosmopolitan. We
  hope to reflect the diversity of
  Hawaii's people, their writers,
  their interests.

Cathy Song, John Unterecker,
  Phyllis Thompson, William
  Stafford, Tony Quagliano.
Payment: one year's subscription,
  upon publication.
Copyright held by Chaminade
  Press; reverts to author upon
  publication.
1987; 2/yr; 350
$10/yr; $18/2 yrs ind & inst;
  $5/ea; 20%
175 pp; 6 x 9
Ad rates: $50/page/4 x 7¼; $25/½
  page/4 x 3⅞
ISSN: 0894-6396

THE CHARIOTEER

Pella Publishing Company
337 West 36th Street
New York, NY 10018-6401
(212) 279-9586

Poetry, fiction, criticism, essays, reviews, plays, translation, graphics/artwork.

Purpose: to bring to English-speaking readers information on, appreciation of, and translations from modern Greek literature, with criticism and reproductions of modern Greek art and sculpture.

Payment: none.

Reporting time: 3 months.

Copyright held by Pella Publishing Company; reverts to author upon request.

1960; 1/yr; 1,500

$15/yr; $28/2 yrs; $40/3 yrs

200 pp; 5½ x 8½

Ad rates: $125/page/4⅛ x 7; $75/½ page/4⅛ x 3½

ISSN: 0577-5574

THE CHARITON REVIEW

Jim Barnes
Northeast Missouri State University
Kirksville, MO 63501
(816) 785-4499

Poetry, fiction, essays, reviews, translation.

Excellence in literature only. We like the old; we like the new.

Jack Cady, Phyllis Barber, Barry Targan, David Ray, Robert Canzoneri, Patricia Goedicke, Gordon Weaver, Steve Heller, Elizabeth Moore.

Payment: $5/page.

Reporting time: 1 week to 1 month.

Copyright held by Northeast Missouri State University; reverts to author upon publication.

1975; 2/yr; 700

$5/yr; $2.50/ea; 0%

100 pp; 6 x 9

Ad rates: $100/page/4 x 7; $50/½ page/4 x 3½

ISSN: 0098-9452

Direct mail and bookstores only

THE CHATTAHOOCHEE REVIEW

Lamar York
DeKalb College
2101 Womack Road
Dunwoody, GA 30338-4497
(404) 551-3019

Poetry, fiction, criticism, essays, reviews, interviews.

THE CHATTAHOOCHEE REVIEW promotes fresh writing and encourages as yet unacknowledged writers by giving them space in print next to their acclaimed peers.

Leon Rooke, Fred Chappell, George Garrett, Jim Wayne Miller, Peter Meinke.

Payment: none.

Reporting time: 6 months.

Copyright held by DeKalb College; reverts to author upon publication.

1980; quarterly; 1,250

$15/yr; $3.50/ea; 30%

100 pp; 6 x 9

Ad rates: $125/page/4½ x 7; $75/½ page/4½ x 3½

ISSN: 0741-9155

CHELSEA

Sonia Raiziss, Alfredo de Palchi, Richard Foerster, Caila Rossi

Box 5880

Grand Central Station

New York, NY 10163

(212) 988-2276

Poetry, fiction, criticism, essays, translations, interviews, photographs, graphics.

Stress on style, variety, originality. No special biases or requirements. Flexible attitudes, eclectic material. Active interest, as always, in crosscultural exchanges, in superior translations. Leaning toward cosmopolitan avant-garde, interdisciplinary techniques, but no

strictures against traditional modes. Annual competition (send for guidelines).

Meena Alexander, Bruce Bawer, Rita Dove, James Laughlin, Robert Phillips, Marjorie Stelmach

Payment: $5/page.

Reporting time: immediately to 4 months.

Copyright held by magazine; reverts to author upon publication.

1958; 1/yr; 1,300

$11/2 issues or 1 double issue; $6/ea

192 pp; 6 x 9

$125/page/4½ x 7½; $75/½ page/4½ x 3½

ISSN: 0009-2185

Bernard DeBoer, Inc.; Faxon; EBSCO

CHICAGO REVIEW

Elizabeth Arnold and Jenny Mueller

Faculty Exchange Box C

University of Chicago

Chicago, IL 60637

(312) 753-3571

Poetry, fiction, criticism, essays, reviews, translation, interviews, photographs, graphics/artwork.

CHICAGO REVIEW is dedicated to contemporary writing of excellence, regardless of stylistic biases or trends. A sure hand, demonstrating originality and precision of language and tone, is the sole requirement for inclusion, overriding formal affiliation, theme, regional basis, or previous history of publication.

Earan Boland, Beth Tasherry Shannon, Turner Cassity, Mark Harris.

Payment: copies/subscription.

Reporting time: 2 months.

Copyright held by magazine; transfers to author upon request.

1946; 4/yr; 1,400

$14/yr ind; $18/yr inst; $4.50/ea; 40%

110 pp; 6 x 9

Ad rates: $145/page/4½ x 7½; $100/½ page/2½ x 7½

ISSN: 0009-3696

CIMARRON REVIEW

Gordon Weaver, Editor; Deborah Bransford, Managing Editor; Jack Myers, Randy Phillis, Sally Shigley, Poetry Editors; Gordon Weaver, Kathy Bedwell, Steffie Corcoran, David Major, Fiction Editors; E.P. Walkiewicz, Nonfiction Editor; Thomas E. Kennedy, European Editor

205 Morrill Hall

Oklahoma State University

Stillwater, OK 74078-0135

(405) 744-9476

Poetry, fiction, essays, reviews. Seeks well-written material, which emphasizes attempts to find value and purpose in a dehumanized and dehumanizing world. Avoids "easy" answers of extremes and would not publish work which espouses any specific religious or political view or advocates simple escapism. It does not publish children's stories; but does publish stories about children aimed at adult understanding.

Payment: none.

Reporting time: 3–4 weeks.

Copyright held by magazine.

1967; 4/yr; 450

$12/yr; $3/ea

96 pp; 6 x 9

ISSN: 0009-6849

CINCINNATI POETRY REVIEW

Dallas Wiebe

English Department, 069

University of Cincinnati

Cincinnati, OH 45221

(513) 475-4484

Poetry.

CINCINNATI POETRY REVIEW sets local writers in a national context. One fourth to one third of each issue is local;

the rest is national. "Local" means about 150 from the city. All types of poetry considered. Poetry contest each issue.

Alvin Greenberg, X.J. Kennedy, David Citino, Laurie Henry, Walter McDonald.

Payment: none.

Reporting time: 4–6 weeks.

Copyright held by magazine; reverts to author upon publication.

1985; 2/yr; 1,000

$3/ea; 40%; 50% for direct purchase by dealers

72 pp; 5½ x 8½

CLOCKWATCH REVIEW

James Plath, Editor; Lynn DeVore, James McGowan, Pamela Muirhead, Associate Editors

Dept. of English
Illinois Wesleyan University
Bloomington, IL 61702
(309) 828-4452, 556-3352

Fiction, poetry, interviews, essays, photographs, graphics/artwork.

CLOCKWATCH REVIEW seeks to present quality work in a format lively enough to attract a popular as well as literary/academic audience. Special feature: an ongoing interview series with contemporary artists and musicians.

Rita Dove, Suzanne Vega, William Stafford, J.W. Major, Rosellen Brown.

Payment: in 2 copies, and a small cash award.

Reporting time: under 2 weeks; up to 2 months if under serious consideration.

Copyright held by author.

1983; 2/yr; 1,500

$8/yr; $4/ea

64 pp; 5½ x 8½

ISSN: 0740-9311

Ingram Periodicals

CLUES: A Journal of Detection

Pat Browne
Journals Department
Popular Press
Bowling Green State University
Bowling Green, OH 43403
(419) 372-2981

Fiction, articles.

A magazine focusing upon detective fiction.

1982; 2/yr; 700

$12.50/yr; $7.75/ea

COLLAGES & BRICOLAGES

Marie-José Fortis
P.O. Box 86
Clarion, PA 16214
or 212 Founders Hall
Clarion University of Pennsylvania

Clarion, PA 16214
(814) 226-2340 or 226-5799

Poetry, fiction, criticism, essays, reviews, plays, translation, interviews, photographs, graphics/artwork.

COLLAGES & BRICOLAGES wants mostly to involve experimental, post-modern writing, anything innovative, whether it is poetry, short fiction, or new criticism. We seek the unusual, the eccentric, the bold, the brave. This includes feminism, satire, parody, avant-garde, surrealism, dada, etc. We believe we live in an empty mirror world. The only image transmitted is the one of despair, decadence, void, nihil. Any writer sensing this vision, and willing to play—humorously—with literary despair, willing to be some kind of neo-dada writer, is welcome. (This will indeed comprise anti-war, anti-nuke, and anti-racist writing.)

Randal Silvis, Christopher Woods, Patricia Flinn, Jane Hoppen.

Payment: 1 or 2 copies/contributor. Extras: $2.50/copy.

1987; 1/yr; 400

$3/ea

80 pp; 11 x 18

Ad rates: $50/page/9 x 16; $30/½ page/5 x 8; $15/¼ page/2½ x 4

COLORADO REVIEW

Bill Tremblay, General Editor;
    David Milofsky, Fiction Editor;
    Mary Crow, Translations Editor
360 Eddy Building
English Department
Colorado State University
Fort Collins, CO 80523

Poetry, fiction, criticism, reviews, translation.

Although published in Colorado, **COLORADO REVIEW** is more than a regional literary magazine. We seek to print the best fiction, poetry, translations, interviews, reviews, and articles on contemporary literary subjects that we receive from a contributorship that is national and international. We continue to be interested in Magical Realist writing, but any writing that is vital, highly imaginative and highly realized in artistic terms and that avoids mere mannerism to embody important human concerns will find support here.

Reg Saner, Patricia Goedicke, Bin Ranke, Carole Oles, T. Alan Broughton, Rita Ciresi, David Huddle; interviews with Carolyn Forche; Gwendolyn Brooks, Gretel Ehrlich.

Payment: when funding permits.

1977; 2/yr 1,000

$5/yr ind/inst; $3/ea; 40%

112 pp; 6 x 9
Ad rates: $100/page/7½ x 5;
$50/½ page

COLUMBIA: A Magazine of Poetry and Prose

Rotating Editors
404 Dodge Hall
Columbia University
New York, NY 10027
(212) 280-4391

Poetry, fiction essays.
Payment: in copies; Editors' awards, also.
Reporting time: 1–2 months.
Copyright reverts to author.
1977; 1–2/yr; 200
$15/3 issues; $11/2 issues; $6 ea
Approx. 220 pp; 5 x 8
Ad rates: on request

CONDITIONS

Cheryl Clarke, Dorothy Randall Gray, Sabrina Williams, Pam Parker, Melinda Goodman, Mariana Romo-Carmona
Box 150056
Van Brunt Station
Brooklyn, NY 11215-0001
(718) 788-8654

Poetry, fiction, criticism, essays, review, translation, interviews, photographs, graphics/artwork.
Writing by women with an emphasis on writing by lesbians, women of color, non-U.S. writers (in or with translation).
Audre Lorde, Mila Aquilar, Jacqueline Lapidus, Julia Alvarez, Cheryl Clarke.
Payment: in copies.
Reporting time: 3 months.
Copyright held by magazine; reverts to author upon publication.
1976; 1/yr; 2,500
$24/ind; $36/inst; $8.95/ea; 40%
225 pp; 5½ x 8½
Ad rates: $200-125/page/4½ x 7; $125-75/½ page/4½ x 3½; $75-50/¼ page/2 x 3½
ISSN: 0147-8311

CONFRONTATION

Martin Tucker
L.I.U. Dept. of English
C.W. Post
Greenvale, NY 11548
(516) 299-2391

Poetry, fiction, criticism, essays, plays, translation, interviews.
We are eclectic in our tastes, preferring a mix of traditional and experimental, of the known and relatively unknown writers. We have no prohibition except that of poor literary quality.
Cynthia Ozick, Wilfrid Sheed, Stephen Dixon, Joyce Carol Oates, Thomas Fleming, Joseph Brodsky.

Payment: $5 to $100.
Reporting time: 6 weeks.
Copyright held by Long Island
University; reverts to author
upon publication.
1968; 2/yr; 2,000
$10/yr ind; $10/yr inst; $6/ea
160–190 pp; 5½ x 8½

CONJUNCTIONS

Bradford Morrow
33 West 9th Street
New York, NY 10011
(212) 477-1136

Poetry, fiction, translation, interviews, photographs, graphics/
artwork, reviews, essays.
CONJUNCTIONS publishes for-
mally innovative writing, with
equal emphasis on fiction and
poetry; also essays on culture
and the arts, book reviews, literary historical materials, special features. Editorial staff:
Walter Abish, Mei-Mei Berssenbrugge, Guy Davenport,
Kenneth Irby, William Gass,
Ann Lauterbach, Nathaniel
Tarn.
Payment: in copies, and $50–100.
Reporting time: 4–6 weeks.
Copyright reverts to author upon
publication.
1981; 2/yr; 7,500
$18/yr paper; $45/yr cloth;
$9.95/ea paper

320 pp; 6 x 9
Ad rates: $350/page/4⅜ x 7½;
$250/½ page
ISSN: 0278-2324
New Writing Foundation

THE CONNECTICUT POETRY REVIEW

James Wm. Chichetto, J. Claire
White
P.O. Box 3783
New Haven, CT 06525
Poetry, criticism, reviews, transla-
tions, interviews, excerpts from
verse plays.
Marge Piercy, John Updike, Mar-
garet Randall, Allen Ginsberg,
Eugenio de Andrade.
Payment: $5/poem; $10/review;
$20/interview; $20/verse play.
Reporting time: 3 months.
1981; 1/yr; 500
$3/ea
50 pp; 5¾ x 9¼
ISSN: 0277-7770

CONNECTICUT RIVER RE-VIEW

Ben Brodinsky, Editor
7 Shawnee Court
Cromwell, CT 06416
(203) 635-0525
Poetry.
The CRR uses highest quality
poetry, in which logic and emo-

tion, picture and sound cohere, making for authentic music. All forms welcome, except haiku. Prefer poems of 40 lines or under; submit no more than 5 poems at a time.
Payment: 2 copies.
Reporting time: 2–8 weeks.
Copyright held by Connecticut Poetry Society; reverts to author upon publication.
1978; 2/yr; 600
$10; $5/ea; 40%
60 pp; 6 x 9

CONTACT II

Maurice Kenny, J.G. Gosciak
P.O. Box 451, Bowling Green
New York, NY 10004
(212) OR4-0911
Poetry, reviews, criticism, translation, interviews, photographs, graphics/artwork.
Contemporary American poetry.
Janice Mirikitani, Charlotte de Clue, Carolyn Stoloff, Shalin Hai-Jew, Karoniaktatie.
Payment: in copies; when payment is cash, $10/poem, $15/review.
Reporting time: 6 months.
Copyright held by Contact II Publications; reverts to author upon publication with credit.
1976; semi-annual; 2,500
$10/ind; $16/inst; $7/ea; 40%; 50% prepaid on 10 or more.

92 pp; 7¾ x 10½
Ad rates: $150/page; $80/½ page; $50/¼ page
ISSN: 0197-6796

CORNFIELD REVIEW

Stuart Lishan, General Ed; Martha Bartter, Fiction; Terry Hermson, Poetry; Larry Sauselen, Art
OSU at Marion
1465 Mt. Vernon Ave
Marion, OH 43302
(614) 389-2361
Poetry, short stories, nonfiction essays; original art (black & white) and photography.
A "little" literary magazine showcasing the Midwest experience (but not limited to that topic). Submissions should be of high quality; fiction and non-fiction should not exceed 3500 words.
David Citano, Donald M. Hassler, Roas Maria DelVecchio, Will Wells.
Payment: 1 copy.
Reporting time: 2–4 months.
Copyright reverts to author.
1976; 1/yr; 1,500
$4.50/ea
64 pp
ISSN: 0363-4574

COTTON BOLL/ATLANTA REVIEW

Mary Hollingsworth
Sandy Springs P.O. Box 76757
Atlanta, GA 30358-0703

Poetry, fiction, essays, profiles, commentaries, interviews, book reviews.

Preference is for reflection of the contemporary South or for general applicability. No pornography, religion, lovelorn or racism, or genres such as sci-fi or romance.

Miller Williams, Gail Galloway Adams, Lawrence Naumoff, Madison Jones, Edward C. Lynskey.

Payment: for short stories is $10.00 per story on publication for stories *accepted after* January 1, 1990. Note: This payment CANNOT apply to stories accepted and/or published *before* January 1, 1990.

Payment for poems is $5.00 per poem on publication for poems *accepted after* January 1, 1990. Note: This payment CANNOT apply to poems accepted and/or published *before* January 1, 1990.

Copyright held by magazine; reverts to author upon publication.

1985; 4/yr; 1,000
$20/yr ind/inst; $5.50/ea; 40%

125 pp; 8½ x 5½
No ads
ISSN: 0886-5051

COTTONWOOD

George Wedge, Editor; Phil Wedge, Poetry Editor; Jane Garrett, Fiction Editor
Box J, Kansas Union
Lawrence, KS 66045
(913) 864-4520

Poetry, fiction, reviews, interviews, photographs, graphics/artwork.

COTTONWOOD uses fiction and poetry with clear images and interesting narratives and reviews of books by writers or from publishers in our area. The magazine welcomes submissions from all parts of the country.

Robert Day, Rita Dove, Patricia Traxler, Gerald Early, William Stafford.

Payment: none.

Reporting time: 2–6 months.

Copyright held by magazine; reverts to author upon publication.

1965; 3/yr; 500
$12/yr; $5/ea; 30%
120 pp; 6 x 9
ISSN: 0147-149X

CRAB CREEK REVIEW

Linda Clifton, Carol Orlock (Fiction)
4462 Whitman Avenue, N.
Seattle, WA 98103
(206) 633-1090
Poetry, fiction, translation, essays, graphics/artwork.
. . . well-crafted and perceptive works . . . technically proficient and sensitive poems . . . powerfully expressed images . . . tightly controlled narrative . . . diverse enough to appeal to a variety of literary tastes . . ." Literary Magazine Review.
William Stafford, Jana Harris, Maxine Kumin, David Lee.
Payment: 2 copies.
Reporting time: 4–8 weeks.
Copyright held by CCR; reverts to author upon publication.
1983; 3/yr; 350
$8/yr; $3/ea; 40%; 50% through distributor Small Changes, 3443 12th W., Seattle, WA 98119
32 pp; 6 x 10
$120/page/6 x 10; $65/½ page/6 x 5; $35/¼ page/6 x 2½; $20/⅛ page/3 x 2½
ISSN: 07380-7008

CRAWL OUT YOUR WINDOW

Melvyn Freilicher, Eleanor Bluestein
4641 Park Boulevard
San Diego, CA 92116
(619) 299-4859 or 454-1098
Poetry, fiction, interviews, photographs, graphics/artwork, experimental prose.
CRAWL OUT YOUR WINDOW is a showcase for the experimental literary and visual art of San Diego; we publish residents of the region and former residents still actively involved here.
Michael Davidson, Melvyn Freilicher, Lydia Davis, Rae Armantrout, Guillermo Gómez-Peña, Emily Hicks.
Payment: none.
Reporting time: several months.
Copyright held by M. Freilicher; reverts to author upon publication.
1974; 1/yr; 500
100 pp; 8½ x 11

CRAZYHORSE

Zabelle Stodola (Managing Editor); David Jauss (Fiction); David Wojahn and Lynda Hull (Poetry); Dennis Vanatta (Criticism)
Poetry Submissions Only
David Wojahn and Lynda Hull
English Department
Ballantine Hall
Indiana University
Bloomington, IN 47405

*Fiction, Criticism, and All Other
Correspondence*
English Department
University of Arkansas at Little
Rock
2801 S. University
Little Rock, AR 72204
(501) 569-3160
Poetry, fiction criticism, reviews,
interviews.
A literary magazine which pub-
lishes quality work by estab-
lished and promising new
writers.
Andre Dubus, Bobbie Ann Ma-
son, Raymond Carver, Jorie
Graham, John Updike.
Payment: 2 copies and $10/page.
Annual fiction and poetry awards:
$500 each.
Reporting time: 2 weeks–1 month.
Copyright reverts to author upon
request.
1960; 2/yr; 900
$8/yr; $4/ea; 25%–40%
135 pp; 6 x 9
Ad rates: $85/page; $50/½ page
ISSN: 0011-0841

CRAZYQUILT

Marsh Cassady
3341 Adams Ave
San Diego, CA 92116
Poetry, fiction, criticism, essays,
plays, photographs, graphics/
artwork.

All kinds of poetry; short stories
with good character development; nonfiction about writers;
literary criticism; one-act plays
and black and white photography and art work. Accept translations of poetry. Publish new
writers as well as established
authors. Annual contest: poetry,
short story; biannual: chapbook
contest in poetry, fiction.
Louis Phillips, Elizabeth Barret,
Brian Clark, Barbara Brent
Brower, Charles Kray.
Payment: 2 copies.
Reporting time: 10–12 weeks.
Copyright held by Crazyquilt
Press; reverts to author upon
publication.
1986; quarterly; 180
$14.95/ind/inst; $4.50 ea; 40%
80 pp
ISSN: 0887-5308

CREAM CITY REVIEW

Ron Tanner, Editor-in-Chief
P.O. Box 413
University of Wisconsin-
Milwaukee
Milwaukee, WI 53201
(414) 229-5041
Poetry, fiction, reviews, essays,
interviews. Will consider: plays,
photographs, graphics/artwork.
The **CREAM CITY REVIEW** is
an eclectic literary magazine

affiliated with the University of Wisconsin-Milwaukee; it strives to publish the best of traditional and non-traditional work by new and established writers. Two NEA-supported special issues forthcoming, one devoted to fiction, the other to poetry.
Eve Shelnutt, Stuart Dybek, Fred Chappell, Denise Levertov, David Ignatow.
Payment: varies with funding.
Reporting time: 2–8 weeks.
Copyright held by the Board of Regents of the University of Wisconsin; reverts to author upon publication.
1975; 2/yr; 1,000
$9/yr; $4.50/ea; 40%
140 pp; 5½ x 8½
Ad rates: $50/page

CREEPING BENT

Joseph P. Lucia
433 West Market Street
Bethlehem, PA 18018
(215) 758-4998 or (215) 691-3548
Poetry, reviews, fiction, essays, translation.
Hewing to no orthodoxies but reflecting an awareness of the broad spectrum of current writing and thought about writing, **CREEPING BENT** is an independent, eclectic, and adventurous magazine for serious (but not solemn or humorless) readers and writers of contemporary literature, with emphasis on poetry.
Bridget Kelly, Charles Edward Eaton, Turner Cassity, Robert Gibb.
Payment: none.
Copyright held by publishers; reverts to author upon publication.
1984; 2/yr; 250
$6/yr ind; $7/yr inst; $3/ea. 40%
No ads
ISSN: 8756-0291

THE CRESCENT REVIEW

Guy Nancekeville
P. O. Box 15065
Winston-Salem, NC 27113
(919) 924-1851
Fiction, art.
A fiction-lover's magazine. Eager to hear from new voices.
Madison Bell, Michael Martone, Stephen Dixon, Tom Whalen, Richard Krawiec, Sally Herrin.
Payment: in copies.
Copyright reverts to author.
1983; 2/yr; 500
$10/yr; $6/ea
132 pp; 6 x 9
Ingram, Faxon

CRITICAL TEXT: A Review of Theory and Criticism

Joe Childers, Jon Anderson, Richard Moye, Martha Buskirk, James Buzard, Ina Lipkowitz, Susan Fraiman, Gary Hentzi, Eric Lott
602 Philosophy Hall
Columbia University
New York, NY 10027
(212) 854-3215

Articles, reviews, translations and interviews dealing with theory in the humanities.

We are an oppositional journal interested in printing articles and reviews on theoretical issues connected with the humanities and social sciences.

Jean Franco, Alexander Argyros, Norman Finkelstein, Bruce Robbins, Sandra M. Gilbert and Susan Gubar.

Payment: none.
Reporting time: 2 months.
Copyright held by **CRITICAL TEXT.**
1982; 3/yr; 850
$9/yr ind; $3.75/ea; $5 back issues
120 pp; 6 x 9
$185/page; $100/½ page
ISSN: 0730-2304
Ubiquity

CROSSCURRENTS

Linda Brown Michelson
2200 Glastonbury Road
Westlake Village, CA 91361
(818) 991-1694
Fiction, graphics.

CROSSCURRENTS features previously unpublished, literary short fiction. Select pieces are highlighted by photos and line drawings. Reading period from May 1 through November 30. Two special issues each year.

Alice Adams, Saul Bellow, Josephine Jacobsen, Joyce Carol Oates, John Updike.

Payment: varies, $35 minimum per story.
Reporting time: 6 weeks.
Copyright reverts to author.
1980; 4/yr; 3,000
$15/yr; $5/ea; 40%
176 pp; 6 x 9
ISSN: 0739-2354
The Faxon Company; EBSCO Subscription Service; Boley Internatinal Subscription Agency; L-S Distributors

CUMBERLAND POETRY REVIEW

Editorial Board
P.O. Box 120128 Acklen Station
Nashville, TN 37212
(615) 371-9078

Poetry, criticism, interviews.

CUMBERLAND POETRY REVIEW is devoted to poetry

and poetry criticism and presents poets of diverse origins to a widespread audience. We place no restrictions on form, subject, or style. Manuscripts will be selected for publication on the basis of the writer's perspicuous and compelling means of expression. We welcome translations of high quality poetry. Our aim is to support the poet's efforts to keep up the language.

Seamus Heaney, Lewis Horne, Emily Grosholz, Francis Blessington, Mairi McInnes.

Payment: in contributor's copies.

Reporting time: 6 months.

Copyright held by Poetics, Inc.; reverts to author upon publication.

1981; 2/yr; 500

$12/yr ind; $15/yr inst; $6/ea; 40%

100 pp; 6 x 9

Ads: accepted only on exchange basis

ISSN: 0731-7980

Faxon, Swets, EBSCO, McGregor

Poetry, primarily; also fiction, essays and interviews.

We lean towards what a decaying world-center like New York does best: Highly sophisticated aestheticism and violent/erotic self-display. We like to beautifully present (via advanced typography & design) a representative (largish) selection from each of the 10–15 writers, half of whom are regular contributors, that we publish per issue.

William Burroughs, Dennis Cooper, Eileen Myles, Richard Hell, John Ashbery, Susie Timmons.

Payment: 5 copies.

Reporting time: 3–6 months.

Copyright reverts to author.

1988; 2/yr; 1,000

$16/4 issues; $3.95/ea + .85 postage; 40%

100 pp; 4¼ x 7

$160/page

CUZ

Richard Myers
437 E. 12th Street
Apt. 25
New York, NY 10009

D

DENVER QUARTERLY

Donald Revell
University of Denver
Denver, CO 80210
(303) 871-2982

Poetry, fiction, reviews, criticism, essays, interviews.

For twenty years the **DENVER QUARTERLY** has been publishing work by distinguished as well as promising new writers. The magazine generally publishes material reflecting on modern culture as it has developed over the past century. It is recognized as the premiere literary publication of the Rocky Mountain region.

James Tate, Carl Dennis, Charles Baxter, Jorie Graham, Rachel Hadas.

Payment: $5/page for fiction essays, reviews; $5/page for poetry.

Copyright held by magazine.

1966; 4/yr; 900

$15/yr ind; $18/yr inst; $5/ea; 30%

160 pp; 6 x 9

Ad rates: $150/page/6 x 9; $75/½ page/6 x 4½

ISSN: 0011-8869

THE DIFFICULTIES

Tom Beckett

596 Marilyn Street

Kent, OH 44240

Criticism, poetry, reviews, interviews.

THE DIFFICULTIES is a journal devoted to new writing.

Typically an issue will focus on an individual—presenting recent examples of his or her work, interviews, critical essays by others and bibliographic materials. The next issue will be a focus on the work of Susan Howe. Inquire before submitting.

Ron Silliman, Charles Bernstein, David Bromige, Michael Davidson, Rae Armantrout.

Payment: in copies.

Reporting time: usually a week. Generally no later than a month.

Copyright held by magazine; reverts to author upon publication.

1980; irreg.; 500

$7/ea; 40%

110 pp; 8½ x 11

No ads

Segue Foundation, Small Press Distribution

DIMENSION

A. Leslie Willson

P.O. Box 26673

Austin, TX 78755

(512) 345-0622

Poetry, fiction, essays, plays, translation, interviews, graphics/artwork, German literature in the original and translation: post 1945.

DIMENSION concentrates on

established and non-established writers from all German-speaking countries, with original works with translations. Few essays.

Friedrich Dürrenmatt, Wolfgang Hildersheimer, Günter Grass, Günter Kunert, Peter Weiss.

Payment: modest, copies for translators.

Reporting time: varies.

Copyright held by magazine.

1968; 3/yr; 1,000

$20/yr ind; $24/yr inst; $10/ea; 20%

200 pp; 6 x 9

DOG RIVER REVIEW

Laurence F. Hawkins, Jr.
5976 Billings Road
Parkdale, OR 97041-0125
(503) 352-6494

Poetry, fiction, reviews, translation, interviews, graphics/artwork.

Poetry, fiction, reviews, satire and art. Experimental and traditional. Descriptive and emotional stressed over the purely intellectual. No pornography. Prefer shorter, to 30 lines, poems, and fiction to 3,000 words. Longer work considered. Black and white art only.

Gerald Locklin, Lyn Lifshin, Judson Crews, David Chorlton, Arthur Winfield Knight.

Payment: in copies.

Reporting time: 2–3 months.

Copyright reverts to author upon publication.

1982; 2/yr; 200

$6/yr; $3/ea; 40%

60 pp; 5½ x 8½

THE DRAMA REVIEW

Richard Schechner
MIT Press Journals
55 Hayward Street
Cambridge, MA 02142
(617) 253-2866

TDR is a quarterly journal of performance with a strong intercultural, intergeneric, and interdisciplinary focus. We consider everything from wrestling to ritual, from Peter Brook's Mahabharata to what is going on at "Downtown Beirut." TDR borrows from the fields of anthropology, performance theory, ethology, psychology, and politics. We combine scholarship and journalism in the form of essays, interviews, letters and editorials.

Payment: 2¢ per word.

Copyright held by MIT Press.

1955; 4/yr; 6,000

$25/yr ind; $55/yr inst; $7/ea

160 pp; 7 x 10
ISSN: 0012-5962

E

**EARTH'S DAUGHTERS: A
Feminist Arts Periodical**

Editors: Kastle Brill, Elizabeth
Conant, Camille Cox, Perrie
Hill, Bonnie Johnson, Joy
Walsh, Joyce Kessel, Robin
Willoughby, Ryki Zuckerman
Box 41
Central Park Station
Buffalo, NY 14215
(716) 837-7778

Poetry, fiction, plays, photographs, graphics/artwork.
EARTH'S DAUGHTERS is a
feminist literary and art periodical published in Buffalo, New
York. We believe ourselves to
be the oldest feminist arts periodical extant, having published
our first issue in February,
1971. Our focus is the experience and creative expression of
women.
Jimmie Canfield, Lyn Lifshin,
Marge Piercy, Kathryn Machan
Aal, Susan Fantl Spivack.
Payment: 2 copies.
Reporting time: 3 months.

Copyright held by magazine; reverts to author upon publication.
1971; 3/yr; 1,000
$12/yr ind; $20/yr inst; $4/ea;
30%
60 pp; 6 x 9
No ads
ISSN: 0163-0989
EBSCO, Faxon, Burroughs Subscription Agencies

**EARTHWISE REVIEW/
EARTHWISE
PUBLICATIONS**

Barbara Holley
P.O. Box 680536
Miami, FL 33168
(305) 653-2875

Poetry, fiction, criticism, essays,
reviews, translations, interviews, photos, artwork, short
stories.
EARTHWISE REVIEW is a bi-
monthly tabloid of poetry, fine
arts, focuses on poetry and environment. Accepts interviews,
critical essays, fiction, children's work and prison projects.
Sponsors four annual competi-
tions including the annual T. S.
Eliot Memorial Chapbook Competition.
The annual **EARTHWISE LIT-
ERARY CALENDAR** appears
for the tenth year and includes

poetry of over 200 poets, quotes and excerpts from longer poems. We feature an annual Artist and this year we have featured Hand Adolf Seeberg of West Germany (Hamburg).
Calendar sells for $8.95. Free copy to members of the Earth Chapter, FSPA, Inc. ($15 annual dues)
Richard Wilbur, Lola Haskins, Galway Kinnell, Jorge Valls, William Stafford.
Payment: $5 and up.
Copyright reverts to author upon publication.
1978; 6/yr; 400
$25/yr ind
60–80 pp; 5½ x 8½
Ad rates: $100/page/4 x 6; $50/½ page/4 x 4; $30/¼ page/2 x 3½
ISSN: 0190-1761

ECHOES

Carol Lambert, Susan McIntosh
Box 365
Wappingers Falls, NY 12590
(914) 471-0226

Poetry, fiction, essays, plays, graphics/artwork.
ECHOES was created by Carol Lamber and Barbara Mindel who believe Hudson Valley Writers Association should and could publish a literary magazine which would showcase unknown area writers. It was designed, therefore, to introduce readers to writers from the Hudson Valley and beyond, to present a balance of notable prose and poetry from those writers, and to invite writers to submit their essays, illustrations, prose and poetry to our quarterly. Its emphasis has now grown to reflect writers from the country at large and the pool of shared writing has grown tremendously in the last four years.
Jodi Sterling, Barbara Mindel, Ken Wibecan, Claire Michaels, David Stalzer.
Payment: one copy, upon publication.
Copyright held by Hudson Valley Writers Association; reverts to author upon publication.
1985; 4/yr; 150
$15/yr ind & inst; $4.50/ea; 40%
44 pp; 8½ x 11
No ads

EIGHTY-NÍNE CENTS, A Journal of Writing

Thomas Avena, Gary Szabo, Ellen Romano, Jennifer Wollin
P.O. Box 11837
San Francisco, CA 94101-7837
(415) 564-5291

Poetry, fiction, photographs, graphics/artwork.

An open-forum journal, **EIGHTY-NINE CENTS** seeks to publish a diverse collection of visions, both from established and emerging artists. We emphasize that we are a journal of writing and therefore don't actively seek visual art, although we would be interested in seeing any submissions. We try to balance the volume of poetry against that of fiction, and then to present varying approaches to literature.

William Dickey, Stephen Mitchell, Charlotte Painter, Carolyn Lau, Essex Hemphill.

Payment: none.

Copyright held by magazine; reverts to author conditionally.

1988; 3/yr; 500

$10/yr ind & inst; $3/ea ($.89 in S.F. Bay Area); 40%

28 pp; 8½ x 11

Ad rates: $400/page/8½ x 11; $200/½ page/ 8½ x 5½; $100/¼ page/4¼ x 5½

EMBERS

Katrina Van Tassel, Mark Johnston, Charlotte Garrett

Box 404

Guilford, CT 06437

(203) 453-2328

Poetry.

A poetry journal. Editors are poets, interested in poets' voices. New writers encouraged. Submit 3–5 poems.

Margaret Gibson, Marilyn Waniek, Walter MacDonald, Brendan Galvin, Sue Ellen Thompson.

Payment: 2 copies.

Reporting time: close to Oct. and Mar.

Copyright held by poets; reverts to author upon publication.

1979; 2/yr; 500

$11/yr; $6/ea; $3/sample

48 pp; 6 x 9

ISSN: 0731-0382

THE EMRYS JOURNAL

Linda Julian

P.O. Box 8813

Greenville, SC 29604

(803) 294-3151

Poetry, fiction, essays.

Our journal is interested in publishing the work of new writers, especially that of women and other minorities. We are interested in maintaining a high literary standard.

Maxine Kumin, Carole Oles, Linda Paston, Amy Clampitt, Pattiann Rogers.

Payment: in copies.

Reporting time: 6 weeks.

Copyright held by The Emrys
Foundation.
1984; 1/yr; 400
$5/ea; 40%
No ads

EPOCH

Michael Koch
251 Goldwin Smith Hall
Cornell University
Ithaca, NY 14853
(607) 255-3385

Poetry, fiction.

EPOCH is primarily a journal of
fiction and poetry and we publish work by a wide range of
writers, some established, some
just beginning their careers.

Harriet Doerr, Sherley Anne
Williams, Stuart DyBek, Ster-
ling Plumpp, Lee K. Abbott,
Cynthia Bond.

Payment: $5/magazine page
(prose); 50¢/line (poetry).

Reporting time: 2 months.

Copyright held by Cornell University; reverts to author upon publication.

1947; 3/yr; 1,000
$11/yr; $4/ea
80 pp; 6 x 9

Ad rates: $180/page/5 x 8;
$100/½ page/3 x 8

ISSN: 0145-1391

B. DeBoer

EVERYWHERE

Greg Booth, Mike Burbach
P.O. Box 5173
Grand Forks, ND 58206-5173
(701) 780-1130 or (701) 780-1242

Poetry, fiction, criticism, photographs, graphics/artwork,
essays.

Thomas McGrath, Jay Meek, Joel
Sartore, Bill Alkofer, Louis
Jenkins, Joan Hoffman.

$8/yr; $3 ea

EXQUISITE CORPSE

Andrei Codrescu
English Department
Louisiana State University
Baton Rouge, LA 70803

Poetry, criticism, essays, reviews,
translation, photographs, graph-
ics/artwork, polemics, letters,
reports from many countries.

A review of books and ideas. We
are a print cafe, hopeful that
vigorous dialogue on general
culture is still possible in Man-
darin U.S.A. We encourage
honesty, combativeness and
openness. We have published
wide-ranging polemics, as well
as essays on various matters of
literary interest. Our foreign
bureaus report on goings-on in
several European and Asian
cities. We also publish translations, and reprint important but

overlooked texts. Our contributors are both famous and unknown.

Lawrence Ferlinghetti, John Cage, James Laughlin, Janet Gray, Janet Hamill.

Payment: some payment to contributors.

Reporting time: 2 weeks.

Copyright held by authors.

1983; monthly; 3,500

$15/yr; $2.50/ea

20 pp; 6 x 15½

ISSN: 0740-7815

Inland Books

F

F MAGAZINE

John Schultz
1405 West Belle Plaine
Chicago, IL 60613
(312) 281-7642

Fiction, criticism, essays, reviews, translations, interviews, photos on quiry.

F MAGAZINE has the unique, contemporary purpose of being devoted to the publication of novels-in-progress that are part of a literary movement toward a synthesis of novelistic techniques, emphasizing story—

content, imagery, character, voice, style, a rich exploration of points of view, forms, dimensions of time, dramatic and self relationships. Award winning fiction.

Andrew Allegretti, Betty Shiflett, Beverlye Brown, Gary Johnson, Shawn Shiflett, John Schultz, Charles Johnson, Harry Mark Petrakis, Cyrus Colter, Paul Carter Harrison.

Payment: varies from $5.00 per page.

Reporting time: 4 months. No reading June 1 – Sept. 1.

Copyright held by magazine; reverts to author upon publication.

2/yr; 1,500

$6.95/ea; 40%

210 pp; 6 x 9

Ad rates available. Contact CLMP for information.

ISBN: 0-936959-00-2

Ingram, DeBoer

FAG RAG

John Wieners, Charles Shively, John Mitgel
Box 331
Kenmore Station
Boston, MA 02215
(617) 661-7534

Poetry, fiction, criticism, essays, reviews, plays, translation, in-

terviews, photographs, graphics/
artwork, gay autobiography.
Gay male journal in search of the
unrestrained aesthetic with emphasis on the striking and aston-
ishing. Prisoners, mental
patients, children, pedophiles
and other poets.
Payment: in copies.
Reporting time: 4–6 months.
Copyright held by magazine; reverts to author upon publication.
1971; 1–2/yr; 5,000
$10/yr ind; $20/yr inst; $5/ea;
40%
28–44 pp; quarterfold tabloid
ISSN: 0046-3167

FARMER'S MARKET

Jean C. Lee, John E. Hughes,
Lisa Ress
P.O. Box 1272
Galesburg, IL 61402
Poetry, fiction, essays, translation,
graphics.
A Midwestern magazine, publish-
ing quality literary work by
Midwestern authors and work
by others that is reflective of
Midwestern values and con-
sciousness.
Michael McMahon, David
Williams, Lloyd Zimpel, Mary
Maddox, Kathleen Peirce, Joe
Survant, Gloria Regalbuto.

Payment: 1 copy.
Reporting time: 4–8 weeks.
Copyright held by author.
1982; 2/yr; 500
$7/yr; $3.50/ea; 40%
78 pp; 5½ x 8½
No ads
ISSN: 0748-6022

THE FEDERAL POET

Frank Goodwyn
P.O. Box 65400
Washington Square Station
Washington, DC 20035

FELL SWOOP

X.J. Dailey
1521 N. Lopez St.
New Orleans, LA 70119
(504) 943-5198
Poetry, fiction, essay, drama, art,
photographs.
The All Bohemian Revue, FELL
SWOOP is a guerilla/gorilla
venture exploring the edge of
'acceptability' in contemporary
writing. We like a good laugh
at anyone's expense, especially
our own.
Richard Martin, Elizabeth
Thomas, Andrei Codrescu,
Normandi Ellis, Clara Talley-
Vincent, R. Speck.
Payment: in copies.
Reporting time: immediately.

Copyright reverts to author upon publication.

1983; 2–3/yr; 1,000
$6/yr; $3/ea
pp varies; 8½ x 11
ISSN: 1040-5607

FICTION INTERNATIONAL

Harold Jaffe, Larry McCaffery
Department of English
San Diego State University
San Diego, CA 92182
(619) 594-5443 or (619) 594-5469

Fiction, reviews, essays, visuals.

FICTION INTERNATIONAL's twin biases are toward postmodernism and progressive politics, either integrated or apart. We especially welcome writing from the "Third World" (both abroad and at home), and we favor writing that cuts through or fuses or ignores the canonical genres. Please note: we read manuscripts between 9/1–1/1 of each year.

Robert Coover, Claribel Alegria, Gerald Vizenor, Michel Serres, Marianne Hauser, Pierre Guyotat, Margaret Randall, Roque Dalton.

Payment: varies.
Reporting time: 1–3 months.
$14/yr ind; $24/yr inst; $8/ea; 40%

DeBoer, Blackwell North American, Faxon, Baker & Taylor

FICTION NETWORK MAGAZINE

Jay Schaefer
P.O. Box 5651
San Francisco, CA 94101
(415) 391-6610

Fiction.

Publishes short fiction by established and undiscovered writers.

Alice Adams, Ann Beattie, Ken Chowder, Lynne Sharon Schwartz, Ron Carlson.

Payment: $25 to $500 and up.
Reporting time: 12–14 weeks.
Copyright held by author.
1983; 2/yr; 6,000
$8/yr; $4/ea; 40%
48 pp; 8½ x 11
Ad rates: $400/page/7 x 10; $240/½ page/7 x 4⅝; $130/¼ page/3⁵⁄₁₆ x 4⅝
ISSN: 0741-6024
DeBoer

FIELD

Stuart Friebert and David Young
Rice Hall
Oberlin College
Oberlin, OH 44074
(216) 775-8408

Poetry, criticism, essays, reviews, translation.

We look for the best in contemporary poetry, poetics and translations and emphasize essays by poets themselves on the craft.
Sandra McPherson, Charles Wright, William Stafford, Jean Valentine, Charles Simic, Dennis Schmitz.
Payment: $20–30/page.
Reporting time: 2 weeks.
Copyright held by Oberlin College; reverts to author upon publication.
1969; 2/yr; 2,150
$10/yr; $16/2 yrs; $5/ea; 30–40%
100 pp; 5½ x 8½

FINE MADNESS

Sean Bentley, Louis Bersagel, John Marshall, Christine Deavel, John Malek
P.O. Box 15176
Seattle, WA 98115
Poetry, fiction, reviews.
We look for poetry that shows wit, imagination, love of language, technical skill and individual style.
Andrei Codrescu; Catherine Sasanov; Leslie Norris; Naomi Shihab Nye; Pattiann Rogers.
Payment: varies.
Reporting time: 3 months.
Copyright held by magazine; reverts to author upon publication.

1980 2/yr; 800
$9/yr; $5/ea
80 pp; 5½ x 8
ISSN: 0737-4704
Small Changes (Seattle); Ubiquity (New York); Homing Pigeon (Elgin, TX); Armadillo & Co. (Venice, CA); Don Olsen Dist. (Minneapolis).

FIVE FINGERS REVIEW

John High, Malcolm Garcia, Aleka Chase, Thoreau Lovell, Ruth Schwartz, Jason Beaubien
553 25th Avenue
San Francisco, CA 94121
(415) 661-8052
Poetry, fiction, essays.
We publish poetry, fiction and essays from a diversity of perspectives and aesthetics, ranging from traditional to experimental. We also welcome work that crosses/falls between genres. Our goal is to present a wide variety of writing that expresses the complexity of the world we live in, in fresh, surprising ways. Although much of our work focuses on social or political concerns, we seek quality writing on any subject.
Philip Levine, Fanny Howe, Molly Giles, Ron Silliman, Juan Felipe Herrera, Marilyn Chin, Denise Levertov.

Payment: in copies.
Reporting time: 3 months. (Query for current deadlines.)
Copyright held by magazine; reverts to author upon publication.
1984; 1–2/yr; 600–1,000
$12/ind; $13/inst; $7/ea; 40%
150 pp; 6 x 9
$150/page/4½ x 7½; $100/½ page/4½ x 3½ or 2 x 7½; $75/¼ page/2 x 3½
Small Press Distribution, Berkeley; L-S Distributors, San Francisco; Anton J. Mikofsky, New York

FLOATING ISLAND

Michael Sykes
P.O. Box 516
Point Reyes Station, CA 94956
(415) 663-1181

Poetry fiction, photography in folio formal, graphics/artwork.
Expansive, eclectic, very wide-ranging with center on West coast of North America— special interest in photography and graphic arts, lyric poetry and experimental prose. Volumes I-IV, First Series is now complete. Second Series to begin in 1992.
Diane di Prima, Gary Snyder, Michael McClure, Robert Bly, Christina Zawadiwsky, Frank Stewart, Lawrence Ferlinghetti, Joanne Kyger, Sam Hamill, Cole Swensen, Arthur Sze
Payment: in copies.
Reporting time: 4 weeks.
Copyright held by publisher; reverts to author upon publication.
1976; irreg; 2,000
All issues $15/ea; 40% 5 or more copies, 20% 1–4 copies
160 pp; 8½ x 11
ISSN: 0147-1686
Small Press Distribution, Bookpeople

THE FLORIDA REVIEW

Pat Rushin, Tom George
English Department
University of Central Florida
Orlando, FL 32816
(305) 275-2038

Poetry, fiction, essays, reviews.
We publish stories with heart that aren't afraid to take risks. Experimental fiction is welcome, so long as it doesn't make us feel stupid. We look for clear, strong poems filled with real things, real people, real emotions, poems that might conceivably advance our knowledge of the human heart.
Stephen Dixon, Jane Ruiter, Liz Rosenberg, Karen Fish, Michael Martone.

Payment: $5/printed page of fiction; $15/poem.
Reporting time: 6–8 weeks.
Copyright held by University of Central Florida; reverts to author upon publication.
1972; 2/yr; 1,000
$7/yr ind; $11/2yrs ind; $9/yr inst; $13/2 yrs inst; $4.50/ea; 40%
128 pp; 5½ x 8½
Ad rates: Exchange ads only
ISSN: 0742-2466

FOLIO

Department of Literature
American University
Washington, DC 20016
(202) 885-2973

Poetry, fiction, reviews, translations, interviews, black & white art & photography.
FOLIO prints quality fiction and poetry by established writers as well as those just starting out. We like to comment on submissions when time permits. Prose limit: 3,000 words. SASE required. Manuscripts read Aug.–April.
Henry Taylor, Simon Perchik, Kermit Moyer, Myra Sklarew, Linda McFerrin, Linda Paston, Anne Louise Kerr.
Payment: prizes of up to $75 awarded for best fiction and poem.

Copyright reverts to author upon publication.
1984; 2/yr; 400
$9/yr; $4.50/ea; 30%
70 pp; 6 x 10
The Bookstall, Common Concerns, Chapters, The Writers Center (Bethesda)

FOOTWORK: The Paterson Literary Review

Maria Mazziotti Gillan
Cultural Affairs Department
Passaic County Community College
College Boulevard
Paterson, NJ 07509
(201) 684-6555

Poetry, fiction, review, graphics/artwork.
FOOTWORK is a high quality literary quarterly.
Laura Boss, Ruth Stone, Sonia Sanchez, William Stafford, Marge Piercy.
Payment: in copies.
Copyright held by Passaic County College; reverts to author upon publication.
Reporting time: 3 months.
1979; 1/yr; 1,000
$5/yr ind; $6/yr inst; $5/ea; 40%
120 pp; 8½ x 11 perfect-bound
Ad rates: $200/page/8½ x 11; $100/½ page/8½ x 5; $50/¼ page/4 x 2½

FOR POETS ONLY

Lillian M. Walsh

P.O. Box 1382

Jackson Heights, NY 11372

(718) 424-7534

Poetry.

Little "little" publishes sincere, serious poet—any subject—no pornography.

J. Bernier, C. Weirich, A.M. Swaim, G. Labocetta, J. Schernitz.

Payment: in copies, plus prize money.

Copyright held by magazine; reverts to author upon publication.

1985; 4/yr; 150

$3/ea

30 pp; 5½ x 8

ISSN: 0087-0896

FORMATIONS

Jonathan Brent, Frances Padorr Brent

Northwestern University Press

625 Colfax St.

Evanston, IL 60201-2807

(708) 491-5313

Fiction, essays, plays, translation, interviews, photographs, graphics/artwork.

FORMATIONS publishes new American fiction in the context of both work being done in other media (painting, music theater) and work being done in foreign countries. Each issue therefore will contain a variety of essays, American fiction, and translations. The aim of the magazine is to become international in focus and to relate current American fiction to broader concerns of world culture.

Raymond Federman, Angela Carter, Milan Kundera, Primo Levi, Edna O'Brien.

Payment: fiction: $100–$500; essays: $100–$300.

Reporting time: 1–3 months.

Copyright held by magazine; reverts to author upon publication.

1984; 3/yr; 1,500

$16/yr ind; $32/yr inst; $6.95/ea; 40%

120 pp; 7 x 10

Ad rates: $200/page/5½ x 8½; $125/½ page/5½ x 4

ISSN: 0741-5702

DeBoer, Ingram

FOUR QUARTERS

John J. Keenan, Editor; John P. Ross, Associate Editor

La Salle Univ.

20th & Olney Avenues

Philadelphia, PA 19141

(215) 951-1610

Poetry, fiction, nonfiction, short dramatic pieces.

A magazine of contemporary culture aimed at college-educated readers. Publishes nonspecialized articles, essays, fiction, and poetry.
Seamus Heaney, Joyce Carol Oates, James Merrill, John Lukacs, John Hollander, J.D. McClatchy.
Payment: on contribution.
Reporting time: 6 weeks.
Copyright held by La Salle Univ.; assignable to author.
1951; 2/yr
$8/yr; $4 each; 40%
64 pp; 7 x 10
$100/full page
ISSN: 0015-9107
La Salle University

FRANK: An International Journal of Contemporary Writing and Art

David Applefield, Editor/Publisher
B.P. 29
94301 Vincennes Cedex
FRANCE
Poetry, fiction, translations, interviews, graphics/artwork, essays, photographs.
FRANK is a highly eclectic journal open to both established and emerging talent which emphasizes internationalism. The journal encourages both literary and visual work that takes risks but does not ignore the value of intellectual traditions.
Italo Calvino, James Tate, Allen Ginsberg, Paul Bowles, Robert Coover, Raymond Carver, Rita Dove, Stephen Dixon, Mavis Gallant.
Contemporary Chinese, Turkish, Nordic, Philippino and Pakistani writing.
Payment: $10/page plus two copies.
Copyright held by author.
1983; 2/yr; 3,000
$25/4 issues ind; $40/4 issues inst; $7/ea; 33%–40%
224 pp; 5½ x 8½
Ad rates: $500/page/5 x 8; $250/½ page/4½ x 3½; $150/¼ page/2½ x 3½
ISSN: 0738-9299

FREE FOCUS

Patricia D. Coscia
224 82nd Street
Brooklyn, NY 11209
(718) 680-3899
Women's Poetry.
FREE FOCUS is a small-press magazine which focuses on the educated women of today and needs stories and poems. The poems can be as long as 2 pages or as short as 3 lines. No X-rated material. Poems should

be single-spaced on individual sheets.
Mary Place, Larry Nicastro, Terry Naudzunas, Richard Murray.
Payment: 1 copy.
Reporting time: 6 months.
Copyright held by editor.
1985; 2/yr; 500
$4/yr; $2/ea
20 pp; 8 x 14
$1/column; $3/page
ISSN: 0447-5667
Thursday's Press

G

GALLERY WORKS
Peter Holland, Jeanne Lance
218 Appleton Dr.
Aptos, CA 95003
(408) 685-9518
Poetry, fiction, photographs, graphics/artwork, short experimental prose.
Solicits a wide range of styles of writing from around the U.S. (and occasionally Canada and England). The editors believe a literary magazine should raise the level of communication among writers and artists. Feminist and language writing.
David Bromige, Beverly Dahlen,
Rosmarie Waldrop, Patrick McGrath.
Payment: two free copies.
Copyright held by magazine; reverts to author upon publication.
1973; 1/2 yrs; 500
$30/ind. issues 1–7; $40/inst. issues 1–7; $5/ea; 40%
64 pp; 5 x 7

THE GALLEY SAIL REVIEW
Stanley McNail
1630 University Avenue, #42
Berkeley, CA 94703
(415) 486-0187
Poetry, reviews.
GSR seeks excellence in contemporary poetry, without regard for schools, cliques, or "movements." It values sincerity and honors craftsmanship. It tries to encourage poetry that speaks to the human condition in this modern world, and to develop a wider appreciation of poetry as an essential art in society.
Martin Robbins, Michael Culross, Laurel Ann Bogen, Harold Witt, Carol Hamilton.
Payment: in copies.
Copyright held by magazine; reverts to author upon publication.
1958; 3/yr; 400

$8/yr ind; $15/2 yr ind; $15/2 yr
  inst; $3/ea; 40%
40 pp; 8½ x 5½
ISSN: 0016-4100

GANDHABBA

Tom Savage
622 East 11th Street
New York, NY 10009
(212) 533-3893
Poetry, translation (of poetry),
  graphics/artwork.
Language, New York School,
  postmodern and emerging poetry. Each issue has a theme.
Allen Ginsberg, John Godfrey,
  Alan Davies, Norman MacAfee,
  Bernadette Mayer.
Payment: none.
Reporting time: 1 year.
Copyright held by magazine; reverts to author upon publication.
1983; 1/yr; 350
$12/ind for 3 issues; $15/inst for 3
  issues; $3.50/ea; 40%. Please
  make all checks payable to
  Thomas Savage.
100 pp; 8½ x 11
No ads

GARGOYLE

Toby Barlow
5825 Colby
Oakland, CA 94618
(415) 655-3949
Fiction, interviews, poetry, reviews, essays, photographs,
  graphics/artwork
As **GARGOYLE** heads into its
  14th year and we all enter the
  fin-de-siècle I find myself thinking this is a time for manifes-
  tos. We at **GARGOYLE** find
  the lyrics of Morrissey, David
  Sylvian and Brian Eno superior
  to most of the poetry published
  today, and the *Love and Rockets*
  comix of Los Bros Hernandez
  more relevant and captivating
  than most contemporary fiction.
Edouard Roditi, Robert Peters,
  Rita Dove, Charles Bukowski,
  Kathy Acker.
Payment: 1 copy; 50% off addi-
  tional copies.
Reporting time: 1 month; closed
  August.
Copyright held by Toby Barlow;
  reverts to authors upon publication.
1976; 2/yr; 2,000
$15/yr ind; $20/yr inst; single
  copy price varies; 40%
Average 300 pp; format varies.
Ad rates: $100 full/$150 inside
  covers/$200 back cover
ISSN: 0162-1149
Bookslinger, Flatland Distribution,
  SPD, Writers & Books

THE GEORGIA REVIEW

Stanley W. Lindberg
University of Georgia
Athens, GA 30602
(404) 542-3481

Poetry, fiction, essays, reviews, graphics/artwork.

An international journal of arts and letters with a special interest in current American literary writing; seeking interdisciplinary thesis-oriented essays—not scholarly articles—and engaging book reviews, plus the best in contemporary poetry and fiction; authors range from Nobel laureates and Pulitzer Prize winners to the as-yet unknown and previously unpublished.

Rita Dove, T.R. Hummer, Eudora Welty, Fred Chappell, Seamus Heaney, Mary Hood, Louise Erdrich.

Payment; $2/line for poetry; $25/printed page for prose.

Reporting time: 8–12 weeks.

Copyright held by University of Georgia; reverts to author upon publication.

1947; 4/yr; 5,500

$12/yr; $5/ea

224 pp; 6¾ x 7½

Ad rates: $250/page/4¾ x 7½; $150/½ page/4¾ x 3⅝

ISSN: 0016-8386

Bernhard DeBoer

THE GETTYSBURG REVIEW

Peter Stitt
Gettysburg College
Gettysburg, PA 17325
(717) 337-6770

Poetry, fiction, essays, graphics/artwork.

THE GETTYSBURG REVIEW is an interdisciplinary magazine of arts and ideas, which features the highest quality poetry, fiction, essays, essay-reviews, and graphics by both beginning and established writers and artists. Two special interests are the publication of serial fiction and the inclusion of a full-color graphics section in each issue. Essays are in a variety of disciplines, with a wide range of subject matter.

Frederick Busch, Paul West, Joyce Carol Oates, Ed Minus, Linda Pastan, Rita Dove, Charles Wright, Deborah Larsen, Donald Hall, Mary Hood.

Payment: $20/page prose; $2/line poetry; upon publication.

Copyright held by Gettysburg College; reverts to author upon publication.

1988; 4/yr; 2,000

$12/yr ind; $12/yr inst; $4/ea; 40%

184 pp; 6 x 10

Ad rates: $150/page/5 x 7½;
   $225/inside cover
ISSN: 0898-4557

GIANTS PLAY WELL IN THE DRIZZLE

Martha King
326-A 4th Street
Brooklyn, NY 11215
(212) 639-3631
Poetry, fiction, essays, reviews,
   graphics/artwork.
With a tip of my hat to *Migrant*
   and *Floating Bear*, I try to keep
   the **DRIZZLE** small, free, an
   delicate. I publish—side-by-
   side—works by writers of
   sometimes vastly different aesthetics. It's the energy I look
   for and hope to share with readers. Very small format. Please
   ask for a sample copy before
   submitting.
August Kleinzahler, Paul Green,
   Kim Lyons, Todd Baron, David
   Rattray, Connie Deanovich.
Payment: none.
Copyright held by **GPWITD**; reverts to author upon publication.
1984; 4/yr; 450
No ads

GIORNO POETRY SYSTEMS

John Giorno
222 Bowery
New York, NY 10012
(212) 925-6372
Poetry.
Magazine in three formats: LP
   record, Compact Disc, and Cassette. Video Pak series is a
   magazine in video format.
Laurie Anderson, William Burroughs, Patti Smith, Diamanda
   Galas, Nick Cave.
Payment: $400 royalty advance,
   and 12% of the retail price of
   each record sold.
1972; 4/yr; 10,000
$8.98/single album; $12.98/double
   album; $8.98/casette; $13.98/
   compact disc CD; $39.95 video
   cassette; 40%, 55% to distributors

GRAB-A-NICKEL

Barbara Smith
Alderson-Broaddus College
Philippi, WV 26416
(304) 457-1700
Poetry, fiction, reviews, photographs, graphics/artwork.
GRAB-A-NICKEL is a tabloid
   journal of poems, fiction, book
   reviews, photographs and drawings. Open submissions; priority
   given to Appalachian writers
   and subject matter. There is
   encouragement of new writers
   of any age or background. It is

a product of a college commu-
nity's writers' workshop.
Barbara Smith, Dawn Norman,
Mark Rowh, T. Kilgore Splake,
Llewellyn McKernan, Jim
Wayne Miller.
Payment: in copies.
Copyright held by author.
1977; 2–3/yr; 1,000
25¢/ea
16 pp; 11½ x 14

GRADIVA

Luigi Fontanella
P.O. Box 831
Stony Brook, NY 11794-3359
(516) 632-7448 or (516) 632-7440
Poetry, essays, reviews, translation, interviews.
GRADIVA is an international
journal of modern Italian literature that focuses on literary criticism and theory. All
contributions are published in
English or Italian. Creative
works written in other
languages are published with
translation.
Umberto Eco, Edoardo Sangui-
neti, Philipe Souppault, Jan
Kott, Andrea Zanzotto.
Payment: in issues, subscription.
Copyright held by Gradiva; reverts
to author upon publication.
1986; 2/yr; 2,500
$20/yr ind; $20/yr inst

100 pp; 5½ x 8½
Ad rates: $100/page/5½ x 8½;
$60/½ page/5½ x 4¼; $35/¼
page/2¾ x 4¼
Distribution: Gradiva

GRAHAM HOUSE REVIEW

Peter Balakian, Bruce Smith
Box 500
Colgate University
Hamilton, NY 13346
(315) 824-100, ext. 262
Poetry, essays, translation, interviews.
We publish the best poetry and
poetry in translation we can get.
We have just begun an interview series and will publish
essays in the future. We pay
scrupulous attention to production, and have an international
interest in selecting material.
Seamus Heaney, Derek Walcott,
Madeline DeFrees, David Wagoner, Maxine Kumin, Carolyn
Forché.
Payment: in copies.
Reporting time: 1–2 months.
Copyright held by magazine; reverts to author upon publication.
1976; 1/yr; 1,750
$7.50/yr ind; $7.50/inst; $7.50/ea;
20%
125 pp; 8½ x 5½

GRAND STREET

Jean Stein

135 Central Park West

New York, NY 10023

(212) 721-3325

Poetry, fiction, criticism, essays, reviews.

Alice Munro, William Trevor, Alice Adams, Alexander Cockburn, James Merrill.

Payment: inquire.

Reporting time: 4–6 weeks.

Copyright held by magazine; reverts to author upon publication.

1981; 4/yr; 4,000

$24/yr ind; $28/yr inst; $28/yr foreign; $6/ea

240 pp; 6 x 9

Ad rates: $250/page

ISSN: 0734-5496

DeBoer.

GREAT RIVER REVIEW

Orval Lund

211 West Wabasha

Winona, MN 55987

(507) 454-6564

Poetry, fiction, criticism, reviews, graphics.

Dedicated to publishing the best in fiction, creative prose, and poetry, and to showcasing the work of new, emerging and established writers. Specially interested in Midwestern writers.

Jack Myers, Lucille Clifton, Tom McGrath.

Payment: in copies.

Reporting time: 1–3 months.

Copyright reverts to author.

1977; 2/yr; 1,200

$9/yr; $4.50/ea

280 pp; 6 x 8

Ad rates: $100/page; $50/½ page; $25/¼ page

EBSCO Subscription Services, Faxon Services, Aquinas Subscription Services

GREAT STREAM REVIEW

Diane Z. Himes, Rick Sutliff

Lycoming College

Box 66

Williamsport, PA 17701

(717) 321-4114

Poetry, fiction, familiar essays, novel excerpts, screen and stage plays, reviews, interviews.

GSR provides a forum for writers engaged in evaluating, confronting and offering alternatives to literary modernism and postmodernism; writers who find the source of their imagination in other than despair, disease and alienation.

Will Baker, Scott Cairns, Pam Houston, Deborah Monroe, Janet Sylvester, Lee Upton.

Payment: $10/page.

Reporting time: 4 weeks.

Copyright held by GSR.
1989; 2/yr; 1,000
$7.50/yr; $4/ea; 40%
100 pp; 6 x 9
ISSN: 1042-8208

GREEN MOUNTAINS REVIEW

Neil Shepard, Poetry; Tony Whedon, Fiction
Johnson State College
Johnson, VT 05656
(802) 635-2356

Poetry, fiction, essays, reviews, interviews, translations, photographs.

GMR publishes work by promising newcomers and well-known writers from across the country. In addition, each issue features the work of one regional writer—either a suite of poems, extended work of fiction, interview or literary essay.

Galway Kinnell, Denise Levertov, Larry Levis, David St. John, Ellen Lesser, David Wojahn.
Payment: in copies.
Reporting time: 1–3 months.
Copyright held by GMR; reverts to author upon publication.
1987; 2/yr; 1,000
$8.50/yr; $4.50/ea; 40%
120+ pp; 6 x 9
$150/page; $75/½ page

ISSN: 0895-9307
Ubiquity

THE GREENSBORO REVIEW

Jim Clark
Department of English
Univ. North Carolina-Greensboro
Greensboro, NC 27412
(919) 334-5459

Poetry, fiction.
Contemporary and experimental. We want to see the best being written regardless of theme, subject or style.

Robert Morgan, Kelly Cherry, Larry Brown, Madison Smartt Bell, Ellen Herman.
Payment: in copies.
Reporting time: 2–4 months.
Copyright held by TGR; reverts to author.
1966; 2/yr; 5–600
$5/yr; $12/3 yrs; $2.50/ea
120 pp; 6 x 9
ISSN: 0017-4084

GULF COAST

Gary McKay, Lisa Lewis, Roger Mullins
Department of English
University of Houston
4800 Calhoun Rd.
Houston, TX 77204-5641
(713) 749-3640

Poetry, fiction, essays, translation, photographs, graphics/artwork.

GULF COAST encourages submission of high-quality, well-crafted and energetic poetry and fiction, with emphasis on subject matter. Contributors may be students in the University of Houston creative writing program, but submission is open to others.

Lisa Zeidner, Charles Baxter, Rosellen Brown, Amy Clampitt, Richard Howard, Rich Bass, Rodney Jones.

Payment: copies.

Copyright held by **GULF COAST**; reverts to author upon publication.

1981; 2/yr; 500+

$8/yr ind; $6/yr inst; $4/ea; 40%

96 pp; 9 x 6

No ads

ISSN: 0896-2251

GULF STREAM MAGAZINE

Lynne Barrett, Editor; Pamel Gross, Assoc. Editor

FIU, North Miami Campus

North Miami, FL 33181

(305) 940-5599

Poetry, fiction, essays.

GSM publishes high quality fiction, poetry and essays. We are open to experimental and mainstream work. No more than 5 poems. Limit prose to 25 pages.

Gerald Costanzo, Ann Hood, Judith Berke.

Payment: in copies.

Reporting time: 2 weeks–2 months.

Copyright held by Gulf Stream—1st North American.

1989; 2/yr; 200

$7.50; $4/ea; 40%

96 pp; 8½ x 5½

H

HAIGHT ASHBURY LITERARY JOURNAL

Joanne Hotchkiss, Alice Rogoff, Will Walker

P.O. Box 15133

San Francisco, CA 94115

(415) 221-2017

The magazine began with six editors of extremely diverse backgrounds. The magazine encompasses diversity of viewpoint, racial, sexual as well as style, tending to confront the difficult and painful of human experiences as well as the higher reaches of emotional experiences.

Eugene Rugghes, Mona Lisa Saloy, Peter Plate, Jack Hierschman, Panco Aquilla.

Payment: in copies.
Reporting time: 2–4 months.
Copyright held by author.
+1980; 1½/yr; 1,600
$25/lifetime subs; $1/ea; 50%
16 pp; 11 x 17¼
Ad rates: $150/page/10 x 17;
$75/½ page/7½ x 9; $50/¼
page/9 x 5

HAMBONE

Nathaniel Mackey
132 Clinton Street
Santa Cruz, CA 95062
(408) 426-3072

Poetry, fiction, criticism, reviews,
plays, translation, interviews,
photographs, graphics/artwork.
Cross-cultural work emphasizing
the centrifugal.
Edward Kamau Brathwaite, Beverly Dahlen, Kenneth Irby,
Leslie Scalapino, Jay Wright.
Payment: copies.
Reporting time: 1–4 months.
Copyright held by magazine; reverts to author upon publication.
1974; 1/yr; 600
$10/2 issues ind; $14/2 issues inst;
$6/ea; 40%
170 pp; 5½ x 8½
ISSN: 0733-6616
Inland Book Company, Small
Press Distribution

THE HAMPDEN-SYDNEY POETRY REVIEW

Tom O'Grady
P.O. Box 126
Hampden-Sydney, VA 23943
(804) 223-8209

Poetry.
A small, carefully-printed correspondence among poets which
attempts to print the unknown
with the known.
David Ignatow, Robert Pack, Patricia Goedicke, David Huddle,
Lewis Turco.
Payment: in copies.
Copyright held by Tom O'Grady;
reverts to author upon publication.
1975; 2/yr; 500
$5/yr ind; $5/yr, $12/3-yr inst;
$5/ea; 40%
60 pp; 5 x 9
No ads

HANGING LOOSE

Robert Hershon, Dick Lourie,
Mark Pawlak, Ron Schreiber
231 Wyckoff Street
Brooklyn, NY 11217
(718) 643-9559

Poetry, fiction, translation, graph-
ics/artwork.
Our interests continue to center on
finding new writers and then
staying with them, often to the

point of book publication.
(Book mss by invitation only.)
Paul Violi, Kimiko Hahn, Steven
Schrader, Chuck Wachtel,
Cathy Cockrell.
Payment: some payment to con-
tributors.
Reporting time: 2–3 months.
Copyright held by magazine; re-
verts to author upon publica-
tion.
1966; 3/yr; 1,500
$9/yr ind; $10.50/yr inst;
$3.50/ea; 20%–40%
80–96 pp; 7 x 8½
ISSN: 0440-2316
Small Press Distribution (Books &
Magazine), Bookslinger, Inland
Book Co. (Books Only)

**HANSON'S: A Magazine of
Literary & Social Interest**
Eric Hanson, Shannon Rogowski
113 Merryman Court
Annapolis, MD 21401
(301) 626-1643
Poetry, fiction, essays, humor,
interviews, dialogues, and various features.
A magazine of general interest,
we are striving to combine the
traditionally separate aspects of
literary and social journals into
one magazine. On the literary
side we tend toward examina-

tions of existence, rather than
ruminations on politics.
Ray Bradbury, Dan Oldenburg,
Mary Ellen Hughes, Dawn
Miller, George Kempis, Edward
Lee.
Payment: $30–$100, plus one
copy.
Reporting time: 6 weeks.
Copyright held by C.C. Unltd.
Publishing; reverts to author.
1988; 4/yr; 3,000
$8/yr; $2/ea; 40%
80 pp; 8½ x 11
$200/page; $100/½ page; $50/¼
page
ISSN: 0251-4316
C.C. Unlimited Publishing

HAPPINESS HOLDING TANK
Albert Drake
1790 Grand River
Okemos, MI 48864
(517) 349-0552
Poetry, very short fiction, essays,
reviews, interviews, etc. . . .
HHT is an eclectic magazine, and
publishes a wide variety of
poetry—free verse, forms, narrative, lyric, found poetry,
visual poetry, etc. . . .
Emphasis is on the well-made
poem that expresses a sense of
humanity.
Earle Birney, Vern Rutsala,
William Stafford, William Mat-

thews, Judith Goren, Lee Upton.
Payment: in copies.
Reporting time: 2 weeks–2 months.
Copyright held by author.
1970; 1/yr; 300
No subs; $2/ea
pages and size varies
Have never had paid ads.

HAWAII REVIEW

Elizabeth Lovell, Editor-in-Chief
UH Manoa
Department of English
1733 Donaghho Road
Honolulu, HI 96822
(808) 948-8548

Poetry, fiction, criticism, essays, reviews, plays, translations, interviews, photographs, graphics/artwork.
Ursule Molinaro, Ian MacMillan, Nell Altizer, John Unterecker, Michael McPherson, William Pitt Root, Frank Stewart.
Payment: $10–75, plus 2 copies; more for cover art.
Reporting time: 30–90 days.
Copyright held by magazine; reverts to author upon request.
1973; 3/yr; 2,000
$12/yr; $20/2 yrs; $5/ea
100–150 pp; 5½ x 9
Ad rates: $75/page
ISSN: 0093-9625

Chaminade University, Hawaii State Library Systems, Northwestern University, Columbia University

HAYDEN'S FERRY REVIEW

Salima Keegan
Matthews Center
Arizona State University
Tempe, AZ 85287-1502
(602) 965-7572

Poetry, fiction, interviews, photography, artwork.
HAYDEN'S FERRY REVIEW is Arizona State University's national literary magazine featuring the best solicited and unsolicited works of well known and new writers.
Bob Shacochis, Frank Stewart, Ron Carlson, Rita Dove.
Interviews with Joseph Heller, John Updike, T.C. Boyle, Richard Ford.
Published bi-annually. Reporting time 6–8 weeks.
Payment: in copies.
Copyright held by the magazine; reverts to author upon publication.
1986; 1/yr; 1,000
1988; 2/yr; 750
$4/1986; $5/1987; $5/1988
125 pp; 6 x 9
ISSN: 0887-5170

HELICON NINE: The Journal of Women's Arts and Letters

Gloria Vando Hickok
P.O. Box 22412
Kansas City, MO 64113
(913) 345-0802

With Issue #20, in the fall of 1989, **HELICON NINE** concluded its publication. The editor will be embarking on a venture called **THE READER**, which will be an Anthology of previously published works from **HELICON NINE**.

HELICON NINE provided a literary forum for women past and present in literature, music, visual and performing arts. **THE READER** will reiterate highpoints from **HELICON NINE'S** ten year history. Contact Gloria Vando Hickok for details.

HERESIES: A Feminist Publication on Art and Politics

Heresies Collective, Inc.
P.O. Box 1306
Canal Street Station
New York, NY 10013
(212) 227-2108

Essays, experimental writing, short fiction, interviews, poetry; page art, photography, graphic art, all visual arts.

HERESIES is the longest-lived feminist art journal still publishing. Thematic, political focus. "We believe that what is commonly called art can have a political impact and that in the making of art and all cultural artifacts our identities as women play a distinct role . . . A place where diversity can be articulated."

Payment: $10.
Reporting time: 4–12 weeks.
Copyright reverts to author upon publication.
1977; 2/yr; 8,000
Four issues - $23/ind; $33/inst; $6.75/ea
96 pp; 8½ x 11
Ad rates: $250/½ page; $125/¼ page
Bookpeople, Inland, Small Changes, Homing Pigeon

HIGH PLAINS LITERARY REVIEW

Robert O. Greer, Jr.
180 Adams Street, Suite 250
Denver, CO 80206
(303) 320-6827

Fiction, essays, poetry, reviews, criticism, interviews.

Designed to "bridge the gap between commercial magazines and an outstanding array of academic quarterlies." A handsomely produced literary magazine that is intended to be more broadly based than academia without being commercially "targeted." A journal designed to display the "absolute best of craft." O. Henry award winning fiction appeared in Vol. 1, No. 1.

Richard Currey, Ron Carlson, Marilyn Krysl, Michael J. Rosen, Julia Alvarez, Rita Dove.

Payment: $5 per page for prose; $10 per page for poetry.

Reporting time: 8 weeks.

Copyright held by High Plains Literary Review; reverts to author upon publicaton.

1986; 3/yr; 900

$20/yr; $7/ea; 40%

135 pp; 6 x 9

Ad rates: $100/page; $50/½ page; $25/¼ page

ISSN: 0888-4153

Total Circulation Services Ubiquity Distrib. Inc.

HIRAM POETRY REVIEW

Hale Chatfield and Carol Donley

Box 162

Hiram, OH 44234

(216) 569-3211

Poetry, criticism, essays, reviews, interviews. Photographs, graphics, and artwork by invitation only.

Reporting time: 8–12 weeks.

Copyright reverts to author upon publication.

1967; 2/yr; 500

$2/ea; 40%–60%

40 pp; 6 x 9

ISSN: 0018-2036

HOBO JUNGLE

Marc Edrich & Ruth Boerger

33 Rucum Rd.

Roxbury, CT 06783

(203) 354-4359

Poetry, fiction, essays, serialized novels; also drawings and music scores.

HOBO JUNGLE seeks poetry, fiction, essays, musical scores and line art. There are no limits on length or subject matter. Simultaneous submissions are acceptable. Manuscripts should be typed.

Payment: $10 and 2 copies.

Reporting time: 8–12 weeks.

Copyright reverts to author upon publication.

1987; 4/yr; 11,000

$12/yr; free at dist. outlets; $3 by mail

64 pp; 8 x 10½

$61/⅛ page; $115/¼ page

ISSN: 1045-2591

Query for lists

THE HOLLINS CRITIC

John Rees Moore
P.O. Box 9538
Hollins College, VA 24020
(703) 362-6317 or 362-8268
Poetry, critical essays, reviews, graphics/artwork.
A non-specialist periodical concentrating on the work of a single contemporary poet, fiction writer or dramatist in each issue. Cover picture, essay of about 5,000 words, brief account of author, check-list of publications, several poems and a section of brief book reviews.
Jean Nordhaus, Carole Simmons Oles, John Whalen, Ramona Weeks, Michael J. Bugeja.
Payment: essays/$200 by permission of editor only; $25/poems.
Copyright held by magazine.
1964; 5/yr; 850
$6/yr; $2/ea
20 pp; 7 x 10
ISSN: 0018-3644

HOME PLANET NEWS

Donald Lev and Enid Dame, Editors
P.O. Box 415
Stuyvesant Station
New York, NY 10009
(718) 769-2854
Poetry, fiction, criticism, reviews, translation, interviews, photographs, news.
We publish poetry, reviews of books, bookstores and poetry readings, news of the literary scene, interviews and fiction. We also have a column which deals with experimental theater, and a "cross-cultural" feature, which includes poetry in translation from such diverse peoples as the Sicilians and the Macedonians.
Judith Malina, Hayden Carruth, Leo Connellan, Cornelius Eady, Norman Rosten, Karen Alvalay, Steve Kowit, William Packard.
Payment: in copies and subscription.
Reporting time: 2–3 months.
Copyright held by magazine; reverts to author upon publication.
1979; 3–4/yr; 1,000
$8/yr ind; $8/yr inst, $15/2 yrs; $2/ea; 40%
24 pp; 10 x 15
Ad rates: $150/page/10 x 15; $75/½ page/10 x 7½; $37.50/¼ page/5 x 7½

HORNS OF PLENTY: Malcolm Cowley and his Generation

William Butts and Yoland Butts
2041 West Farragut Ave.

Chicago, IL 60625
(312) 728-4671
Poetry, criticism, essays, inter-
views, reviews, graphics/art-
work, photographs, memoirs.
Focuses on the work and influence
of poet/critic/literary historian
Malcolm Cowley (1898–1989)
and his contemporaries who
came of age in the 1920's. Also
special issues devoted to se-
lected writers such as Kenneth
Burke, Lewis Mumford and
Kay Boyle.
Gay Wilson Allen, Robert B.
Heilman, Helga Sandburg,
Philip L. Gerber, and Bernard
Bergonzi.
Payment: in copies.
Reporting time: 6 weeks.
Copyright reverts to author upon
publication.
1988; 4/yr; 200
$15/ind; $20/inst; $4/ea; 15%
60 pp; 5½ x 8½
No advertising
ISSN: 0896-9965
Faxon, Faxon Europe, Boley In-
ternational

HOW(ever)
Myung Mi Kim
Meredith Stricker
1171 E. Jefferson
Iowa City, IA 52245
(319) 351-6361

Poetry, reviews.
HOW(ever) hopes to create a
place in which women poets
can talk to scholars through poems and working notes on these
poems, as well as through commentary on neglected women
poets who were/are making tex-
tures and structures of poetry in
the tentative region of the un-
tried.
Barbara Guest, Daphne Marlatt,
Maureen Owen, Gail Sher, Lisa
Pater Faranda.
Payment: none.
Copyright reverts to author.
1983; 4/yr; 400
$10/4 issues ind; $12/4 issues inst
16 pp; 8½ x 11

HOWLING DOG
Mark Donovan
8419 Rhode
Utica, MI 48087
(313) 254-5334

Poetry, fiction, graphics/artwork.
Our purpose is to have an effect
similar to the howl of a dog
with its foot caught in a fence.
We desire something that may
not be pleasant or permanent,
but will still be heard by every-
one in the neighborhood.
Arthur Knight, Alan Catlin, John
Sinclair, Keith Wilson, Jay
Dougherty.

Payment: in copies.
Reporting time: 6 months or more.
Copyright held by authors.
1985; 2/yr; 500
$10/yr; $5/ea; 40%
64 pp; 6 x 9
Ad rates: $80/page/4 x 8; $40/½
page/4 x 4; $20/¼ page/2 x 4
ISSN: 0888-3521

THE HUDSON REVIEW
Paula Deitz, Frederick Morgan
684 Park Avenue
New York, NY 10021
(212) 650-0020
Poetry, fiction, criticism, essays, reviews.
We publish both new and established writers. We have no university affiliation, and we are not committed to any narrow academic aim or to any particular political perspective. We focus on the area where literature and poetry bear on the intellectual life of the time.
Payment: 2½¢/word for prose; 50¢/line for poetry.
Reporting time: 1–3 months.
Copyright held only on assigned reviews.
1948; 4/yr; 3,000
$20/yr; $6/ea
160 pp; 6 x 9¼
Ad rates: $300/page/4½ x 7½;

$200/½ page/4½ x 3⅝; $150/¼ page/2⅛ x 3⅝
ISSN: 0018-702X
Eastern News Distributors

HUNGRY MIND REVIEW
Bart Schneider, Editor
1648 Grand Avenue
St. Paul, MN 55105
(612) 699-2610
Essays, reviews, interviews, photographs and woodcuts.
HUNGRY MIND REVIEW publishes book reviews, essays, and forums on particular focuses. HUNGRY MIND REVIEW reviews large, small, and university presses, focusing on mid- and backlist titles.
Clark Blaise, Robert Bly, Rosellen Brown, Doris Grumbach, Lewis Hyde, W.P. Kinsella, Herbert Kohl, Phillip Lopate, William Stafford. Interviews with Noam Chomsky and Art Spiegelman.
Payment: varies.
Copyright held by David Unowsky, dba HUNGRY MIND REVIEW.
1986; 4/yr; 30,000
$7/yr ind; $10/yr Canada and inst; free/ea
48 pp; 9¾ x 15
Ad rates: $995/page; $550/½ page; $300/¼ page; $180/⅛ page; $110/¹⁄₁₆ page

ISSN: 0887-5499
We distribute to 300 independent
bookstores across the U.S. and
Canada.

HURRICANE ALICE: A Feminist Quarterly

Martha Roth
207 Church Street, S.E.
Minneapolis, MN 55408
(612) 625-1834
Reviews, essays, criticism, fiction, poetry, graphics/artwork.
HURRICANE ALICE provides a feminist review of culture. It prints reviews of books by and about women, critical essays having a feminist perspective—especially essays on literature, film, dance, and the visual arts—fiction, some poetry and graphics.
Alice Walker, Toni McNaron, Peter Erickson, Meridel Le Sueur, Susan Griffin.
Payment: in copies.
Reporting time: 1–3 months.
Copyright reverts to author upon publication.
1983; 4/yr; 700
$10/yr; $8/yr students/seniors; $2.50/ea
14 pp; 11 x 17
Ad rates: $45/3 x 4; $20/3 x 2; $75/⅙ page

Ubiquity, L-S Distributor, Don Olson Distributors

I

ICE RIVER

David Memmott, Managing Editor
953 N. Gale
Union, OR 97883
(503) 562-5638
Poetry, fiction, reviews, essays, interviews.
IR is a magazine of speculative writing, fantastic art and contemporary music. Focus is on surrealism, literary SF, literature of the fantastic, dark fantasy, magic realism, futurism, experimental. Artwork with an element of the fantastic. Electronic music reviews.
Lance Olsen, Louis Phillips, Richard Kostelanetz, Andrew Joron, Ivan Arguelles, Edward Mycue.
Payment: copies, $5 poem, $15 short story.
Reporting time: 8–10 weeks.
Copyright reverts to author.
1987; 3/yr; 300–500
$9; $4/ea; 40%
60 pp; 6½ x 8
Ad rates: $25/page; $17/½ page; $12.50/¼ page
ISSN: 1043-7010

IKON

Susan Sherman
P.O. Box 1355
Stuyvesant Station
New York, NY 10009
Poetry, fiction, essays, translation, interviews, photographs, graphics/artwork.

IKON is a cultural, political, feminist magazine, showing the experiences of third world, lesbian, Jewish and working women, all women in the diversity of our experience. IKON is about making connections through the words and images of women themselves in their essays, articles, paintings, photographs, fiction, art, songs and poems.

Audre Lourde, Kimiko Hahn, Beth Brant, Grace Paley, Adrienne Rich.
Payment: $15 and two copies.
Reporting time: 90 days.
Copyright held by magazine; reverts to author upon publication.
1982; 2/yr; 1,750
$10/yr ind; $15/yr inst; $6/ea; 40%
140 pp; 7 x 9

ILLINOIS WRITERS REVIEW

Kevin Stein, Jim Elledge
P.O. Box 1087
Champaign, IL 61820
(217) 424-6267
Essays, reviews.
We publish reviews by and about Illinois writers, particularly those published by small presses. In addition we seek reviews about publications of national import and offer our readers essays of interest to fiction writers and poets.
Payment: $25–35.
Reporting time: 1 month.
Copyright held by author.
1981; 2/yr; 500
$15/yr ind; $20/yr inst; 40%
24 pp; 5 x 8
Ad rates: $100/page/4½ x 7; $50/½ page/4½ x 4
ISSN: 0733-9526
Illinois Literary Publishers' Association

IMAGES

Gary Pacernick, Dorothea Pacernick
Wright State University
English Department
Dayton, OH 45435
(513) 873-2443
Poetry, photographs.
An inexpensive tabloid in an attractive format specializing in the best poems and photos the editor can find.
Marge Piercy, Roy Bentley, Wal-

ter McDonald, Imogene Bolls, Chris Bursk.
Payment: none.
Reporting time: 1 month.
Copyright held by editors; reverts to author upon publication.
1974; 3/yr; 1,000
$3/yr; $1/ea
12 pp; 11½ x 15
No ads

Copyright held by magazine; reverts to author upon publication.
1976; 3/yr; 1,200
$12/yr ind; $15/yr inst; $5/ea
120 pp; 6 x 9
Ad rates: $100/page/6 x 9; $60/½ page/6 x 4½
ISSN: 0738-386X
Ingram Periodicals

INDIANA REVIEW
Jon Tribble, Renée Manfred
316 North Jordan Avenue
Bloomington, IN 47405
(812) 855-3439
Fiction, poetry, essays.
We have no prejudices of style or content, but will publish only those poems and short stories which demonstrate: 1) keen sense of craft; 2) insight into the human condition. Writers should send their best work only. We prefer stories of rich texture to those that depend on a gimmick.
Naomi Shihab Nye, Robert Lacy, Andrew Hudgins, Antonya Nelson, Christopher Gilbert, Charles Johnson, Eleanor Wilner.
Payment: $5 per page poetry; $25 per story.
Reporting time: 3 weeks–3 months.

INK
Debora Ott
111 Elmwood Avenue
Buffalo, NY 14201
(716) 885-6400
Poetry, fiction, translation, photographs, graphics/artwork.
INK is a focus for new writing, primarily in English, though the sources are literally worldwide.
Robert Creeley, Tom Pickard, Tom Raworth, Jennifer Dunbar, Alice Notley.
Payment: $20.
Reporting time: varies.
Copyright held by author.
1974; 1/yr; 750
$3.50/ea; 30%–40%
100 pp; 5½ x 8½

INNISFREE
Rex Winn
P.O. Box 277
Manhattan Beach, CA 90266

(213) 545-2607

Fiction, poetry, essays, graphics/
artwork.

We provide an open medium for
artists to express their thoughts
and relate their experiences.
Home grown magazine, professional quality.

Payment: awards.

Copyright held by author.

1981; 6/yr; 120

$18/yr ind; $2.50/ea

40 pp; 8½ x 11

INTERIM

A. Wilber Stevens, Editor; James
Hazen, Arlen Collier, Joe Mc-
Cullough, Associate Editors

Department of English
University of Nevada
Las Vegas, NV 89154

Poetry, fiction, reviews.

INTERIM prints the best poetry
and short fiction we can find,
plus occasional reviews. It is
the revival, under its original
editor, of the magazine published and edited in Seattle in
1944–55.

William Stafford, John Heath-
Stubbs, X.J. Kennedy, Stephen
Stepanchev, Gladys Swan.

Payment: contributor's copies plus
a two-year subscription.

Copyright held by magazine; reverts to author upon publication.

1944; 2/yr; 750

$10/3 yrs; $5/yr ind; $8/yr inst;
$3/ea; 40%

48–64 pp; 9 x 6

ISSN: 0888-2452

INTERNATIONAL POETRY REVIEW

Evalyn P. Gill, Alice Rice, Clare
Rosen

Box 2047

Greensboro, NC 27402

(919) 273-1711

Unpublished translation with contemporary original language
poem. Contemporary English
language poetry, graphics.

Willis Barnstone, Catherine Sav-
age Brosman, Charles Edward
Eaton, Mary C. Snotherly,
William Stafford.

Payment: in copies.

1975; 2/yr; 400

$4/ea; 40%

136 pp; 6 x 9

Ad rates: $100/page; $50/½ page

INTERSTATE

Loris Essary, Mark Loeffler

P.O. Box 7068

University Station

Austin, TX 78713

(512) 928-2911

Poetry, fiction, criticism, essays, reviews, plays, translations, interviews, photographs, graphics/artwork; experimental art in all genres and non-genres.

INTERSTATE has a special focus on non-traditional, experimental writing and art, particularly visual literature, mixed media and work for theatre. There is a strong non-U.S. content.

Charles Brownson, Robert Coover, Brian Eno, Karl Kempton, Dan Raphael.

Payment: in copies.

Reporting time: immediately, occasionally longer.

Copoyright reverts to author upon publication.

1974; 1/2 yrs; 500

$10/2 issues; 40%

92 pp

ISSN: 0363-9991

INVISIBLE CITY

John McBride and Paul Vangelisti

P.O. Box 2853

San Francisco, CA 94126

(415) 527-1018

Poetry, criticism, translation, graphics/artwork, visual poetry.

A book series, formerly tabloid, of poetry, translation, visuals and statements published whenever enough good material is available: focusing on current U.S. writing, some concrete poetry and Italian writing—focused on "the internal tension of language."

Adriano Spatola, Giulia Niccolai, Ernst Meister, John Thomas, Stanislaw Baranczak, Antonio Porta, Emilio Villa.

Payment: copies and then some.

Reporting time: 2 months.

Copyright reverts to author upon publication.

1971; 1–2/yr; 1,000

$10/yr ind; $15/yr inst·

80+ pp; 5 x 9

ISSN: 0034-2009

IO

Richard Grossinger, Lindy Hough

North Atlantic Books

2800 Woolsey St.

Berkeley, CA 94705

(415) 652-5309

Poetry, essays, translations, interviews, photographs, graphics/artworks, prose.

IO does special issues on subject matters ranging among geographical/ecological concerns, hermetic studies (alchemical symbolism), sports literature (baseball, basketball), literature (issues on Melville, Blake, contemporary poets), and psychological/anthropological issues (dreams, American Indian mythology).

Michael McClure, James Broughton, John Updike, Diane Di Prima, Joanne Kyger.

Payment: some payment to contributors.

Reporting time: immediately.

Copyright held by author.

1964; irreg; 2,000

$25/4 issues; $5–$12.95/ea; 20%–50%

300 pp; 6 x 9

ISSN: 0021-0331

THE IOWA REVIEW

David Hamilton

308 EPB

University of Iowa

Iowa City, IA 52242

(319) 335-0462

Poetry, fiction, criticism, essays, reviews, interviews.

We look for new as well as established writers and are usually pleased, on the whole, with what we are able to publish.

Payment: $1/line for poetry; $10/page for prose.

Reporting time: 2–3 months.

Copyright held by the University of Iowa; reverts to author upon publication.

1970; 3/yr; 1,500

$15/yr ind; $20/yr inst; $6.95/ea; 30%

180 pp; 6 x 9

Ad rates: $150/page/5½ x 8½

ISSN: 0021-065X

Ingram Periodicals

IOWA WOMAN

Carolyn Hardesty; Sandra Witt, poetry

P.O. Box 680

Iowa City, IA 52244

(319) 338-9858

Fiction, essays, reviews, interviews, poetry, news briefs, features, advertisements, graphics/artwork.

Rooted in the Midwest, **IOWA WOMAN** publishes the writings of women from all over the country. Our subscribers—one third outside of Iowa—often send fan letters.

Judy Ruiz, Jane Ruiter, Ingrid Hill, Alice Friman, Natalie Kusz.

Payment: in copies and subscription.

Reporting time: 6–8 weeks.

Copyright held by magazine; reverts to author upon publication.

1980; quarterly; 1,000

15/yr; $17/yr Canada and Pan-Amer.; $20/other; $4/ea; 30%

48 pp; 8⅛ x 10⅞

ISSN: 0271-8227

THE ITHACA WOMEN'S ANTHOLOGY

Alicia Dowd, Joyce Gross
P.O. Box 582
Ithaca, NY 14850

Poetry, fiction, translation, photographs, graphics/artwork, criticism.

THE ITHACA WOMEN'S ANTHOLOGY was originally established as an annual collection of creative work, by, for and about women. The types of work we publish include essays, interviews, criticism, journal entries, translations, fiction, and poetry as well as graphics of all kinds. Our commitment is to provide a medium for women to creatively express their concerns, to coin varied and new voices, while emphasizing the highest in artistic quality.

Phyllis Janowitz, Alice Fulton, Lisa Ress, Carolyn Beard Whitlow, Beth French (Lorden).

Payment: none.

Copyright held by magazine; reverts to author upon publication.

1976; 1/yr; 350

$2.80/yr; $3/ea; 40%

Borealis Book Store, Smedley's Book Shop, Triangle Book Store

J

JACARANDA REVIEW

Cornel Bonca
Department of English
University of California
Los Angeles, CA 90024
(213) 825-4173

Poetry, fiction, essays, reviews translation, interviews.

We try to publish the best fiction, poetry, and essays we can find. A potential contributor should read an issue or two to see what we mean by that. We feature in each issue an interview with a major writer and, usually, a supplement featuring work of special interest to us.

Jorge Luis Borges, Carolyn Forché, Alfred Corn, Ed Minus, Joscha Kessler.

Payment: three copies.

Copyright held by University of California; reverts to author upon publication.

1985; 2/yr; 1,000

$7/yr ind; $10/yr inst; $3.50/ea; 40%

120 pp; 5½ x 8

Ad rates: $75/page/5½ x 8; $50/½ page/5½ x 4; $25/¼ page/2¾ x 4

JAMES WHITE REVIEW

G. Baysans, P. Willkie
P.O. Box 3356

Traffic Station
Minneapolis, MN 55403
(612) 291-2913

Poetry, fiction, criticism, reviews, plays, photographs, graphics/ artwork.
We are a gay men's literary quarterly.
Robert Peters, Robert Gluck, James Broughton, Felice Picano, Harold Norse.
Payment: none.
Reporting time: 6–8 weeks.
Copyright held by magazine; reverts to author upon publication.
1983; 4/yr; 2,000
$12/yr ind; $12/yr inst; $2/ea; 40%
16 pp; 11 x 15
Ad rates: $400/page; $200/½ page; $120/¼ page

JOURNAL OF IRISH LITERATURE

Robert Hogan, Kathleen Danaher
P.O. Box 361
Newark, DE 19715
(302) 764-8477

Poetry, fiction, criticism, reviews, graphics.
Irish literature past and present is of central interest, and new or previously unpublished creative material forms the majority of works published.

Mervyn Wall, Mary Rose Callaghan, Thomas Sheridan, Mary Manning, W.J. Lawrence.
Payment: none.
Reporting time: about 2 months.
Copyright reverts to author.
1972; 3/yr; 600
$12/yr ind; $18/yr inst; $4.50/ea
60 pp; 5½ x 8½
Ad rates: $100/page; $50/½ page; $25/¼ page
ISSN: 0047-2514

K

KALEIDOSCOPE: International Magazine of Literature, Fine Arts, and Disability

Darshan C. Perusek, Ph.D., Editor-in-Chief; Gail Willmott, Senior Editor
United Cerebral Palsy and Services for the Handicapped
326 Locust Street
Akron, OH 44302
(216) 762-9755

Poetry, photographs, graphics/artwork, fiction, essays, reviews.
KALEIDOSCOPE addresses the experience of disability through literature and the fine arts by publishing unsentimental

disability-related fiction, poetry, and visual art.

Anne Finger, Nancy Mairs, Ellen Hunnicutt, Leonard Kriegel, Christopher Hewitt.

Payment: $25–$100 fiction, up to $25 for body of poetry.

Reporting time: 6–12 weeks.

Copyright held by Kaleidoscope; reverts to author upon publication.

1979; 2/yr; 1,500

$9/yr, $16/2 yrs ind; $12/yr, $20/2 yrs inst; $4.50/ea; 40%; agency discount 20% of price

64 pp; 8½ x 11

ISSN: 0748-8742

Ubiquity, Trinity News Co.

KALLIOPE: A Journal of Women's Art

Mary Sue Koeppel
Florida Community College
3939 Roosevelt Boulevard
Jacksonville, FL 32205
(904) 387-8211

Poetry, fiction, essays, reviews, interviews (3 annually), photographs, graphics/artwork.

Purpose of **KALLIOPE** is to offer support and encouragement to women in the arts. We are open to experimental forms of drama, fiction, poetry, prose and art as well as traditional formats. Editors like to see work that chal-

lenges the reader and addresses the complex relationships women have with each other, men, children and society.

Marge Piercy, Ruthann Robson, Roberta Allen, Sylvia Sleigh, Vee Watts.

Payment: 3 copies or 1 yr subscription to writers and artists.

Reporting time: 2–3 months.

Copyright held by magazine; reverts to author upon request.

1978; 3/yr; 1,000

$10.50/yr ind; $18/yr inst; $7/ea last issues; $4/ea early issues; 40%

90 pp; 7¼ x 8½

No ads

ISSN: 0735-7885

Ingram Periodicals, DeBoer

KANSAS QUARTERLY

Harold Schneider, Ben Nyberg, W.R. Moses, John Rees, Paul McCarthy
Denison Hall 122
Kansas State University
Manhattan, KS 66506-0703
(913) 532-6716

Poetry, fiction, criticism, translation, interviews, photographs, graphics/artwork.

A cultural arts and literary magazine emphasizing but not restricted to the culture, history, art and writing of Mid-America but with international interests. David Kirby, John Bovey, Stephen Dixon, Jonathan Holden, Peter LaSalle, Susan Fromberg Schaeffer, Jerry Bumpus, Lex Williford, Annabel Thomas.

Payment: 2 copies and two series of annual awards.

Reporting time: 2–6 months.

Copyright held by magazine; reverts to author upon request.

1968; 4/yr; 1,500

$20/yr; $6/ea; 10%–40%

152+ pp; 6 x 9

Ad rates: $100/page/4½ x 7½; $60/½ page/4½ x 3¾; $35/¼ page/2¼ x 3¾

ISSN: 0022-8745

Available to bookstores at 40% discount on consignment.

THE KENYON REVIEW

Terry Hummer, Editor; Philip Church, Senior Editor

Kenyon College

Gambier, OH 43022

(614) 427-3339

Poetry, fiction, essays, reviews, plays, translation, memoir.

THE KENYON REVIEW seeks excellent writing more than any particular kind or style; essays which combine actual analysis with aesthetic, philosophical, and cultural issues of signifi-cance; fiction that exploits "viewpoint" and the arts of storytelling; poetry of all kinds, though with a respect for the verse-line; we invite offers to review books.

Lee K. Abbott, Cynthia Huntington, Philip Levine, Lynne Mc-Mahon, Reginald McKnight, Reynolds Price.

Payment: $10/page, prose; $15/page, poetry.

Reporting time: 3 months.

Copyright reverts to author.

1979; 4/yr; 4,500

$15/yr ind; $18/yr inst; $5/ea; 25%

144 pp; 7 x 10

ISSN: 0163-075X

Bernard DeBoer, Nutley, NJ

KEY WEST REVIEW

William J. Schlicht, Jr., Ph.D.

9 Avenue G

Key West, Florida 33040

(305) 296-1365

Poetry, fiction, essays, interviews, photographs, graphics/artwork, folktale, editorial.

We are a traditional literary magazine, but with important differences, including extraordinary emphasis on publishing prestigious writers along with excellent less well-established authors, aggressive marketing aimed at an audience beyond the usual scope of literary magazines, an interest in dialogue between authors and readers, and a particular focus on the Florida Keys.

Peter Taylor, Richard Eberhart, George Starbuck, Richard Wilbur, James Merrill.

Payment: none.

Copyright held by magazine; reverts to author upon publication.

1988; 2/yr; 2,000

$17/yr ind & inst; $5/ea; 40% (sometimes 20%)

100 pp; 6 x 9

Ad rates: $100/page/5½ x 8; $50/½ page/5½ x 3¾; $300/inside front cover; $200/inside back cover

ISSN: 1041-5254

KIOSK

Stephanie Foote, Marten Clibbens
English Department
302 Clements Hall
SUNY at Buffalo
Buffalo, NY 14226
(716) 886-0533

Poetry, fiction, essays, interviews.

KIOSK is interested in publishing quirky, unconventional, experimental, polished and/or well-crafted fiction and poetry. We are looking also for essays and criticism, where appropriate.

Carol Berge, Ted Pelton, Fritz Bacher, Beverly Sanford, as well as Raymond Federman.

Payment: none.

Copyright held by KIOSK; reverts to author upon publication.

1986; 1/yr; 1,000

Free with large SASE

100 pp; 5½ x 8½

No ads

L

LA NUEZ

Rafael Bordao, Celeste Ewers
P.O. Box 1655
New York, NY 10276
(212) 260-3130

Poetry, fiction, criticism, essays, interviews, plays, reviews, photographs, and artwork.

LA NUEZ is an international quarterly magazine of literature and art published entirely in Spanish. We publish established, as well as new and emerging writers and artists.

Reinaldo Arenas, Clara Janes, Justo Jorge Padron, Amparo Amoros, Frank Dauster, Kathleen March.

Payment: 2 copies.
Reporting time: 6–8 weeks.
Copyright reverts to author upon
publication.
1988; 4/yr; 500
$12/ind; $15/inst; $18/foreign; $3/
ea; 40%
32 pp; 8½ x 11
$200/page; $115/½ page; plus
smaller
ISSN: 0898-1140

LACTUCA

Michael Selender
P.O. Box 621
Suffern, NY 10901
Poetry, fiction, black and white
art.
Our bias is toward work with a
strong sense of place or experience. Writing with an honest
emotional depth and writing that
is dark or disturbing are pre-
ferred over safer material. Work
with a quiet dignity is also de-
sired. Subject matter is wide
open and work can be rural or
urban in character. We don't
like poems that use the poem,
the word, or the page as images
or writing about being a poet/
writer (though work about dead
poets/writers is o.k.).
David Cope, David Chorlton, Barbara Henning, Alan Catlin, Joe
Cardillo.

Payment: in copies.
Copyright held by magazine; reverts to author upon publication.
1986; 3/yr; 500
$10/yr ind; $10/yr inst; $3.50/ea;
40% bookstores, 60% distributors
60 pp; 7 x 8½
Ad rates available. Contact CLMP
for information.

LAKE EFFECT

Jean O'Connor Fuller
Oswego Art Guild
Oswego Civic Arts Center
P.O. Box 315
Oswego, NY 13126
Poetry, fiction, essays, reviews,
translations, photo essay, black
and white art, nonfiction.
LAKE EFFECT, a regional quarterly of arts and comment, is
published four times a year by
Lake County Writers Group. It
seeks to provide residents of the
lake country region of Upstate
New York with nonfiction, fiction, poetry, and art of interest
to them and to publish the
works of writers and artists who
live in the area. The magazine
also includes the works of artists in other parts of the country.

Katharyn Machan Aal, Lyn Lifshin, Louis McKee.
Payment: $25/review; $25–$50/nonfiction on assignment; $25/fiction; $5/poems; $25/photo essay; $5/incidental photo/art.
Acquired First Serial Rights.
1986; 4/yr; 9,000
$5/yr ind; $5/yr inst; $2/ea
24–32 pp; 11½ x 17
Ad rates available. Contact CLMP for information.
ISSN: 0887-4492
We distribute direct mail to 2,000 and 7,000 free in the region of Lake Ontario.

LAKE STREET REVIEW

Kevin Fitzpatrick
Box 7188
Powderhorn Station
Minneapolis, MN 55407
Poetry, fiction, essays, interviews, graphics/artwork.
An annual literary publication interested in poems, stories, songs (with musical notation) and drawings (black and white).
Jonathan Sisson, Dorian Brooks Kottler, Gregory W. Bitz, Beryle Williams, Ethna McKiernan, Tom Disch.
Payment: 2 copies.
Reporting time: 2 months after

annual deadline of 9/15 of each year.
Copyright held by magazine; reverts to author upon publication.
1975; 1/yr; 600
$4/2 issues ind; $8/2 issues inst; $2/ea
40 pp; 7 x 8½
ISSN: 0889-6410
Bookslinger Distribution

LATIN AMERICAN LITERARY REVIEW

Yvette E. Miller
University of Pittsburgh
Department of Hispanic Languages
2300 Palmer Street
Pittsburgh, PA 15218
(412) 351-1477
FAX #: (412) 351-6831
Poetry, fiction, plays, in translation. Criticism, essays, interviews, reviews.
The Journal in English devoted to the literatures of Latin America. It contains feature essays and translations of poetry (Bilingual format), plays, and short stories.
Gabriel Garcia Marquez, William Gass, Margaret Sayers Peden, Severo Sarduy, Mario Vargas Llosa.
Payment: varies.

Reporting time: 3 months.

Copyright held by magazine.

1972; 2/yr + Special double issue; 1,200

$18/yr ind; $32/yr inst; $34/yr foreign; $16/ea; 10%

150 pp; 250 pp special issue; 6 x 9

Ad rates: $200/page/4½x 7½; $125/½ page/4½ x 3¾; $80/¼ page/4½ x 2¼

ISSN: 0047-4134

Ebsco, Faxon, McGregor, Turner

LAUREL REVIEW

Craig Goad, William Trowbridge, David Slater

GreenTower Press

Department of English

Northwest Missouri State University

Maryville, MO 64468

(816) 562-1559

Poetry, fiction.

LAUREL REVIEW is national in scope and prints the best work received, regardless of style or author's reputation.

Stephen Dunn, Sydney Lea, Katherine Soniat, Carol Bly, Albert Goldbarth.

Payment: two copies and subscription.

Reporting time: 1 week–4 months.

Copyright held by GreenTower Press; reverts to author upon request.

1960; 2/yr; 800

$8/yr; $14/2 yrs; $5/ea; 40%

124 pp; 6 x 9

Exchange ad rates: $80/page/6 x 9; $50/½ page/6 x 4½

ISSN: 0023-9003

THE LEDGE POETRY AND PROSE MAGAZINE

Timothy Monaghan

64-65 Cooper Ave.

Glendale, NY 11227

(718) 366-5169

Poetry, fiction, prose.

THE LEDGE is meant to publish all types and forms of well-written fiction or poetry, by both established and young or little-known writers on the contemporary scene. We're independent and will make no move for compromise.

Jim Brodey, Les Bridges, Bob Holman, Margueritte, Ken DiMaggio, Brigid Murnaghan.

Payment: in copies.

Reporting time: 6 to 8 weeks.

Copyright reverts to author.

1988; 2/yr; 450

$13.50/6 issues; $3/ea; 40%

70 pp; 5 x 7

$50/page; $30/½ page

ISSN: 1046-2724

No dist. as of yet.

LIPS

Laura Boss
P.O. Box 1345
Montclair, NY 07042
(201) 662-1303
Poetry.
LIPS publishes the best contemporary poetry submitted. No biases.
Michael Benedikt, Gregory Corso, Maria Gillan, Allen Ginsberg, Robert Phillips, Marge Piercy, Ishmael Reed.
Payment: in copies.
Reporting time: 1 month.
Copyright held by magazine; reverts to author upon publication.
1981; 3/yr; 1,000
$9/yr ind; $12/yr inst; $3/ea; 40%
65 pp; 5½ x 8½
ISSN: 0278-0933
Anton Mikofsky

THE LITERARY REVIEW

Walter Cummins, Martin Green, Harry Keyishian, William Zander
Fairleigh Dickinson University
285 Madison Avenue
Madison, NJ 07940
(201) 593-8564
Poetry, fiction, criticism, essays, reviews, translation, interviews, graphics/artwork.
New writing in English and translation. We're looking for a unique blend of craft and insight.
Geraldine C. Little, Anthony Bukoski, Krystyna Lars, Sandor Csoori.
Payment: 2 copies.
Reporting time: 4–8 weeks.
Copyright held by Fairleigh Dickinson University; reverts to author upon publication.
1957; 4/yr; 1,800
$18/yr; $5/ea; 40%
128 pp; 6 x 9
Exchange ads
ISSN: 0024-4589

LITERATI

Sharon Lonergan
P.O. Box 15245
East Providence, RI 02915
Poetry, fiction, essays, humorous commentary, cartoons, black and white art.
LITERATI seeks to publish work of innovative form and artistic quality. Well crafted submissions of any reasonable length, subject or style are welcome. Admittedly biased against rhyming poetry and trite sentiments. Committed to becoming a major voice in literary publishing and to keeping our sense of humor.
Dionisio D. Martinez, April

Selley, Millie Mae Wicklund, John Grey, Ben Haes.
Payment: in copies.
Reporting time: 1–3 months.
Copyright reverts to author upon publication.
1989; 2/yr; 500
$10/yr; $5/ea; 40%
100 pp; 8½ x 11
$100/page; $50/½ page; $25/¼ page
ISSN: Pending
Literati Publications

LONG POND REVIEW

Russell Steinke, William O'Brien, Anthony Di Franco
Suffolk Community College
533 College Road
Selden, NY 11784
(516) 451 4153

Poetry, fiction, essays, reviews, interviews, photographs, graphics/artwork.

LONG POND REVIEW publishes the finest work submitted by established, emergent, and beginning writers. **LPR** has been recognized as an outstanding small press in **The Pushcart Prize II** (1977–78), **IV** (1979–80), **V** (1980–81), **VI** (1981–82), **VII** (1982–83), and **IX** (1984–85).

Fred Chappell, David Citino, Colette Inez, Linda Pastan, Jim

Barnes, William Stafford, Michael Blumenthal.
Payment: one contributor's copy.
Reporting time: 2–6 months.
Copyright held by author.
1975; 1/yr; 500
$3/ea ind; $5/ea inst
72–88 pp; 6 x 9
Ad rates: $75/page; $40/½ page

LONG SHOT

Daniel Shot, Caren Lee Michaelson, Jack Wiler
P.O. Box 6231
Hoboken, NJ 07030

Poetry, fiction, photographs, graphics/artwork.

"The most exciting literary magazine in America."

Charles Bukowski, Allen Ginsberg, Amiri Baraka, June Jordan, Sean Penn.
Payment: in copies.
Reporting time: 6 weeks.
Copyright held by magazine; reverts to author upon plublication.
1982; 2/yr; 1,000
$20/2 yrs; $5/ea; 40%
128 pp; 5 x 8½
Ad rates: $125/page/5 x 8½; $75/½ page/5 x 4¼
ISSN: 0895-9773
B. DeBoer & Co.; Ubiquity Distributors; Invisible Records

THE LONG STORY

R. Peter Burnham
11 Kingston Street
North Andover, MA 01845
(508) 686-7638

Fiction.

We are interested strictly in long stories (8,000–20,000 words, or roughly 20–50 pages)—bias is left wing and concern for human struggle for dignity etc.; but quality is the main criterion.

Payment: 2 copies.

Reporting time: 2 weeks–2 months.

Copyright held by magazine; reverts to author upon publication.

1983; 1/yr; 500
$5/yr; $5/ea; 40%
200 pp; 5½ x 8½
ISSN: 0741-4242
Ingram

LOOK QUICK

Joel Scherzer, Robbie Rubinstein
P.O. Box 222
Pubelo, CO 81002

Poetry, fiction, reviews, photographs.

Emphasis is on free verse, blues lyrics and brief vignettes. We have also published material relating to the Beats. Not reading unsolicited manuscripts.

Payment: in copies.

Copyright held by Quick Books; reverts to author upon publication.

1975; irreg; 200
Single issue only, $3/ea
24–32 pp; 5½ x 8½

LOUISIANA LITERATURE:
Literature/Humanities Review

Tim Gautreaux, Editor; William Parrill, Associate Editor; Norman German, Assistant Editor
Box 792
Southeastern Louisiana University
Hammond, LA 70402
(504) 549-5022

Poetry, fiction, reviews of Louisiana-related books, articles on LA writing and culture.

We are interested in publishing essays and photo articles on Louisiana writing, history or art, but no college term papers or anything full of jargon. Creative work we will take from anywhere on any topic.

Lewis P. Simpson, Elton Glaser, Katharyn Machan Aal, Sue Owen, Ann Dobie.

Payment: in copies.

Reporting time: 1 month.

Copyright held by author.

1984; 2/yr; 650
$7.50; $3.75/ea; 40%
92 pp; 6½ x 9½

Query for ad rates
ISSN: 0890-0477

LYRA

Lourdes Gil, Iraida Iturralde
P.O. Box 3188
Guttenberg, NJ 07093
(201) 861-1941 or (201) 869-2558

Poetry, fiction, criticism, interviews, essays, photographs, graphics/artwork.

We publish in English, French, Spanish, Italian, as we are committed to raising the level of communication among contemporary writers and artists in North America and other parts of the world.

Jim Sagel, Elizabeth Macklin, Carlota Caulfield, Robert Lima, Tom Whalen.

Payment: in copies.

Copyright held by magazine; reverts to author upon publication.

1987; 4/yr; 700
$15/yr ind; $18/yr inst; $4/ea; 40%
32 pp; 8½ x 11
Ad rates: $200/page; $125/½ page; $70/¼ page. Also, on exchange.
ISSN: 0897-6716
Faxon, SLUSA, Giralt

THE LYRIC

Leslie Mellichamp
307 Dunton Drive SW
Blacksburg, VA 24060
(703) 552-3475

Poetry.

We use rhymed verse in traditional forms, for the most part, about 36 lines max. We print only poetry, no opinions, no reviews. Our themes are varied, ranging from religious ectasy to humor to raw grief, but we feel no compulsion to shock, embitter, or confound our readers.

John Robert Quinn, Gail White, Amy Jo Schoonover, Alfred Dorn, Rhina P. Espaillat, Sarah Singer, Charles B. Dickson.

$600 in prizes annually.
$8/yr; $2/ea

M

THE MACGUFFIN

Arthur J. Lindenberg
Schoolcraft College
18600 Haggerty Road
Livonia, MI 48152-2696
(313) 462-4400 ext 5292

Poetry, fiction, essays, photographs, graphics/artwork.

We publish poetry, fiction, and

essays of the highest quality. We have no biases with regard to style, but we are committed to seeking excellence. Prose submissions should be less than 4,000 words.

Joe Schall, Tom Sheehan, Dan Dervin, David Sosnowski, Curtis Zahn.

Payment: 2 copies.

Reporting time: 8 weeks.

Copyright held by Schoolcraft College; reverts to author upon publication.

1984; 3/yr; 500

$10/yr ind; $8/yr inst; $3.75/ea; 40%

128 pp; 5½ x 8½

No ads

MANHATTAN POETRY REVIEW

Elaine Reiman-Fenton
36 Sutton Place South
New York, NY 10022
(212) 355-6634
Also:
FDR Box 8207
New York, NY 10150
Poetry.

MANHATTAN POETRY REVIEW is dedicated to a celebration of excellence in contemporary American poetry, welcomes unsolicited manuscripts, and presents a balance of new and established poets in each issue. It was founded as a community of poets and readers to demonstrate the diversity of fine poetry in America today.

Marge Piercy, Judith Farr, Theodore Weiss, Diane Wakoski, David Ignatow.

Payment: none.

Reporting time: 12–16 weeks.

Copyright reverts to author.

1982; 2/yr; 500–1,000

$12/yr; $7/ea (domestic, in U.S.$)

60–72 pp; 5½ x 8½

ISSN: 885-9205

THE MANHATTAN REVIEW

Philip Fried
440 Riverside Drive, #45
New York, NY 10027
(212) 932-1854
Poetry, interviews, photographs, reviews.

We try to compare and contrast American and foreign writers, and we focus on foreign writers with something to offer the current American scene. We like to think of poetry as a powerful discipline engaged with many other fields.

Peter Redgrove, Paul Ricoeur, Christopher Bursk, A.R. Ammons, Stanislaw Baranczak, Thomas Kinsella.

Payment: none.

Reporting time: 8–10 weeks.
Copyright held by Philip Fried.
1980; 1/yr; 500
$8 per volume (two issues)
64 pp; 5½ x 8½/page; 5½ x
4¼/½ page horizontal
ISSN: 0275-6889

THE MASSACHUSETTS REVIEW

Mary Heath, Paul Jenkins, Fred
Robinson
Memorial Hall
University of Massachusetts
Amherst, MA 01003
(413) 545-2689

Poetry, fiction, criticism, plays,
translation, interviews, photographs, graphics/artwork.
A quarterly of literature, the arts
and current affairs; special art
sections and special issues devoted to Feminism, Black literature, Ethnicity, Latin America,
contemporary Ireland, etc. oca-
sionally featured.
Ariel Dorfman, Marilyn Hacker,
Seamus Heaney, Joyce Carol
Oates, Octavio Paz.
Payment: $50 prose; 35¢/line po-
etry ($10 min.).
Reporting time: 3 months.
Copyright held by magazine; reverts to author upon publication
when requested.
1959; 4/yr; 1,700

$14/ind; $17/inst; $4.50/ea +
50¢/postage; 40%
172 pp; 6 x 9
Ad rates: $125/page 4⅛ x 7;
$75/½ page/4⅛ x 3½
Special university press rate:
$100/2 full pages
ISSN: 0025-4878
DeBoer

METAMORFOSIS

Erasmo Gamboa, Lauro Flores
Chicano Studies Program
American Ethnic Studies Dept.
B523 Padleford Hall, GN-80
University of Washington
Seattle, WA 98195
(206) 543-5401

Poetry, fiction, criticism, essays,
reviews, translation, interviews,
photographs, graphics/artwork.
METAMORFOSIS welcomes
submissions of poetry, drama,
critical articles, book reviews,
and artwork (black and white 8
x 10 photographs) with SASE.
Shifra Goldman, Pedro Rodriguez,
Alfredo Arreguin, Margaret
Randall, Bobby Paramo.
Payment: none.
Copyright held by the Center; reverts to author upon publication.
1977; 2/yr; 500
$10/yr ind; $15/yr inst; $5/ea
50 pp; 8 ½ x 10

ISSN: 0273-1606

MICKLE STREET REVIEW
Geoffrey M. Sill
328 Mickle Street
Camden, NJ 08103
(609) 541-8280
Poetry, essays, reviews, criticism,
translations, interviews, photographs, graphics/artwork.
The **MICKLE STREET
REVIEW** is published from
Walt Whitman's home on
Mickle Street in Camden by the
association which maintains his
house as a historic site. Material
reflecting Whitman's influence
on American letters is welcome.
James Dickey, Stanley Kunitz,
Richard Eberhart, Philip Dacey,
Antler.
Payment: $100 annual Walt Whit-
man Award.
Reporting time: 3 months.
Copyright held by magazine; reverts to author upon publication.
1979; 1/yr; 800
$10/ind; $20/inst; $5/ea; 40%
150 pp; 6 x 9
ISSN: 0194-1313

MID-AMERICAN REVIEW
Ken Letko
English Department
Bowling Green State University
Bowling Green, OH 43403
(419) 372-2725
Poetry, fiction, translations, essays, book reviews, interviews.
MAR publishes poetry using
strong, evocative images and
fresh language; fiction which is
both character and language-
oriented; translations of contemporary writers; essays and book
reviews on contemporary authors.
Cid Corman, Eve Shelnutt, Lee
Upton, Rolf Jacobsen, Margaret
Gibson, Dan O'Brien.
Payment: copies and $7/page, up
to $50.
Reporting time: 1–4 months.
Copyright held by MAR; reverts
to author upon publication.
1979; 2/yr; 1,000
$6/yr; $10/2 yrs; $4.50/ea; 40%
200 pp; 5½ x 8½
Exchange ads, 5 x 8
ISSN: 0747-8895

MILDRED
Ellen Biss, Kathryn Poppino
P.O. Box 9252
Schenectady, NY 12309
(518) 783-8849
Poetry, fiction, reviews, inter-
views, photographs, graphics/
artwork.
MILDRED is a biannual maga-

zine of poetry, fiction, art and photography with an emphasis on psychological realism.

MILDRED is not limited to female contributors.

Robert Bly, Christopher Bursk, James Freeman, Joseph Bruchac, Gary Fincke, Madeline Tiger, Louis Little, Coon Oliver, Rachel deVries.

Payment: in 2 copies.

Copyright held by Mildred Publishing: reverts to author upon publication.

1987; 2/yr; 500

$12/yr ind; $14/yr inst; $6/ea; 30%—1–4 copies; 40%—5–19 copies; 60%—20+ copies

100–150 pp; 6 x 9

No ads

ISSN 0892-5267

MINDPRINT REVIEW

Ron Pickup

P.O. Box 62

Soulsbyville, CA 95372

(209) 532-7045

Poetry, fiction, photographs, translations, graphics/artwork.

We publish quality prose, fiction, poetry, translations, B&W photography and graphics of both well-established and emerging writers, artists and photographers. Our submission base is Northern California, but our publication reflects a national/international cross section of work. Each issue forms a thematic focus pertaining to humanity or philosophy, but submissions are never limited to any subject, style or persuasion. Quality is our criteria for acceptance.

Rosalie Moore, John Oliver Simon, Lo Fu, Agusti Bartra, Jack Hirschman.

Payment: in copies only, upon publication.

Copyright held by Mindprint Review; reverts to author upon publication.

1983; 1/yr; 600

$7/yr ind; $7/yr inst; $6.50/ea; $7.50 by mail; 40%; consignment

128 pp; 6 x 9

Ad rates: $240/page/4 x 7¾; $120/½ page/4½ x 4; $60/¼ page/4½ x 2½ or 2½ x 3¾

ISSN: 1040-2233

Bookpeople

THE MINNESOTA REVIEW

Helen Cooper, Michael Sprinker, Susan Squier

SUNY Stony Brook

Department of English

Stony Brook, NY 11794

(516) 246-5080

Poetry, fiction, criticism, essays, reviews, translation, interviews.

THE MINNESOTA REVIEW is a journal of committed writing. We are particularly interested in new work that is progressive in nature, with special commitment to the areas of socialist and feminist writing.

Jonathan Holden, Jean Franco, Joan Joffe Halle, Marge Piercy, Fredric Jameson.

Payment: in copies.

Reporting time: 60–90 days.

Copyright held by magazine; reverts to author upon publication.

1960; 2/yr; 1,000

$8/yr ind; $15/yr inst; $4.50/ea

160 pp; 5½ x 8 ½

Ad rates: $80/page/5 x 7; $50/½ page/5 x 3½ ; $30/¼ page/ 2 x 3

ISSN: 0026-5667

MISSISSIPPI MUD

Joel Weinstein

1336 S.E. Marion Street

Portland, OR 97202

(503) 236-9962

Poetry, fiction, photographs, graphics/artwork.

MISSISSIPPI MUD presents lucid, elegant writing and art from the *ne plus ultra* of the American scene.

Tama Janowitz, Joyce Thompson, Fred Pfeil, Todd Grimson, Christina Zawadiwsky.

Payment: in copies.

Reporting time: 3 months.

Copyright held by magazine; reverts to author upon publication.

1973; 2–3/yr; 1,500

$19/4 issues, $5 ea

44 pp, 11 x 17

MISSISSIPPI REVIEW

Frederick Barthelme

Southern Station, Box 5144

Hattiesburg, MS 39406

(601) 266-4321

Fiction, poetry, criticism, translation, interviews.

MISSISSIPPI REVIEW is a nonregional literary magazine published by the Center for Writers at the University of Southern Mississippi. The editors combine solicited and unsolicited works of well-known as well as new writers in an innovative format, producing three numbers a year. Although **MR** publishes mostly fiction and poetry, the editors are interested in literature in translation, interviews, and literary criticism.

Elizabeth Tallent, William Gibson, E.M. Cioran, Amy Hempel, Tama Janowitz.

Payment: in copies.
Reporting time: 8–12 weeks.
Copyright held by magazine; reverts to author upon publication.
1976; 2/yr; 2,000
$15/yr; $7.50/ea
120 pp; 5½ x 8½
Ad rates: $100/page; $50/½ page; exchange
ISSN: 0047-7559
Bernhard DeBoer

MISSISSIPPI VALLEY REVIEW

Forrest Robinson, Loren Logsdon, John Mann
Department of English
Western Illinois University
Macomb, IL 61455
(309) 298-1514

Although an expression of outgrowth of Midwest's commitment to literary art, **MVR**'s eclectic editorial philosophy makes possible a wide variety of styles and concerns.
Laurence Lieberman, Lucien Stryk, Daniel Curley, John Knoepfle, Susan Fromberg Schaeffer.
Payment: in copies.
Reporting time: 3 months.
Copyright held by author.
1971; 2/yr; 500
$6/yr; $3/ea

64 pp; 9 x 6
ISSN: 0270-3521

MISSOURI REVIEW

Speer Morgan, Greg Michalson
University of Missouri
107 Tate Hall
Columbia, MO 65211
(314) 882-6066

Poetry, fiction, essays, reviews, interviews, special features of literary interest, cartoons.
Payment: $10/page.
Reporting time: 10–12 weeks.
Copyright held by the University of Missouri; reverts to author upon request.
1978; 3/yr; 2,300
$12/yr; $5/ea; 40%
224 pp; 6 x 9
Ad rates: $50/page
ISSN: 0191-1961

MODERN HAIKU

Robert Spiess
P.O. Box 1752
Madison, WI 53701
(608) 233-2738

Haiku, essays, reviews.
We publish only quality haiku in which felt-depth, insight and intuition are evident. Good university and public library subscription list includes foreign.
Dr. Paul O. Williams, Gunther

Klinge, Ann Atwood, Alexis Rotella, Virginia B. Young, Geraldine Little, William J. Higginson.

Payment: $1/haiku on acceptance; $5/page for articles.

Reporting time: 2 weeks.

Copyright held by Robert Spiess; reverts to author upon publication.

1969; 3/yr; 625

$11.65 yr; $4.25/ea

100 pp; 5½ x 8½

ISSN: 0026-7821

THE MONOCACY VALLEY REVIEW

William Heath, Editor

P.O. Box 547

Frederick, MD 21701

(301) 662-4190

Fiction, poetry, photographs, graphics, artwork, criticism, interviews, essays.

Holly St. John Bergon, Roser Caminals, Mary Noel, John Grey, Robert Bevington, Barbara Petoskey, Maxine Combs.

Payment: $25 for each poem, story, or artwork accepted (funds permitting).

Submission deadlines: Sept. 15 and March 15

$5/yr; $3/ea

Distributors: Frederick Arts Council; Square Corner Bookshop

MOTHEROOT JOURNAL

Anne Pride, Paulette J. Balogh

P.O. Box 8306

Pittsburgh, PA 15218

(412) 731-4453

Reviews, interviews.

Reviews of small press books of interest to women; interviews and essays.

Virginia Scott, Judy Hogan, Felice Newman, Doris Davenport.

Payment: none.

Reporting time: 6 weeks.

Copyright held by magazine; reverts to author upon publication.

1978; 3/yr; 1,000

$5/yr ind; $7/yr inst; $1.25/ea; 40%

8 pp; 9 x 16

Ad rates: $250/page; $125/½ page; $75/¼ page; column size: 2¼ x 16

ISSN: 0739-5272

MR. COGITO

John M. Gogol, Robert A. Davies

U.C. Box 627

Pacific University

Forest Grove, OR 97116

(503) 226-4135; 233-8131

Poetry, photographs, graphics/artwork.

Poetry in English, including translations; photographs, graphics. We like poems that surprise us with their language, sound and invention.

Dian Million, Elizabeth Woody, Tomasz Jastrun, Ann Chandonnet, W.D. Ehrhart.

Payment: 1 copy.

Reporting time: 1–3 months.

Copyright held by magazine; all but anthology rights revert to author upon publication.

1973; irregular; 500

$6/3 issues; $2/ea

24–28 pp; 4¼ x 11

ISSN: 0740-1205

EBSCO; Faxon; Acquinas

MUSCADINE

Lucille Cyphers

1940 Walnut St., #418

Boulder, CO 80302

(303) 443-3243

Poetry, fiction, essays, graphics/ artwork.

Old (60 yrs) people celebrating all aspects of life.

Segmund Weiss, Grace Young, Mary Olson.

Payment: 1 copy and $1.

Reporting time: 3 weeks.

Copyright held by magazine; reverts to author upon publication.

1977; quarterly; 400

$6/yr ind; $1.50/ea

28 pp; 8½ x 11

N

NANTUCKET REVIEW

Richard Burns, Richard Cumbie

P.O. Box 1234

Nantucket, MA 02554

(617) 228-3883

Poetry, fiction, translation, interviews, graphics/artwork.

THE NANTUCKET REVIEW publishes fiction primarily, some poetry, translations, when we can get them. 60–80 pp; perfect bound, offset, high quality paper.

Robert Luhn's interviews with Nathaniel Benchley, R.H.W. Dillard, Denise Levertov.

Payment: in copies.

Reporting time: 3 months.

Copyright held by author.

1974; 2–3/yr; 700

$5.50/yr; $2/ea

60–80 pp; 5½ x 8½

Ad rates: $75/page/5 x 8; $40/½ page/5 x 4½

THE NEBRASKA REVIEW

Richard Duggin (fiction), Art Homer (poetry)

215 ASH

University of Nebraska–Omaha

Omaha, NE 68182-0324

(402) 554-2771

Poetry, fiction.

TNR publishes quality literary fiction and poetry, material that transcends mere technical proficiency.

Carolyne Wright, Stephen Dixon, Joan Joffe-Hall, Elizabeth Evans, David Hopes, Vern Rutsala.

Payment: 1 year subscription plus contributer's copies.

Reporting time: 3–4 months (longest for poetry.)

Copyright held by magazine; reverts to author upon publication.

1972; 2/yr; 500

$6/yr; $3.50/ea; 40%

65 pp; 5½ x 8½

Ad rates: $45/page/3⅝ x 6¼; $25/½ page/3⅝ x 3

ISSN: 8755-514X

NEGATIVE CAPABILITY

Sue Brannan Walker, Ron Walker

62 Ridgelawn Drive, East

Mobile, AL 36608

(205) 460-6146

Poetry, fiction, essays, reviews, interviews, photographs, graphics/artwork, original music, bagatelles.

NEGATIVE CAPABILITY is a creative journal whose emphasis is joy—not merely laughter, though we encourage humor, but the joy that arrives through insight into oneself and others, the world and our all too human condition.

Richard Eberhart, X.J. Kennedy, Denise Levertov, Marge Piercy, John Updike, Marvin Bell.

Payment: in copies.

Reporting time: 8 weeks.

Copyright held by magazine; reverts to author upon publication.

1981; 3/yr; 1,000

$12/yr ind; $16/yr inst; $4/ea; 40%

180 pp; 5¼ x 8¼

Ad rates: $100/page/4½ x 8; $50/½ page/4 x 4; $25/¼ page/4 x 2½

ISSN: 0277-5166

NEW AMERICAN WRITING

Maxine Chernoff, Paul Hoover

2920 West Pratt

Chicago, IL 60645

(312) 764-1048

Poetry, fiction, essays, plays, graphics.

NAW is open to work that presents a progressive and lively point of view.

Robert Cooper, Ned Rorem, Lyn Hejinian, Charles Simic, Ron Padgett, Bob Perelman, Kenneth Koch.

Payment: $5/page, when available.

Reporting time: 1–3 months.
Copyright held by OINK! Press,
Inc.; reverts to author upon
publication.
1971; 2/yr; 1,500
$12/yr; $6/ea; 40%
120 pp; 5½ x 8½
Ad rates: $100/page/5 x 8; $50/½
page/2¼ x 4
ISSN: 0893-7842
DeBoer, Ingram Periodicals, SBD,
Illinois Publishing Project

NEW DELTA REVIEW

Kathleen Fitzpatrick, Editor;
David Starkey, Poetry; David
Racine, Fiction
c/o Department of English
Louisiana State University
Baton Rouge, LA 70803
(504) 388-4079

Poetry, fiction, interviews.

The **NEW DELTA REVIEW** is a
literary journal published by the
creative writing program of the
English Department of Louisiana State University. We at
NEW DELTA REVIEW are
most interested in promoting
"new" writers and exploring
new directions in poetry and
fiction. We offer The Eyster
Prizes, given with each issue to
the contributors of the "best"
new pieces of fiction and poetry. The Eyster Prizes honor
author and teacher Warren Eyster, who served for many years
as advisor to **NEW DELTA
REVIEW**'s predecessors, *Man-
chac* and *Delta*. Judges for
these prizes last year were Virgil Suarez and Kay Murphy.
Thomas E. Kennedy, Anselm
Hollo, Jay Blumenthal.
Payment: in copies, upon publication.
Copyright held by **NEW DELTA
REVIEW**—First North American Serial Rights; reverts to
author upon publication.
1984; 2/yr; 450
$7/2 issues; $4/ea; 40%
80 pp; 6 x 9
No ads

NEW ENGLAND REVIEW AND BREAD LOAF QUARTERLY

T.R. Hummer, Maura High
Middlebury College
Middlebury, VT 05753
(802) 388-3711 ext 5075

Fiction, poetry, essays, reviews,
translation, interviews, plays,
graphics/artwork.

NER/BLQ is a lively, eclectic
journal of contemporary poetry
and fiction, translations, criticism, and ruminations on society and the arts. We look for
writing that is distinguished by

its intelligence, craft, and engagement with the world, and that is of interest to both the general reader and the specialist.

John Engels, Albert Goldbarth, Toi Derricotte, Rosellen Brown, Miroslav Holub.

Payment: $5/page; $10/minimum.
Reporting time: 4–6 weeks.
Copyright held by author.
1978; 4/yr; 3,300
$12/yr ind; $18/yr inst; $4/ea; 40%
128 pp; 6 x 9
Ad rates: $275/page/4⅝ x 7⅛; $125/½ page/4⅝ x 3½; $80/¼ page/2¼ x 3½
ISSN: 0736-2579

NEW LAUREL REVIEW

Lee Meitzen Grue, Calvin A. Claudel
828 Lesseps Street
New Orleans, LA 70117
(504) 947-6001

Poetry, fiction, criticism, essays, reviews, translation, interviews, graphics/artwork, whatever is interesting.

NEW LAUREL REVIEW publishes poetry, fiction, translation, articles; work of sound scholarship which is alive. We hope to continue showing the best writing by nationally accepted writers with that of fresh new talent not seen before.

Enid Shomer, Sue Walker, Martha McFerren, Dixie Partridge, Yevgeny Yevtushenko.

Reporting time: varies.
Copyright held by author.
1971; 500
$8/yr ind; $10/yr inst
85 pp; 6 x 9
ISSN: 0145-8388

NEW LETTERS

James McKinley, Editor; Robert Stewart, Managing Editor; Glenda McCrary, Administrative Assistant
University of Missouri—Kansas City
Kansas City, MO 64110
(816) 276-1168; 276-1120

Poetry, fiction, reviews, photographs, graphics/artwork.

NEW LETTERS, an international literary quarterly, publishes contemporary writing, including that of well-known writers and fresh, new talents. Also publishes photographs and graphics; notable discoveries of overlooked gems. e.g., Theodore Roethke interview, Countee Cullen memoir, archival treasures.

Theodore Roethke, Joyce Carol Oates, William Stafford,

Thomas Berger, William Burroughs, Rosellen Brown, Lisel
Mueller.
Payment: small honorarium and
copies.
Reporting time: 6 weeks.
Copyright held by magazine; reverts to author upon publication.
1934; 4/yr; 2,500
$15/yr ind; $18/yr inst; $4/ea;
40%–50%
128 pp; 6 x 9
Ad rates: $150/page/4 x 6⅞;
$100/½ page/4 x 3⅛
Ingram Periodicals Inc.

NEW MYTHS: MSS
Robert Mooney
SUNY Binghampton
Box 530
Binghampton, NY 13901
(607) 777-2168
Poetry, fiction, essays,
photographs, graphics.
Special emphasis on publishing
the best work of young and
unestablished writers with the
work of well-known writers.
Andrew Hudgins, Dianne Bene-
dict, Gerald Stern, William
Stafford, Linda Pastan.
Payment: whenever funds allow.
Reporting time: 2–8 weeks.
Copyright reverts to author upon
publication.

1961; 2/yr; 1,000
$8.50/yr ind; $14/yr inst; $5.50/ea
$500/page; $250/½ page

THE NEW PRESS
Bob Abramson
75-28 66 Drive
Middle Village, NY 11379
Poetry, fiction, criticism, essays,
interviews, photographs, graph-
ics/artwork, letters, biographies.
We publish articles based on the
writers' enthusiasm about writing them. Illustrations should be
representational. Essays should
be informative. Poetry and fiction should be accessible. We
are always looking for new
writers and new markets.
Howie Rapp, Tom Ho, Estelle
Disch, Jill Heyman, Brett Bee-
man.
Payment: 3 copies.
Reporting time: 2 months.
Copyright held by author.
1985; 4/yr; 700
$8/yr; $2/ea
32 pp; 8 x 10
Ad rates: $50/page; $30/½ page;
$20/¼ page

the new renaissance
Louise T. Reynolds, Harry Jackel,
James E.A. Woodbury
9 Heath Road

Arlington, MA 02174
(617) 523-5700, ext. 159
Poetry, fiction, criticism, essays, reviews, translation, photographs, graphics/artwork, articles, illustrations.

We provide a forum for idea/opinion pieces on political/sociological issues; we have international interests and publish work on its merits, whether by recognized or new writers. We take a classicist position in the arts and avoid fashions and trends. Wide diversity in fiction, poetry and nonfiction focusing on the human condition.

B. Wongar, John Bovey, Faiz Ahmed Faiz (Agha Shahid Ali, translator), Valerie Hobbs, Jeanne Schinto, Eugeny Zanyatin, Joseph Turenon, Joanne Speridel, Marc Hudson, M.E. McMullen, John Wheatcraft, Darri Appel, Juan Ramon Jimenez.

Payment: after publication.

Reporting time: 8–20 weeks, poetry; 16–34 weeks, prose. Suspending submissions from 7/89 through 12/31/90.

Copyright held by magazine.

1968; 2/yr; 1,300

$11.50/3 issues; $6/sample; 20%–33⅓%

120–136 pp; 6 x 9

ISSN: 0028-6575

NEW VIRGINIA REVIEW

Bob Shacochis, Henry Taylor
1306 East Cary Street, 2A
Richmond, VA 23219
(804) 782-1043
Poetry, fiction, essays.

NEW VIRGINIA REVIEW: an annual collection of new poetry, fiction, and essays that strives to publish the best possible work being done by contemporary authors. Guest editors change yearly and accept material from unknown as well as widely recognized writers.

Richard Bausch, David Bradley, Mary Lee Settle, Roland Flint, Dave Smith.

Payment: $10 per printed page, $25 minimum for poems, upon publication.

Copyright held by NVR, editor, and individual writers; reverts to author upon publication.

1979; 1/yr; 1,800

$13.50/ea; 50% w/no return; 40% w/12 mo. return; discount on back issues w/ current volume

300 pp; 6½ x 10

No ads

ISSN: 0-939233-00-2

THE NEWPORT REVIEW

Michele F. Cooper
46 Second Street
Newport, RI 02840

(401) 849-3278

Poetry, fiction, essays, plays, photographs, graphics/artwork, original music.

A journal of art, literature, and ideas which provides an outlet for gifted writers and artists of all backgrounds from Newport and other areas of Rhode Island.

Ruth Whitman, Charles Norman, Edwin Honig, Alan Pryce-Jones, Fritz Eichenberg.

Payment: $5 per contributor.

Reporting time: 3 months.

Copyright held by magazine; reverts to author upon publication.

1979; 1/yr; 1,000

$10/2 issues; $5/ea

88 pp; 8¼ x 10¼

Ad rates: $400/page; $200/½ page; $100/¼ page

ISSN: 0276-5241

NIMROD: International Journal of Fiction & Poetry

Francine Ringold

Arts and Humanities Council of Tulsa

2210 South Main

Tulsa, OK 74114

(918) 584-3333

Poetry, fiction, translation, photographs, graphics/artwork, interviews.

NIMROD seeks vigorous writing that is neither wholly of the academy nor of the streets. Fall issues feature the winners and finalists of the Nimrod Literary Awards Competition and spring issues are thematic. Past thematic issues include Arabic Literature, China Today, "India: A Wealth of Diversity" and "Oklahoma Indian Markings." "Soviet Literature: The Remarkable Assemblage" is slated for 1990.

Wendy Stevens, Tess Gallagher, Denise Levertov, Gish Jen, Sharon Sakson, Alvin Greenberg.

Payment: in copies; also $1,000 to first place winners in our fiction and poetry competition, $500 for second place.

Reporting time: 3 weeks–3 months.

Copyright held by the Arts & Humanities Council of Tulsa.

1956; semi-annual; 1,500–2,500

$10/yr; $5.50/ea

112 pp; 6 x 9

Ad rates: $150/page; $75/½ page

ISSN: 0029-053X

NIT & WIT

Harrison McCormick, Marie Aguirre

P.O. Box 627

Geneva, IL 60134
(312) 232-9496
Poetry, fiction, essays, reviews,
  interviews, photographs,
  graphics/artwork.
NIT & WIT is a full-spectrum
  cultural arts magazine with regular features on art, music,
  dance, theatre, film, architecture, photography, reviews, essays, fiction and poetry.
Philip Graham, June Brinder, Gordon Lish, Sharon Sheehe Stark.
Payment: none.
Reporting time: 2–3 weeks.
Copyright held by author.
1977; 6/yr; 6,000
$12/yr; $2/ea; 40%–50%
68 pp; 8½ x 11
Ad rates: $750/page/7⅛ x 10;
  $390/½ page/4¹¹⁄₁₆ x 7⅜;
  $210/¼ page/3½ x 4¹⁵⁄₁₆

THE NORTH AMERICAN
REVIEW

Robley Wilson
University of Northern Iowa
Cedar Falls, IA 50614
(319) 273-2681, 266-8487
Poetry, fiction, criticism, essays,
  reviews, graphics/artwork.
Oldest magazine in North Amer-
  ica, publishing fiction and non-
  fiction, poetry and reviews.
  Winner in 1981 and 1983 of
  National Magazine Award for

fiction. Non-fiction frequently
  has ecological/environmental
  slant.
Payment: $10/published page;
  50¢/line for poetry.
Reporting time: 1–3 months.
Copyright held by University of
  Northern Iowa; reverts to author
  upon publication.
1815; 4/yr; 4,300
$11/yr; $3/ea
72 pp; 8⅛ x 10⅞
Ad rates: $250/page/7 x 10;
  $90/⅓ page/2¼ x 10
ISSN: 0029-2397
Eastern News

NORTH DAKOTA
QUARTERLY

Robert W. Lewis, Editor; William
  Borden, Fiction Editor; Jay
  Meek, Poetry Editor
University of North Dakota, Box
  8237
Grand Forks, ND 58202
(701) 777-3321
Poetry, fiction, criticism, essays,
  reviews, graphics.
An interdisciplinary journal in the
  arts and humanities. Recent and
  forthcoming special issues on
  cinema studies, Tom McGrath,
  women's research, Native
  American studies, Canadian
  culture, rural America, plea-
  sure, travel/travail.

Sherman Paul, Peter Nabokov,
Kathleen Woodward, Daniel
Curley, Thomas McGrath.
Payment: in copies.
Reporting time: 1–3 months.
Copyright by University of North
Dakota.
1909; 4/yr; 1,000
$10/yr; $4/ea; 20%
200 pp; 6 x 9
ISSN: 0029-277X

THE NORTHERN REVIEW

Richard Behm, Larry Watson
018 LRC
University of Wisconsin/Stevens
Point
Stevens Point, WI 54481
(715) 346-3568
Essays, poetry, fiction, interviews,
reviews, graphics/artwork.
Mary Baron, X.J. Kennedy, Allen
Hoey, Bret Lott, T.K. Chang
$8/yr; $15/2 yrs; $21/3 yrs; $4/ea;
40%

THE NORTHLAND
QUARTERLY

Jody Wallace
51 E. 4th St., Suite 412
Winona, MN 55987
(507) 452-3686
Poetry, fiction, criticism, essays,
reviews, plays, interviews, photographs, graphics/artwork.

Jennifer Lagier, Mark Vinz,
Mitchell Tomfohrde, Tom
Padgett, Mark Maire.
Payment: in copies, upon publication.
Reporting time: 2–4 weeks.
Copyright held by magazine; reverts to author upon publication.
1988; 4/yr; 500
$20/yr ind & inst; $4.95/ea; 40%;
20% to college bookstores; 30%
on ind. orders over 100
Ad rates: $300/page/5½ x 8½;
$150/½ page/5½ x 4¼; $75/¼
page/2¾ x 4¼; advertising accepted on barter system
ISSN: 0899-708X
Don Olson, Minneapolis, MN

NORTHWEST REVIEW

John Witte, Cecelia Hagen
369 PLC
University of Oregon
Eugene, OR 97403
(503) 686-3957
Poetry, fiction, criticism, essays,
reviews, translation, interviews,
graphics/artwork.
NORTHWEST REVIEW is a
tri-annual publishing poetry,
fiction, artwork, interviews,
book reviews and comment.
We have no other criterion for
acceptance than that of

excellence. We are devoted to representing the widest possible variety of styles and perspectives (experimental, feminist, political, etc.), unified within a humanist framework. "A publication to which the wise and honest, and literate, may repair!"—William Stafford.

Joyce Carol Oates, Madeline De-Frees, Alan Dugan, Morris Graves, Raymond Carver.

Payment: in copies.

Reporting time: 8–10 weeks.

Copyright held by magazine; reverts to author upon request.

1957; 3/yr; 1,100

$11/yr; $4/ea; 20%–40%

160 pp; 6 x 9

Ad rates: $160/page/6 x 9

ISSN: 0029-3423

NOTEBOOK/CUADERNO: A Literary Journal

Ms. Y. Zentella

P.O. Box 170

Barstow, CA 92312-170

Fiction, poetry, essays, reviews, graphics/artwork, editorial columns, environment, occasional chapbooks.

Literary journal with focus on humanist literature by all Black writers, especially Americans, Asian Americans, Arab Americans; very special emphasis on Latino-Americans.

Antonia Pigno, Carmen M. Pursifull, Aisha Eshe, Walt Phillips, Arthur W. Knight.

Payment: 1 copy.

Reporting time: 6–12 weeks.

Copyright held by magazine; reverts to author upon publication.

1985; 2/yr; 200

$12/yr ind; $16/yr inst; $6/ea ind; $8/ea inst; 40%

100 pp; 5½ x 8½

Query for ad rates

ISSN: 0883–6337

Read More, Faxon, ZVF International, Subs

NOTUS new writing

Pat Smith

2420 Walter Dr.

Ann Arbor, MI 48103

(313) 747-1680

Poetry, fiction, reviews, translations.

NOTUS is a semi-annual magazine focusing on experimental and non-traditional writing. Its emphasis is two-fold: to publish new work from writers who already have an audience and to help introduce the work of younger writers. We also have a special interest in publishing translations.

Ed Sanders, Robert Kelly,
Nathanial Tarn, Clayton Eshle-
man, Leslie Scalapino.
Payment: none.
Copyright held by OtherWind
Press, Inc.; reverts to author
upon publication.
1986; 2/yr; 300
$10/yr ind; $20/yr inst; $5/ea;
40%
96 pp; 8½ x 11
No ads
ISSN: 0889-0803
Small Press Distribution, Segue
Foundation, Small Press Traffic

trations, and a *small* amount of
poetry.
Lewis Gesner, Payan Kennedy,
Bonnie Jo Campbell, Michael
McInnis.
Payment: in copies.
Reporting time: 4 months. Read
fiction & poetry, Jan. 1–June
30; art submissions/Jan.–Dec.
Copyright held by magazine; reverts to author upon publication.
1985; 4/yr; 325
$10/yr; $3.50/sample copy
60 pp; 7 x 8½
Ad rates: $50/page/7 x 8½; $30/½
page/7 x 4¼
ISSN: 0894-7899

O

OAK SQUARE

Philip Borenstein; Anne E. Pluto,
Fiction; Laura Haun, Poetry;
Geoff Aronson, Art
Box 1238
Allston, MA 02134
(617) 547-1032
Fiction, photographs, poetry,
graphics/artwork.
We are interested in well written
short stories (3,000 words) by
new and emerging writers. We
are more interested in craft
rather than theme or plot. We
also publish photographs, illus-

OBSIDIAN II: Black Literature In Review

Gerald Barrax, Karla Holloway
Box 8105
Department of English
North Carolina State University
Raleigh, NC 27695-8105
(919) 737-3870
Poetry, fiction, criticism, essays,
reviews.
OBSIDIAN II is a tri-annual review for the study and cultiva-
tion of creative works in
English by Black writers worldwide, with scholarly critical
studies by all writers on all aspects of Black literature, book

reviews, poetry, short fiction, interviews, bibliographies, bibliographical essays, and very short plays in English.

Houston A. Baker, Jr., Gayl Jones, Wanda Coleman, Raymond R. Patterson, Gerald Early.

Payment: none.

Copyright held by Department of English, North Carolina State University; reverts to author upon publication.

1986; 3/yr; 500

$12/yr ind; $12/yr inst; $5/ea; 40%

130 pp; 6 x 9

Ad rates: $200/page/4½ x 7⅛; $100/½ page/4½ x 3½

ISSN: 0888-4412

ODESSA POETRY REVIEW

Jim Wyzard

RR 1, Box 39

Odessa, MO 64076

Poetry.

Ester Leipen, Rod Kessler, Rochelle Lynn Holt, Marian Park.

Payment: varies with quality of work.

Copyright held by Jim Wyzard; reverts to author upon publication.

1984; 4/yr; 500–700

$16/yr; $4/ea; 40%

150 pp; 5½ x 8½

No ads

THE OHIO REVIEW

Wayne Dodd

209 C Ellis Hall

Ohio University

Athens, OH 45701-2979

(614) 593-1900

Poetry, fiction, essays, reviews.

THE OHIO REVIEW publishes the best in contemporary American poetry, fiction, book reviews, and essays.

Sandra Agricola, Hayden Carruth, Roger Mitchell, William Stafford, Layle Silbert.

Payment: $1/line (poetry), $5/page (prose).

Reporting time: 90 days.

Copyright held by magazine; reverts to author upon request.

1971; 3/yr; 2,000

$12/yr; $30/3yrs; $4.25/ea; 40%

144 pp; 6 x 9

Ad rates: $175/page/4¼ x 7¼; $100/½ page/4¼ x 3¼

ISSN: 0360-1013

Ingram Periodicals, DeBoer, L.S. Distributors, Small Press Traffic

ONTARIO REVIEW

Raymond J. Smith, Joyce Carol Oates

9 Honey Brook Drive
Princeton, NJ 08540

Poetry, fiction, criticism, essays, translation, interviews, photographs, graphics.

Maxine Kumin, Albert Goldbarth, Russell Banks, Alicia Ostriker, Tom Wayman.

Payment: $10/page.

Reporting time: 6 weeks.

Copyright held by magazine; reverts to author upon publication.

1974; 2/yr; 1,100

$10/yr; $4.95/ea; 40%

112 pp; 6 x 9

Ad rates: $125/page/4¼ x 7; $75/½ page/4¼ x 3¼; $50/¼ page/2 x 3¼

ISSN: 0316-4055

Ingram Periodicals, Ubiquity Distributors

OPEN MAGAZINE

Greg Ruggiero, Stuart Sahulka, Paul Pinkman, Sylvia Muller
215 North Avenue West, Suite 21
Westfield, NJ 07090
(201) 249-0280

Fiction, poetry, essays, photographs, graphics/artwork, plays, interviews.

OPEN works with uninhibited forms of writing and art that inspire change—be they targeted at social processes or the consciousness of the individual. We are fast to accept work that pioneers form, questions the given, risks discussing the intimate or proposing the radical. New emphasis on essays. Special interest in dissident writing, women's issues, media, information & culture.

Margaret Randall, Noam Chomsky, Sylvia Plachy, John Cage, Claribel Alegria, Sesshu Foster.

Payment: copies and up to $50, depending upon presence of grant money.

Reporting time: 1 month.

Copyright held by magazine; reverts to author upon publication.

1985; 2/yr; 1,000

$15/3 issues/ind; $20/3 issues/inst; $5/ea; 40%

60 pp; 8½ x 11

Ad rates: $400/page/8½ x 11; $200/½ page/7½ x 5; $100/¼ page/3¾ x 5

Ad & Issue Swaps with other CLMP publications.

ISSN: 0894-265X

DeBoer, Inc.

ORO MADRE

Loss Glazier, Jan Glazier
4429 Gibraltar Drive
Fremont, CA 94536

Poetry, fiction, criticism, reviews, graphics.

ORO MADRE seeks to present fine poetry and fiction with attention to social and international themes, and also focuses on non-fiction coverage of the small press world through numerous reviews, interviews, and articles on literary bookstores, the art of small press, activities and trends.

Charles Bukowski, A.D. Winans, Alejandro Muguia, Luke Breit, Jack Hirschman.

Payment: in copies.

Reporting time: 2 months.

Copyright held by author.

1981; irreg; 500

$12/yr ind; $16/yr inst; $3.50/ea; 40%

48 pp; 5½ x 8

Ad rates: $40/page/5 x 7½; $25/½ page/5 x 3¾

OSIRIS

Andrea and Robert Moorhead

Box 297

Deerfield, MA 01342

(413) 774-4027

Poetry, photographs, graphics/artwork.

OSIRIS is a multi-lingual poetry journal publishing contemporary work in English, French, Italian and Spanish. Poetry in other languages such as Polish, Latvian and Danish appears in a bilingual format.

Robert Marteau, Sandor Weores, Simon Perchik, Emma Pretti, Claude Beausoleil, Piotr Sommer.

Payment: in copies.

Reporting time: 4 weeks.

Copyright reverts to author upon publication.

1972; 2/yr; 500

$8/yr; $4/ea

32–40 pp; 6 x 9

Ad rates: $60/page/5½ x 8½; $35/½ page/5½ x 4¼

ISSN: 0095-019X

OTHER VOICES

Dolores Weinberg, Founding Editor/Publisher; Lois Hauselman, Sharon Fiffer

820 Ridge Road

Highland Park, IL 60035

(312) 831-4684

Fiction, interviews.

A Prize-winning (IAC), independent market for quality fiction, we are dedicated to original, fresh, diverse stories and novel excerpts. We've won 11 IAC awards in 5 years, plus a CCLM/GE Younger Writers Award in 1988.

David Evanier, Rolaine Hochstein, Edith Pearlman, Stephen Dixon.

Payment: $50+/story;
$150/transcribed interview.
Reporting time: 10–12 weeks.
Copyright held by magazine; reverts to author upon publication.
1985; 2/yr; 1,500
$16/ind; $18/inst; $4.95/ea; 40%, 50% to distributors
225 pp; 7 x 9
Ad rates: $100/page/7 x 9; $75/½ page/3½ x 4½
ISSN: 87565-4696
OLPA

OUTERBRIDGE
Charlotte Alexander
The College of Staten Island
A324-715 Ocean Terrace
Staten Island, NY 10301
(212) 390-7779
Poetry, fiction.
Craft first. Regular special themes, i.e., urban, rural, Southern. Slight bias to new voices and less published writers. Personal replies. Anti pure polemic. Theme projects: interdisciplinary (biology, physics, music, astronomy, etc.); the city, immigrant, migrant experience, best humor, wit nature, children's stories.
John Woodruff, Walter McDonald, Candida Lawrence, Linda Bierds, Susan Astor.

Payment: 2 copies.
Reporting time: 2–2½ months, except July–Aug.
Copyright held by magazine; reverts to author upon publication.
1975; annual issue; 800
$5/yr; $5/ea
120 pp; 8½ x 5
ISSN: 0739-4969

OYEZ REVIEW
Patty Magierski
Roosevelt University
430 South Michigan Avenue
Chicago, IL 60605
(312) 341-2017
Poetry, fiction, photographs.
OYEZ REVIEW is an award-winning, university-based magazine in its 22nd year of publication. Each issue contains a number of poems and short stories written by people from various parts of the country and many different walks of life. The writings are diverse in content; all have universal appeal.
Ronald Wallace, David Martin, Barry Silesky, John Jacob, Brooke Bergen.
Payment: none.
Reporting time: 3 months.
Copyright held by magazine; reverts to author upon publication.

1967; annual; 400
$4/ea; 40%
96 pp; 5½ x 8½
No ads

P

THE PACIFIC REVIEW

Ilona Eubanks, Editor; B.H. Fairchild, Faculty Editor
Department of English
California State University
5500 University Pkwy.
San Bernardino, CA 92407-2397
(714) 880-5824; (714) 880-5831

Poetry, fiction, criticism, essays, reviews, plays, translation, interviews, photographs, graphics/artwork.

THE PACIFIC REVIEW is an academic-based journal of the verbal and visual arts, edited by graduate and undergraduate students at CSUSB. An annual publication now in its eighth year, **THE PACIFIC REVIEW** attempts to reflect aspects of its unique position in Southern California whenever possible, but without compromising its goal to serve as a vehicle for both emerging and established creative voices—from and about any area. Increasingly, **THE PACIFIC REVIEW** wishes to attract submissions of short drama and works in nontraditional genres.

Gabriela Mistral, Don Welch, Yang Mu, Michael Harper, Eugenio Montale.

Payment: in copies, upon publication.

Copyright held by magazine; reverts to author upon publication.

1983; 1/yr; 750
$4/yr ind; $6.50/inst; $4/ea; 40%
102 pp; 6 x 9
Ad rates: $150/page/5 x 7½; $100/½ page/5 x 3¾; $50/¼ page/2½ x 3¾

PAINTBRUSH: A Journal of Poetry, Translations, and Letters

Ben Bennani
Division of Language and Literature
Northeast Missouri St. University
Kirksville, MO 63501
(816) 785-4185

Poetry, criticism, essays, reviews, interviews, translation, photographs, graphics/artwork.

Publishes serious but innovative poetry, translations from any language—especially neglected ones—and interviews, book

reviews, and other readable stuff. The focus is always on quality and novelty.
William Stafford, Richard Eberhart, Colette Inez, Kathleen Spivack, Charles Edward Eaton.
Payment: in copies or $10/page when available.
Reporting time: 4–6 weeks.
Copyright held by magazine; reverts to author upon publication.
1974; 2/yr; 500
$9/yr ind; $12/yr inst; $7/ea; 40%
65 pp; 5½ x 8½
Ad rates: $150/page
ISSN: 0094-1964

**PAINTED BRIDE
QUARTERLY**
Louis Camp and Joanna Di Paolo
230 Vine Street
Philadelphia, PA 19106
(215) 925-9914
Poetry, fiction, criticism, essays, reviews, plays, photographs, graphics/artwork.
**PAINTED BRIDE
QUARTERLY** is a journal of literary and visual arts associated with the Painted Bride Art Center in Philadelphia. We publish both local and national writers and artists; the emphasis is on quality. We like crafted, articulate writing in any genre.

Naomi Shibab Nye, Eugene Howard, Etheridge Knight, Tina Barr, Robert Bly, Marnie Mueller.
Payment: in copies and 1 year subscription.
Reporting time: 2 weeks–2 months.
Copyright reverts to author.
1973; 4/yr; 1,000
$12/yr ind; $16/yr inst; $5/ea; 50%
80 pp; 5 x 8½
Ad rates: $75/page; $50/½ page; $25/¼ page

PANDORA
Meg MacDonald, Editor
2844 Grayson
Ferndale, MI 48220
Poetry, fiction, essays, reviews, graphics/artwork.
Character-oriented science fiction and fantasy by new and established writers. We emphasize role-expanding plots & characters and do not consider work that is racist, sexist, or x-rated. No horror or glorification of violence. Give us work about characters we can care about!
T. Jackson King, Ardath Mayhar, Deborah Wheeler, Wade Tarzia, Heather Gladney
Payment: 1¢-2¢/word; $7 and up

on illos; $3.50 and up on car-
toons and fillers.
Reporting time: 4–6 weeks.
Copyright held by author. Buy 1st
NA Serial Rights usually.
1978; 4/yr; 500
$15/6 issues; $3.50/ea; $6/2 (US);
$20/6 Canada; $25/6 other foreign
48 pp; 5½ x 8½
Display ad rates: $40/page/4½ x
7½; $25/½ page/4½ x 3¾;
$16.50/¼ page/2¼ x 3¾;
$11/⅛ page; ($10 per 25 words
non-display)
ISSN: 0275-519X
Faxon

PANHANDLER

Michael Yots
English Department
University of West Florida
Pensacola, FL 32514
(904) 474-2923
Poetry and short fiction.
THE PANHANDLER is a magazine of contemporary poetry and
fiction. We want poetry and
stories rooted in real experience
of real people in language with
a strong colloquial flavor.
Works that are engaging and
readable stand a better chance
with us than works that are self-
consciously literary.
Walter McDonald, Malcolm

Glass, Enid Shomer, David
Kirby, Joan Colby.
Payment: in copies
Reporting time: 1–2 months.
Copyright held by University; re-
verts to author upon publica-
tion.
1976; 2/yr; 500
$5/yr; $8/2 yr; 40%
64 pp; 6 x 9
ISSN: 0738-8705
EBSCO Subscription Services
(Birmingham, AL)

PANOPLY

Tim Houghton, Barbara Bolz
P.O. Box 85751
Lincoln, NE 68501
Poetry, graphics/artwork.
We seek to publish the best poetry, whether it is written by
well-known poets or more ob-
scure poets. We are particularly
interested in publishing poetry
that is more figurative than lit-
eral, more illustrative than descriptive. We feel too many
poets have been ignored because their works demand close
attention.
A.R. Ammons, David Ignatow,
William Stafford, Colette Inez,
David Ray.
Payment: varies, for solicited material only.

Copyright held by magazine; reverts to author upon request.
1987; 2/yr; 500
$5/yr; $8/2 yrs; $2.50/ea; 40%; bulk discount available upon request.
82 pp; 6 x 9
No ads

PAPER AIR MAGAZINE
Gil Ott
P.O. Box 40034
Philadelphia, PA 19106
(215) 925-9914
Poetry, fiction, criticism, essays, translation, interviews, graphics/artwork.
Now in its second decade, **PAPER AIR** has maintained its independence while exploring issues vital to contemporary poetry, both in the United States and abroad.
Jackson MacLow, Rosmarie Waldrop, Charles Bernstein, Cid Corman, Diane Ward, Lyn Hejinian.
Payment: varies.
Reporting time: 4–6 weeks.
Copyright held by Gil Ott; reverts to author upon publication.
1976; 1/yr; 1,000
$12/3 issues ind; $24/3 issues inst; $7/ea; 40%
128 pp; 8½ x 11
Ad rates: $120/page/8 x 10½;

$70/½ page/8 x 5 or 4 x 10½; $40/¼ page/4 x 5
ISSN: 0890-4359
Segue, Small Press Distribution, Spectacular Diseases (U.K.), Edge Distribution

PARABOLA: The Magazine of Myth & Tradition
Rob Baker
656 Broadway
New York, NY 10012
(212) 505-6200
Essays, reviews, interviews, photographs, graphics/artwork.
PARABOLA's focus is on myth and the world's cultural and spiritual traditions. Accordingly, **PARABOLA**'s approach to literature involves an emphasis on myths, legends, folktales, and oral transmission. **PARABOLA** primarily publishes articles and interviews which deal with mythology, comparative religion, and contemporary spirituality. Each issue focuses on a central theme.
P.L. Travers, Peter Brook, Eknath Easwaran, Frederick Franck, Amadou Hampâté Bâ, Laurence Rosenthal, Edwin Birnbaum.
Payment: $250 for articles; $75 for reviews; $50 for retelling of traditional stories.
Reporting time: 6 weeks.

Copyright held by author.
1976; 4/yr; 35,000
$18/yr; $5.50/ea; 40%
128 pp; 6¾ x 10
Ad rates: $735/page/5¹⁄₁₆ x 8⁵⁄₁₆;
$495/½ page/5¹⁄₁₆ x 4⅛;
$285/¼ page/2⁷⁄₁₆ x 4⅛
ISSN: 0362-1596

PARAGRAPH

Walker Rumble, Karen Donovan
1423 Northampton Street
Holyoke, MA 01040
(413) 533-8767
Prose paragraphs only.
We publish paragraphs of 200
words or less on any subject.
We are very selective and tend
to like paragraphs that have an
innovative topic and an arrest-
ing tone. Both fiction and non-
fiction welcome.
Joel Dailey, Wanda Coleman,
John Gilgun, Laurel Speer,
Gary Fincke, Jessica Treat,
Conger Beasley Jr.
Payment: in contributors copies.
Copyright held by Oat City Press;
reverts to author upon publication.
1985; 3/yr; 500
$8/3 issues; $3/sample; 40%
Ad rates: negotiable

THE PARIS REVIEW

George Plimpton, James Linville,
Patricia Storace
541 East 72nd Street
New York, NY 10021
(212) 861-0016
Fiction, poetry, interviews, graph-
ics/artwork.
Interviews, fiction, poetry, art
portfolio, and literary features.
Charles Wright, Joseph Brodsky,
Czeslaw Milosz, E.L.
Doctorow, Alice Munro.
Payment: varies.
Reporting time: 8–10 weeks.
Copyright held by Paris Review
Inc.; reverts to author upon
publication.
1953; 4/yr; 9,700
$20/yr; $6/ea; 40%
240 pp; 4 x 7½
Ad rates: $250/page/4 x 7½
ISSN: 0031-2037

PARNASSUS

Herbert Leibowitz
41 Union Square West, Room 804
New York, NY 10003
(212) 463-0889
Criticism, essays, reviews, photographs, graphics/artwork.
Devoted to the in-depth analysis
of contemporary books of poetry. PARNASSUS seeks essays
and reviews that are themselves
works of art. The ideal reviewer
is a poet with his or her own
particular point of view. PARN-
ASSUS publishes special issues

on music, poetry in translation, the long poem; includes paintings, illustrations and photographs.

Seamus Heaney, Zbigniew Herbert, Helen Vendler, Joseph Brodsky, Virgil Thomson.

Payment: $25–$250.

Reporting time: varies.

Copyright held by Poetry in Review Foundation; reverts to author upon request.

1972; 2/yr; 2,500

$15/yr ind; $30/yr inst; $10/ea

350 pp; 6 x 9¼

Ad rates: $200/page/6 x 9¼; $125/½ page/5 x 4; $100/¼ page/2½ x 4

ISSN: 0048-3028

Bookslinger, Small Press Traffic, Spectacular Diseases (England)

PARTISAN REVIEW

William Phillips

236 Bay State Road

Boston, MA 02215

(617) 353-4260

Poetry, fiction, criticism, essays, reviews, translation, interviews.

PARTISAN REVIEW examines the central issues of contemporary culture and social thought. It publishes critical essays on the arts and politics, new fiction and poetry, and book reviews.

Joseph Brodsky, Eugene Good-

heart, Pearl K. Bell, Elisabeth Young-Bruehl, Jed Perl.

Payment: varies.

Reporting time: 3 months.

Copyright held by Partisan Review, Inc; reverts to author upon publication.

1937; 4/yr; 8,150

$18/yr ind; $28/yr inst; $5/ea; 15%

160 pp; 6 x 9

Ad rates: $200–$250/page/4¼ x 7⅜; $120/½ page/4¼ x 3½; $75/¼ page/2 x 3½

ISSN: 0031-2525

DeBoer, Nutley, NJ; Capitol News, Boston, MA; L-S Distribution, San Francisco, CA; Ingram Periodicals, Nashville, TN

PASSAGES NORTH

Ben Mitchell

Kalamazoo College

1200 Academy

Kalamazoo, MI 49007

Poetry, fiction, essays, interviews, photographs, graphics/artwork.

PASSAGES NORTH publishes high quality poetry and fiction, along with graphic arts, twice yearly in tabloid size. The magazine not only publishes established writers, but also encourages students in writing programs. It fosters interchange

between the Upper Midwest and other parts of the nation.
Jack Driscoll, Gary Gildner, Judith Minty, Gloria Whelan, Alice Fulton.
Payment: $20/poem, $50/short story, frequent prizes.
Reporting time: 3 weeks–3 months.
Copyright held by magazine; reverts to author upon publication.
1979; 2/yr; 2,000
$2/yr; $5/3 yrs; $1.50/ea; 50%
24 pp; 11½ x 14½
Ad rates: $200/page/9¾ x 12¼; $100/½ page/9¾ x 6¼; $50/¼ page/4¾ x 6¼
ISSN: 0278-0828

PASSAIC REVIEW

Richard Quatrone
Forstmann Library
195 Gregory Avenue
Passaic, NJ 07055
Poetry, fiction, plays, photographs, graphics/artwork.
PASSAIC REVIEW is an independent magazine that publishes the best work submitted to it. Emphasis is on strong, clear, direct writing.
Antler, Ronald Baatz, Amiri Baraka, Allen Ginsberg, Eliot Katz, Wanda Phipps.
Payment: none.

Reporting time: 1–52 weeks.
Copyright held by magazine; reverts to author upon publication.
1979; 2/yr; 500
$6/yr ind; $10/yr inst; $3.75/ea; 40%
48–54 pp; 5 x 8½
Ad rates: $80/page/5 x 8½; $40/½ page/2¾ x 4¼; $20/¼ page/1⅜ x 2⅛
ISSN: 0731-4663

PEMBROKE MAGAZINE

Shelby Stephenson
Box 60, PSU
Pembroke, NC 28372
(919) 521-4214, ext. 433
Poetry, fiction, criticism, reviews, plays, interviews, graphics/artwork.
Open to poetry, fiction, essays, interviews, and artwork.
A.R. Ammons, Fred Chappell, Carson McCullers, Robert Morgan, Betty Adcock.
Payment: none
Reporting time: up to 3 months.
Copyright held by magazine; reverts to author upon publication.
1969; 1/yr; 500–800
$5/yr; $5/ea; surface mail $5.50/yr; $5.50/ea; 40%
250 pp; 6 x 9
Ad rates: $40/page; $25/½ page

THE PENNSYLVANIA REVIEW

Lee Gutkind
English Department, 526 CL
University of Pittsburgh
Pittsbury, PA 15260
(412) 624-6506
Poetry, fiction, criticism, essays, reviews, plays, translation, interviews, graphics/artwork.
Publishing the finest contemporary fiction, poetry, non-fiction and illustrations. *Choice* calls **THE PENNSYLVANIA REVIEW** a "fine small literary magazine . . . highly recommended".
Gordon Lish, Edward Abbey, Linda Pastan, Maxine Kumin, Paul West.
Payment: $5/page for prose; $3/page for poetry.
Reporting time: 6–10 weeks.
Copyright held by Univ. of Pittsburgh; reverts to author upon publication.
1985; 2/yr; 750
$9/yr; $15/2 yrs; $5/ea; 40%
100 pp; 7 x 10
Ad rates: $100/page/6 x 9; $65/½ page/6 x 4
ISSN: 8756-5668

PEQUOD

Mark Rudman
N.Y.U. English Dept., 2nd floor
19 University Place
New York, NY 10003
Poetry, fiction, criticism, essays, translation.
Past issues of **PEQUOD** have featured Irish, Scandinavian, Russian, Israeli, and Ukranian poetry. Future issues will include a special issue on literature and the visual arts and a selection of recent British poetry.
C.K. Williams, Zbigniew Herbert, Deborah Digges, Lydia Davis, Gustaf Sobin.
Payment: some payment to contributors.
Copyright held by PEQUOD.
1974; 2/yr; 1,000–2,000
$10/yr ind; $18/2 yrs ind; $17/yr inst; $30/2 yrs inst; $100/lifetime; $5/ea; $10/double issues
128 pp; 5½ x 8½
Ad rates: $150/page/5½ x 8½; $200/2 pp
ISSN: 0149-0516
DeBoer

PEREGRINE: The Journal of Amherst Writers & Artists

Kate Gleason, 1989 Editor
Pat Schneider, Contact at Amherst Writers & Artists
P.O. Box 1076
Amherst MA 01004
(413) 253-3307; (413) 253-7764

Poetry, fiction, cover graphics/art-
work.

PEREGRINE is the journal of
Amherst Writers & Artists, an
organization dedicated to the
belief that good writing is honest and unpretentious. We believe literature is related to the
speech of home and workplace,
and to the meanings discovered
in ordinary lives without the
bias of sex, race or class.
Katharyn Machan Aal, A.D. Winans, Jane Yolen, William Packard, Noemi Escandell.
Payment: in copies, and
occasional prizes, upon publication.
Copyright held by Amherst Writers & Artists Press, Inc.; reverts
to author upon publication.
1983; 1/yr; 500
$4.50/ea; 40%
64 pp; 5½ x 8¼
Ad rates: contact magazine for
information
ISSN: 0890-662X

PERMAFROST
Ellen Moore
Department of English
University of Alaska
Fairbanks, AK 99775
(907) 474-5247
Poetry, fiction, essays,
photographs, graphics/artwork.

PERMAFROST seeks to promote
excellence in contemporary literature and welcomes submissions in this vein.
Payment: 2 copies.
Reporting time: 4 months.
Copyright held by author.
1975; 2/yr; 500
$7/yr; $4/ea; 30%
80 pp; 5 x 8
No ads

PHOENIX
Joan S. Isom
College of Arts & Letters
Northeastern State University
Tahlequah, OK 74464
(918) 456-5511, ext. 3616
Poetry, fiction, essays, criticism.
We focus on contemporary poetry,
fiction, and essays. Please
query first. We do thematic is-
sues occasionally.
William Stafford, Maurice Kenny,
Louis Phillips, Ruth Schechter.
Payment: in copies.
Copyright held by Northeastern
State University; reverts to au-
thor upon publication.
1964; 1/yr; 300
$7/yr ind & inst; 20%
No ads
ISSN: 0-9615355

PIEDMONT LITERARY REVIEW

Gail White
P.O. Box 3656
Danville, VA 24543
(804) 793-0956
Poetry, fiction, criticism, essays, photographs, graphics/artwork, newsletter.
We publish mainly poetry, short stories; approximately 60 poems, 2 short stories. We need short stories of around 1,500 to 2,000 words. Traditional to avant-garde poetry—we publish established poets and many first timers.
William Matthews, Robert Wrigley, John Timmerman, Kurt Rheinheimer, Judson Jerome.
Payment: in copies.
Reporting time: 2 days–3 months.
Copyright held by magazine; reverts to author upon publication.
1976; 4/yr; 400
$10/yr; $2/ea
50 pp; 5½ x 8½
ISSN: 0257-357X

PIG IRON

Jim Villani, Naton Leslie, Rose Sayre
P.O. Box 237
Youngstown, OH 44501
(216) 783-1269
Poetry, fiction, essays, translation, interviews, photographs, graphics/artwork.
Special emphasis on popular culture, genres, and new literature in a highly visual and cerebral format. Publishes issues around special themes: recent issues have featured Third World, Humor, Psychological Literature, Viet Nam Era, Surrealism, Science Fiction, and Baseball. Forthcoming issues include "Labor in the Post-Industrial Age" and "Epistolary Fiction and the Letter as Artifact."
Back issues available.
Joe Bruchac, Terry Stokes, Dallas Wiebe, Lowell Jaeger, Miguel Ángel Asturias, Lamia Abbas Amara, Margot Treital, Soleida Ríos, Carlos Cumpían.
Payment: $2 per published page.
Reporting time: 3 months.
Copyright held by editors; reverts to author upon publication.
1975; 1/yr; 1,000
$5/1 issue; $9/2 issues; $12/3 issues.
$7.95/ea; 40%
96 pp; 8½ x 11
ISSN: 0362-5214
Available through publisher only; distributor queries accepted.

PIKESTAFF FORUM

Robert D. Sutherland, James R.
  Scrimgeour, James McGowan,
  Curtis White
P.O. Box 127
Normal, IL 61761
(309) 452-4831

Poetry, fiction, criticism, essays,
  reviews, plays, translation,
  interviews, photographs,
  graphics/artwork, editorial profiles.

We welcome original literary
  works, of a traditional or experimental sort, from established
  and non-established writers; we
  particularly enjoy giving launch-
  pad exposure to new talent.

Special features: Young Writers,
  Editors' Profiles (of other publications), The Forum—in which
  anyone may speak out on matters of concern to contemporary
  literature and small press.

Linnea Johnson, J.W. Rivers, Jeff
  Gundy, Constance Pierce, John
  Knoepfle.

Payment: in copies.
Reporting time: 3 months.
Copyright held by authors and
  artists.
1978; irreg; 1,500
$10/6 issues; $2/ea
36–40 pp; 11½ x 17½
ISSN: 0192-8716

PIVOT

Martin Mitchell
250 Riverside Drive #23
New York, NY 10025
(212) 222-1408
Poetry.
Now in its 38th year, **PIVOT**
  publishes the work of both sea-
  soned and new poets. It has a
  reputation for "firsts" of admi-
  rable performance.
Philip Appleman, David Ignatow,
  Eugene J. McCarthy, Willliam
  Matthews, Craig Raine, Robert
  Wrigley.
Payment: in copies.
Copyright held by Sibyl Barsky
  Grucci; reverts to author upon
  publication.
1951; 1/yr; 1,500–3,000
$5/ea
76 pp; 6 x 9
Ad rates: $125/page; $70/½ page;
  $40/¼ page

PLAINS POETRY JOURNAL

Jane Greer
P.O. Box 2337
Bismarch, ND 58502
Poetry, criticism, essays.
PLAINS POETRY JOURNAL is
  a forum for poetry using traditional poetic conventions:
  meter, rhyme, alliteration, asso-
  nance, painstaking attention to
  sound. No prosaic, conversa-
  tional "free verse." No Hall-

mark verse. Will publish one essay per issue: serious criticism, or humorous or serious essays on poetry. Widely published and unpublished poets receive same consideration.
Rhina Espaillat, Jack Butler, Johnny Wink, Gail White, R.S. Gwynn, Geoffrey Wagner.
Payment: none.
Reporting time: 1 week.
Copyright held by magazine; reverts to author upon publication.
1982; 4/yr; 500
$18/yr; $32/2 yrs; $4.50/ea; negotiable
44 pp; 5½ x 8½
ISSN: 0730-6172

PLAINSWOMAN
Elizabeth Hampsten
P.O. Box 8027
Grand Forks, ND 58202
(701) 777-8043

Essays, fiction, reviews, interviews, poetry, photographs, graphics/artwork.
PLAINSWOMAN publishes articles, interviews, fiction, poetry and graphics. We encourage clear writing by both academic and unpracticed writers, and we work with prospective contributors.

Emily Rhoads Johnson, Enid Shomer, Susan Strayer Deal.
Publication has been temporarily suspended, with Jan. 1991 as the anticipated date of resumption.
Payment: $5 to $50, or more if funds allow.
Reporting time: 1 week–1 month
Copyright held by magazine; reverts to author upon publication.
1977; 10/yr; 600
$20/yr; $2/ea; 40%
20 pp; 8 x 11
ISSN: 0146-902X

PLOUGHSHARES
DeWitt Henry, Don Lee, Joyce Pegeroff, David Daniel
Emerson College
100 Beacon St.
Boston, MA 02116
(617) 926-9875

Poetry, fiction, criticism, essays, reviews, translation, interviews.
A magazine of new writing edited on a revolving basis by professional poets and writers to reflect different and contrasting points of view.
Rita Dove, Sven Birkerts, Mona Simpson, Seamus Heaney, Joseph Brodsky.
Reporting time: 5 months.

Copyright held by magazine; reverts to author upon request.
1971; 3/yr; 3,500
$15/yr ind; $18/yr inst; $5/ea; 20%–40%
200 pp; 5½ x 8½
Ad rates: $200/page/4½ x 6½; $125/½ page/4½ x 3¼; $80/¼ page/2¼ x 3¼
ISSN: 0048-4474
Bernhard DeBoer; L-S Distributors

POEM

Nancy Frey Dillard
English Department
University of Alabama in Huntsville
Huntsville, AL 35899
(205) 895-6320
Poetry.
High quality mature poetry. No bias as to form or theme. Particular regard given to less well known poets.
Charles Edward Eaton, John Ditsky, Stephen Lang, R.T. Smith, Alison Reed.
Payment: in copy.
Reporting time: 1 month.
Copyright held by Huntsville Literary Association.
1967; 2/yr; 400
$10/yr; $5/ea
70 pp; 4½ x 7½
No ads

POET AND CRITIC

Neal Bowers
203 Ross Hall
Iowa State University
Ames, IA 50011
(515) 294-2180
Poetry, criticism, reviews.
POET AND CRITIC publishes poems, essays on contemporary poetry and/or poetics (3,000 words or less), and reviews of current poetry books. We try to be receptive to all types of poetry, asking only that the work display a sense of language.
Greg Kuzma, Barry Sparks, Edward Kleinschmidt, Ann Struthers, Malcolm Glass, Wendy Bishop.
Payment: 1 copy.
Reporting time: 3 days–2 weeks.
Copyright held by Iowa State University; reverts to author upon publication.
1964; 3/yr; 400
$16/yr ind; $20/yr inst; $6/ea; 40%
48 pp; 6 x 9
Ad rates: exchanges with other magazines
ISSN: 0032-1958

POET LORE

Sunil Freeman, Managing Editor
7815 Old Georgetown Road
Bethesda, MD 20814

(301) 654-8664

Poetry, criticism, essays, reviews, translation, graphics/artwork.

POET LORE publishes original poems of all kinds. The editors continue to welcome narrative poetry and original translations of contemporary world poets. **POET LORE** publishes reviews of poetry collections and critical essays of contemporary poetry.

Walter McDonald, Robert Peters, Leonard Nathan, Susan Astor, Albert Goldbarth.

Payment: 2 copies.

Reporting time: 3 months.

Copyright held by The Writer's Center; reverts to author upon publication.

1889; 4/yr; 600

$12/yr ind; $20/yr inst; $4.50/ea; 40%

64 pp; 6 x 9

Ad rates: $100/page/5½ x 8; $55/½ page/5½ x 4

ISSN: 0032-1966

The Faxon Co., Inc.; EBSCO; McGregor Subscription Service, Inc.; Boley Subscription Agency, Inc.

POETIC SPACE: POETRY AND FICTION

Don Hildenbrand

P.O. Box 11157

Eugene, OR 97440

(503) 485-2278

Poetry, fiction, reviews, interviews, graphics/artwork.

Maia Peufold, Tom Strand, Patty McDonald, Lyn Lifshin, Sesshu Foster, Barbara Henning.

$15/yr; $2 ea

Fiction: 1,500 word limit

POETICS JOURNAL

Lyn Hejinian, Barrett Watten

2639 Russell Street

Berkeley, CA 94705

(415) 548-1817

Criticism, essays, reviews.

POETICS JOURNAL is a triquarterly journal of contemporary poetics by poets and prose writers as well as by other artists, critics, linguists, and political theorists. It features essays, articles, and investigatory reviews. Individual issues focus on topics including "close reading", "poetry and philosophy", "women and modernism", "non-narrative", etc.

Ron Silliman, George Lakoff, Rae Armantrout, Ted Pearson, Jackson MacLow.

Payment: in copies.

Reporting time: 2–4 weeks.

Copyright held by author.

1982; 3/yr; 600

$20/yr; $7.50/ea; 25%–40%
144 pp; 6 x 9
ISSN: 0731-5236
Small Press Distribution; Inland
Book Co.; Segue

POETPOURRI

Comstock Writer's Group; Kathleen Bryce Nichols, Coordina-
tor; Jennifer B. MacPherson,
President
P.O. Box 3737 Taft Rd
Syracuse, NY 13220
(315) 451-1406
Poetry only.
Perfect-bound 75–100 pp, put out
twice yearly. We accept poetry
on the basis of quality, not reputation. We do not accept
porno, sentimental, greeting
card verse and very few haikus
or religious verse. Well crafted
poetry, free or formal, written
in understandable, grammati-
cally correct English—
metaphor, fresh, vivid imagery
enjoyed.
Joseph Bruchac, Kathryn Machan
Aal, Robt. Cooperman, A.D.
Winans, Scott Sanders, Gayle
Elen Harvey.
Payment: copy, prize $.
Reporting time: usually 2–4
weeks, with comments.
Copyright reverts to author.
1986; 2/yr; 500

$8/yr; $15/2 yrs; $4/ea
75–100 pp; 5½ x 8½

POETRY

Joseph Parisi
60 West Walton Street
Chicago, IL 60610
(312) 280-4870
Poetry, reviews, essays.
For 75 years **POETRY** has been
the most widely read monthly
of verse. From Auden to Ashbery, Pound to Pinsky, Stevens
to Soto—voices famous and
new.
David Wagoner, James Merrill,
Linda Pastan, Amy Clampitt,
Raymond Carver.
Payment: $2/line for verse;
$20/page of prose.
Reporting time: 6–8 weeks.
Copyright held by Modern Poetry
Association; reverts to author
upon request.
1912; 12/yr; 7,300
$25/yr ind; $27/yr inst; $2.50/ea
64 pp; 5½ x 9
Ad rates: $266/page/3¾ x 7;
$165/½ page/3¾ x 3½; $105/¼
page/1¾ x 3½
ISSN: 0032-2032
B. DeBoer, Inc.; Ingram Periodi-
cals; Illinois Literary Publishers
Association

POETRY EAST

Richard Jones, Kate Daniels
Dept. of English, De Paul University
802 W. Belden Ave.
Chicago, IL 60014
(312) 935-5986
Poetry, fiction, criticism, essays, reviews, translation, interviews, photographs, graphics/artwork.
Stanley Kunitz, Amiri Baraka, Philip Levine, Carolyn Forche, Sharon Olds, Gerald Stern, Muriel Rukeyser, Thomas Mc-Grath.
Payment: in copies. Occasional grants allow for small honorarium.
Reporting time: 3 months.
Copyright reverts to author upon request.
1980; 3/yr; 1,500
$10/yr; $3.50/ea single issue; $6/ea double issue
112–300 pp; 5½ x 8½
Ad rates: $100/page/7¾ x 4¾
ISSN: 0197-4009
B. DeBoer

POETRY FLASH

Joyce Jenkins; Richard Silberg, Associate Editor
P.O. Box 4172
Berkeley, CA 94704
(415) 548-6871
Criticism, essays, reviews, interviews, photographs, poetry.
POETRY FLASH, the Bay Area Poetry Review and Literary Calendar, publishes the most complete literary calendar of the area available. Also reviews of books, magazines, readings, and events, as well as interviews, occasional essays, photos, general commentary and information on submissions and publications for poets.
Steve Kowit, Anselm Hollo, Marilyn Chin, Ivan Arguelles, Jack Marshall.
Payment: subscription to $25; $100 for a special essay series.
Reporting time: 3 months.
Copyright held by author.
1972; 12/yr; 15,000; free to public placcs
$10/yr ind; $12/yr inst
16–24 pp; 11½ x 15
Ad rates: $400/page/10 x 13¾; $200/½ page/10 x 7; $100/¼ page/6½ x 5 or 5 x 7 ($105)
ISSN: 0737-4747

POETRY/LA

Helen Friedland, Barbara Strauss
P.O. Box 84271
Los Angeles, CA 90073
(213) 472-6171
Poetry.

POETRY/LA is a semiannual anthology of poems by Los Angeles-area poets. We publish poetry by both well-known and previously unpublished poets, and will consider poems of every length, style and subject matter.

Charles Bukowski, Mark McCloskey, Kate Braverman, Gerald Locklin, Wanda Coleman.

Payment: 1–5 copies.

Reporting time: 2 weeks–6 months.

Copyright held by magazine; reverts to author upon request.

1980; 2/yr; 500

$8/yr; $4.25/ea; 40%

128 pp; 5½ x 8½

No ads

ISSN: 0275-1739

THE POETRY MISCELLANY

Richard Jackson, Michael Panori

University of Tennessee at Chattanooga

Department of English

Chattanooga, TN 37402

(615) 624-7279 or 755-4629

Poetry, essays, reviews, translation, interviews.

We are very much a miscellany in the traditional sense of that word; we publish a variety of "types" of poetry.

John Ashbery, Marvin Bell, Carolyn Forche, William Stafford, Mark Strand.

Payment: none.

Reporting time: 6 weeks.

Copyright held by magazine; reverts to author upon publication.

1971; 2/yr; 1,100

$3/yr ind; $2/yr inst; $3/ea

130 pp; 6 x 9

Ad rates: $100/page/5 x 8; $65/½ page/5 x 4½; $40/¼ page/5 x 2

POETRY PROJECT NEWS-LETTER

Tony Towle

The Poetry Project

St. Mark's Church

Second Avenue and 10th Street

New York, NY 10003

(212) 674-0910

Poetry, criticism, essays, reviews, listings.

Bernadette Mayer, Anselm Hollo, Robert Creeley, Paul Violi, James Schuyler.

Payment: none.

Reporting time: 2 weeks.

Copyright held by author.

1967; 4/yr; 3,000

$20/yr

24 pp; 8½ x 11

Ad rates: $250/page/7 x 10; $130/½ page/7 x 5; $35/¼ page/3½ x 5

POETS ON

Ruth Daigon
29 Loring Avenue
Mill Valley, CA 94941
(415) 381-2824
Poetry.
POETS ON is a semi-annual poetry magazine. Theme-oriented, exploring basic human concerns through insightful, significant, well-crafted poetry. We publish recognized poets as well as unknown poets.
Linda Pastan, Charles Edward Eaton, Seamus Heaney, Joseph Bruchac, Marge Piercy, Philip Booth.
Payment: in copies.
Reporting time: 2–3 months.
Copyright reverts to author.
1977; 2/yr; 500
$6/yr; $3.50/ea
48 pp; 5½ x 8½

THE PORTABLE LOWER EAST SIDE

Kurt Hollander
463 West Street, #344
New York, NY 10014
Fiction, poetry, photography, essays.
PORTABLE LOWER EAST SIDE is a literary magazine involved with New York City. Strong emphasis on ethnic and cultural diversity, and on social

issues. Latest issue: "Crimes of the City". Forthcoming: Asian-New York.
Hubert Selby, Margaret Randall, Luisa Valenzuela, Willie Colon, Edward Limonov.
Payment: in copies and small sums.
Reporting time: 2 months.
Copyright reverts to author.
1984; 2/yr; 2,000.
$11/yr ind; $20/yr inst; $7/ea; 40%
175 pp; 5½ x 7
Ad rates: $100/page; $75/½ page
Inland Books, DeBoer

PORTLAND REVIEW

Nancy Row, Ken Angelo
P.O. Box 751
Portland, OR 97207
(503) 725-4468
Fiction, poetry, essays, plays, photographs, graphics/artwork.
The **PORTLAND REVIEW** is the annual Arts and Literature Magazine of Portland State University. It draws material mainly from the Pacific Northwest, but is open to submissions from outside the region.
Payment: 1 copy.
Reporting time: 1–2 months.
Copyright held by author.
1953; 3/yr; 1,000

$15/subscription; $4.00/ea +
$1.00 postage
80 pp; 9 x 12
Ads

$7.50/yr; $4/ea; 40%
75 pp; 6 x 9
Ad rates: $100/page/6 x 9; $60/½
page/6 x 4½
ISSN: 0894-2730

THE POUGHKEEPSIE REVIEW

Kip Kotzen, Editor; Ashley Mc-
Neely, Poetry Editor
165 Avenue A, #6
New York, NY 10009
(212) 477-5324
Fiction, poetry.
THE POUGHKEEPSIE REVIEW is dedicated to publishing the very best in contem-
porary fiction and poetry. We
aim to provide a forum not only
for established writers but also
for emerging talents. Though
we celebrate our origins in the
Hudson Valley, we consider
ourselves a national rather than
purely regional literary magazine. The magazine is about
voices talking— in small towns
and valleys, as well as in the
limelight, the large cities.
Madison Smartt Bell, Carole
Maso, Nancy Willard, Eamon
Grennan, Tom Spanbauer.
Payment: varies.
Reporting time: 3 weeks.
Copyright held by magazine; reverts to author upon request.
1987; 2/yr; 500

PRAIRIE SCHOONER

Hilda Raz
201 Andrews Hall
University of Nebraska
Lincoln, NE 68588-0034
(402) 472-3191
Poetry, fiction, essays, reviews,
translation.
PRAIRIE SCHOONER, a literary quarterly, publishes the best
writing available from beginning and established writers:
short stories, poems, interviews,
imaginative essays of general
interest, and reviews of current
books of poetry and fiction.
Scholarly articles requiring foot-
note references are generally not
published by **PRAIRIE SCHOONER**.
Marianne Boruch, Philip Dacey,
Brian Swann, Jeanne Murray
Walker, Pat Mora, Dabney Stuart.
Payment: 12 annual writing prizes
and grant funds, when available.
Reporting time: 2–3 months.
Copyright held by Prairie Schoo-

ner; reverts to author upon request.

1927; 4/yr; 2,000
$15/yr ind; $19/yr inst; $4/ea; 40%
144 pp; 6 x 9
Ad rates: $100/page/4¾ x 7½; $50/½ page/4¾ x 3½
ISSN: 0032-6682
Ingram Periodicals, Inc., Total Circulation Services

PRIMAVERA

Editorial Board
1212 East 59th Street
Chicago, IL 60637
(312) 684-2742

Poetry, fiction, photographs, graphics/artwork.

PRIMAVERA focuses on the experiences of women; publishes both established and unknown writers.

Julie Fay, Alice Fulton, Claire Nicolas White.

Payment: in copies.

Reporting time: 2 weeks–3 months.

Copyright held by magazine; reverts to author upon publication.

1975; 1/yr; 1,000
$5/yr; $5/ea
8½ x 11
Ad rates: $150/page/7½ x 10; $80/½ page/7½ x 5; $45/¼ page/4 x 5

ISSN: 0364-7609

PROVINCETOWN ARTS

Christopher Busa
650 Commercial Street
Provincetown, MA 02657
(508) 487-3167

Essays, interviews, visual art projects, poetry, fiction, photographs.

PA is an annual magazine focused on the artists and writers who inhabit or visit the tip of Cade Cod. It seeks to consolidate the voices and images of the nation's foremost summer art colony, placing contemporary creative activity in a context that draws upon a 75-year tradition of literature, visual art, and theater.

Olga Broumas, Douglas Huebler, Justin Kaplan, Stanley Kunitz, Susan Mitchell, Robert Motherwell.

Payment: Prose $100–300; Poetry/Art $25–300.

Reporting time: 2 months.

Copyright held by PA; reverts to author.

1985; 1/yr; 5,000
$6 annual issue; $5/ea; 40%
84 pp; 9 x 12
$650/page; $400/½ page; $200–$250/¼ page
ISBN: 0-944854-

Ingram, DeBoer, Interstate, Cape
News

PUCKERBRUSH REVIEW

Constance Hunting
76 Main Street
Orono, ME 04473
(207) 581-3832
Fiction, poetry, reviews, criticism,
interviews, essays, graphics/art-
work, photographs.
The special focus is on Maine literature and literary figures such
as Elizabeth Hardwick, Mary
McCarthy. Louis Coxe, Phillip
Booth. The intent is to publish
fiction, poetry and reviews by
contemporary Maine writers.
The purpose is both to reveal
and to encourage the literary
energy in this isolated state.
"Puckerbrush" = new growth.
Angelica Garnett, Kris Larsen,
Sonya Dorman, Farnham Blair,
Sanford Phippen.
Payment: in copies.
Copies held by magazine; reverts
to author upon publication.
1978; 2/yr; 450
$4/yr; $2/ea; 40%
50 pp; 8½ x 11
Ad rates: inquire

PUERTO DEL SOL

Kevin McIlvoy
New Mexico State University
Box 3E
Las Cruces, NM 88003
(505) 646-3931
Poetry, fiction, novel sections,
criticism, essays, reviews,
translation, interviews, photographs, graphics/artwork.
Though our emphasis is on the
Southwest, forty percent of each
issue is the poetry, short fiction,
artwork, etc. of artists from all
over the United States.
Naomi Shihab Nye, Richard
Russo, William Stafford, Susan
Thornton, Dagoberto Gilb.
Payment: none.
Reporting time: 8–12 weeks.
Copyright held by magazine; reverts to author upon publication.
1960; 1–2/yr; 1200
$6.75/semi-annual ind; $6/semi-
annual inst; $5/ea; 40%
150 pp; 6 x 9
Ad rates: $150/page; $90/½ page;
$60/¼ page
ISSN: 0738-517X

Q

QUARRY WEST

Kenneth Weisner
c/o Porter College
University of California

Santa Cruz, CA 95064
(408) 429-2155; (408) 429-2951
(messages)
Poetry, fiction, essays, graphics/
artwork.

QUARRY WEST combines quality design, graphics, production with about 95 pages of poetry and fiction, plus essays and reviews. We value linguistic and social centeredness, intensity of voice and variety in form, content, intent. "A controversy of poets." We do symposiums, also: #22, Rexroth; #25, Neruda.

Brenda Hillman, Yehuda Amichai, Robert Bly, Lucille Clifton, Bruce Weigl.
Payment: two contributor's copies.
Copyright held by magazine; reverts to author upon request.
1971; 2/yr; 1,000
$12/yr; $5/ea; 40%
110 pp; 6¾ x 8¼
Ad rates: inquire
ISSN: 0736-4628

THE QUARTERLY

Gordon Lish, Ellen F. Torron,
Rick Whitaker
201 E. 50th St.
New York, NY 10022
(212) 572-2128; 872-8231
Poetry, fiction, essays, humor.
A wide-open venue with particular hospitality for the unaffiliated. Fastest, fairest readings.
Payment: varies.
Copyright held by **THE QUARTERLY**; reverts to author upon publication.
1987; 4/yr; 15,000
$36/yr ind & inst; $47/yr Canada ind & inst; $8.95/ea; 40%
256 pp; 5¼ x 8
No ads
ISSN: 0893-3103
Random House

QUARTERLY REVIEW OF LITERATURE

Contemporary Poetry Series
Theodore and Renee Weiss
26 Haslet Avenue
Princeton, NJ 08540
Poetry.

QRL, a new concept in poetry, publishes 4 to 6 prize-winning collections of poetry in each volume, chosen through international competition. Called "the most significant event in years" and "the best bargain in poetry" and applauded as "brilliant." Each issue includes: poetry, long poems, poetic plays, poetry translation, plus introductory essays, photographs, and biographies of each author. Wislava Szymborska, David Schu-

bert, Nancy Esposito, Larry
Kramer, Julia Mishkin.
Payment: $1,000 per accepted
manuscript. Reading period:
May and November. Please
write for more information,
with SASE.
Reporting time: 2 months or less.
Copyright held by QRL.
1943; 1/yr; 3–5,000
$20/2 volumes ind; $20/cloth volume inst; $10/ea; 10%
350 pp; 5½ x 8½
Ad rates: $200/page; $125/½ page
ISSN: 0033-5819

QUARTERLY WEST
C.F. Pinkerton, Tom Schmid
317 Olpin Union
University of Utah
Salt Lake City, UT 84112
(801) 581-3938
Fiction, poetry, reviews, translation.
We try to publish the best in
poetry and fiction, both mainstream and experimental. We
conduct a biennial novella competition and also publish reviews and translations. We're
not a western genre magazine.
We accept multiple submissions
(just tell us, please) and read
MSS year-round.
Andre Dubus, Ron Carlson, Mar-

vin Bell, Stephen Dobyns,
William Stafford.
Payment: fiction $25; poems and
reviews $15 each + 2 copies
and 1 yr. sub.
Reporting time: 2–8 weeks.
Copyright held by magazine; reverts to author upon request.
1976; 2/yr; 1,000
$8.50/yr; $4.50/ea; 25%–40%
140 pp; 6 x 9
Ad rates: $150/page/4⅜ x 7⅞;
$85/½ page/4⅜ x 4
ISSN: 0194-4231

QUILT
Ishmael Reed, Al Young
1446 Sixth Street, Suite D
Berkeley, CA 94710
(415) 527-1586
Poetry, fiction, criticism, essays,
interviews, graphics/artwork.
QUILT is a book-length literary
journal which represents the
quality and diversity of contemporary writing. **QUILT** is multicultural in focus (featuring
Asian, Afro, Hispanic, European and Native American authors) and gives voice to new as
well as established talent.
Cecil Brown, Frank Chin, Adrienne Kennedy, Harryette
Mullen, Cyn Zarco.
Payment: none.
Copyright reverts to author.

1981; 1/yr; 1,000
$7.95/yr; $7.95/ea; 40%
200 pp; 5½ x 8½
No ads
ISSN: 0277-593X

QUIXOTE

Morris Edelson, Melissa Bondy
1812 Marshall
Houston, TX 77098
(713) 529-7944
Poetry, fiction, criticism, essays,
   translation, interviews.
Social criticism/satire/mucking
   around.
Sesshy Foster, Pablo Neruda,
   Jerry Blatz, Steve Kowitt, Curt
   Johnson.
Payment: in copies.
Reporting time: 6 months.
Copyright held by author.
1965; 12/yr; 500
$15/yr; $2/ea
40–100 pp; 4 x 5–11 x 17

R

RACCOON

David Spicer
P.O. Box 111327
Memphis, TN 38111-1327
(901) 323-8858

Poetry, fiction, criticism, essays,
   reviews, translation, interviews,
   photographs.
A journal of contemporary litera-
   ture, with poetry, fiction, essay.
Maurya Simon, Pattiann Rogers,
   David Romtvedt, Jay Meek,
   Frank Russell.
Payment: 1 year subscription/po-
   etry; $50/prose, 1 copy.
Reporting time: 6 weeks–3
   months.
Copyright reverts to author upon
   publication.
1977; 3/yr; 500
$12.50/yr; $5/ea; 40%
ISSN: 0148-0162
Small Press Distribution, EBSCO,
   Faxon

RAG MAG, Black Hat Press

Beverly Voldseth, Editor, Pub-
   lisher
Box 12
Goodhue, MN 55027
(612) 923-4590
Poetry, fiction, essays, reviews,
   plays, photographs, graphics/
   artwork.
Small lit mag. No special focus.
Pat McKinnon, Dew Harding,
   Paul Scott, Greg Grummer, Su-
   san M. Cosens.
Payment: in copies.
Reporting time: 1 week–2 months,
   reads Nov. 1–Feb. 1

Copyright held by magazine; reverts to author upon publication.
1982; 2/yr; 150
$8/yr. $4.50/ea
64 pp; 5½ x 8½
Ad rates: $35/page/4 x 7⅜; $20/½ page/4 x 3½; $10/¼ page/4 x 1¾
ISSN: 0742-2768

RAMBUNCTIOUS REVIEW

M. Dellutri, N. Lennon, R. Goldman, E. Hausler
1221 West Pratt Boulevard
Chicago, IL 60626
(312) 338-2439

Poetry, fiction, photographs, graphics/artwork.

We are an annual literary arts magazine devoted to the publication of new and established writers and artists. We sponsor annual poetry and fiction contests and theme issues. Our next issue is focused on "City of Dreams."

Elizabeth Eddy, Richard Calisch, Hugh Fox, Richard Kostelanetz.
Payment: 2 issues.
Copyright held by magazine; reverts to author upon publication.
1986; 2/yr; 450
$10/3 issues; $4/sample
48 pp; 7 x 10

No ads
Ingram Periodicals

RARITAN

R. Poirier, Editor; Suzanne K. Hyman, Managing Editor
165 College Avenue
New Brunswick, NJ 08903
(201) 932-7887 or 7852

Criticism, essays, reviews, poetry, fiction. A comprehensive critique of contemporary culture.
Denis Donoghue, Clifford Geertz, James Merrill, Elaine Showalter.
Payment: $100/article.
Reporting time: 2 months.
Copyright reverts to author in 6 months.
1981; 4/yr; 3,500
$16/yr, $26/2 yrs ind; $20/yr, $30/2 yrs inst; $5/ea; $6/back issues; 40%–50%
160 pp; 6 x 9
Ad rates: $250/page/4½ x 7½
ISSN: 0275-1607
DeBoer, Ingram

RED BASS

Jay Murphy
2425 Burgundy Street
New Orleans, LA 70117
(504) 949-5256

Poetry, essays, graphics/artwork, criticism, reviews, translation, interviews, fiction, plays, photographs.

RED BASS seeks to illuminate the interface between art and politics with a provocative mix of visual art/literature/music and reviews, with a special emphasis on translations and international work. We have published emerging artists and those, such as John Cage or Allen Ginsberg, whose reputations are assured.

Kathy Acker, Etel Adnan, James Purdy, Carolee Schneemann, Sue Coe.

Payment: in copies, sometimes in cash as funds allow.

Reporting time: 3 months.

Copyright held by magazine; reverts to author upon publication.

1981; 2/yr; 2,000

$10/yr ind; $15/yr inst; $4/ea; 40%

72–80 pp; 8 x 11

Ad rates: $200/page/8 x 10½; $100/½ page/8 x 5¼; $50/¼ page/4 x 5¼

ISSN: 0883-0126

Ubiquity, Flatland, Homing Pigeon, Armadillo

THE RED CEDAR REVIEW

Susan Parker
Department of English
325 Morrill Hall
Michigan State University
East Lansing, MI 48824
(517) 355-7570

Poetry, fiction, graphics/artwork photography.

Take risks, avoid the mainstream; love, sex, death as always. Oddities. Humor. Originality comes first. SASE required.

Carol Cavallaro, Craig Cotter, Lyn Lifshin, Hannah Stein.

$10/yr; $5/ea; $2/sample, 40%

Faxon, EBSCO

THE REDNECK REVIEW OF LITERATURE

Penelope Reedy
P.O. Box 730
Twin Falls, Idaho 83303
(208) 734-6653

Fiction, essays, poetry, book reviews.

REDNECK is a magazine of contemporary western American literature involved in the development of the region's literature through publishing high quality fiction, poetry, essays, and criticism.

Edward Abbey, Clay Reynolds, Charlotte Wright, Florence Blanchard, Leslie Leek, Harald Wyndham, William Studebaker.

Payment: in copies.

Copyright reverts to author.

1975; 2/yr
$14/yr; $32/3 yrs; $7/ea
100 pp; 5½ x 8½. Some special
 exceptions (Fall 89 is tape and
 8½ x 11 booklet.)

REPRESENTATIONS

Stephen Greenblatt, Svetlana Al-
 phers, Co-Chairs, Editorial
 Board
English Department
University of California
Berkeley, CA 94720
(415) 642-9044

Criticism, essays, translations.

REPRESENTATIONS publishes
 critical essays on interdisciplinary topics; disciplines included
 are literature, political theory,
 art history, and anthropology,
 and roughly 50 percent of the
 work published is literary criticism. Of the balance, literary
 methodology is a substantial
 influence in essays in other
 fields such as history, political
 theory, anthropology, etc.

R. Howard Bloch, Joan DeJean,
 Pierre Nova, Leo Bersani, Ro-
 salind Krauss, Denis Hollier,
 Anne M. Wagner, Steven
 Knapp.

Payment: none.

Reporting time: 6–8 weeks.

Copyright held by University of
 California Press.

1983; 4/yr; 2,200
$22/yr ind; $44/yr inst
152 pp; 7 x 9¾
Ad rates: $150/page
ISSN: 0734-6018
B. DeBoer, others

RESONANCE

Evan and Patty Pritchard
P.O. Box 215
Beacon, NY 12508
(914) 838-1217

Essays, graphics/artwork, poetry,
 review, photographs, fiction,
 interviews, music and humor.

RESONANCE is a journal of all
 forms of creative expression
 inspired by personal spiritual
 experience. It strives to create a
 popular forum for communication between artists, scientists
 and the spiritual community,
 however it does not promote or
 denigrate any other organiza-
 tions, spiritual, educational or
 otherwise. It is a forum for individual spiritual insight.

Heather Hughes-Calero, Susan
 Hanniford Crowley. Interviews
 with Chris Williamson,
 Madeleine L'Engle, Arun Gan-
 dhi, Pete Seeger, David Lanz,
 Joan Houston, others.

Payment: 1 copy.

Reporting time: 8 weeks.
Copyright held by Evan and Patty Pritchard—compilation only; reverts to author upon publication.
1987; quarterly; 2,000
$12/yr; $3/ea; 40%
52 pp; 8½ x 11
$100/½ page; $50/¼ page; $25/⅛ page
Ubiquity Dist., NY; Homing Pigeon, TX; Armadillo, CA; L-S, San Franciso; Book Tech Dist.; New Leaf Dist. (USA)

REVERSE

Jan McLaughlin and Bruce Weber
221 NE 104th St
Miami Shores, FL 33138
(305) 756-6038
Essays, poetry.
Devoted almost exclusively to essays by poets focusing on issues relevant to poetry. Themes of revent issues: censorship of literature; state of poetry in Florida; forgotten poets. Planning an issue on problems in translation. Includes avante-garde and academic points of view. Often deals with controversial subjects. A poetry journal that thinks.
Carolyn Forche, Barbara Holley, Yvonne Sapia, Jan McLaughlin, Bruce Weber, Lenny DellaRoca.
Payment: $20 upon publication.
Reporting time: 3–4 months.
Copyright held by author.
1988; 2/yr; 300
$6/yr; $3.50/ea; 40%
16 pp; 8½ x 11
$50/¼ page; $25/⅛ page

REVIEW

Alfred J. Mac Adam, Daniel Shapiro, Editors
Americas Society
680 Park Avenue
New York, NY 10021
(212) 249-8950
Fiction, poetry, criticism, essays, reviews, translations, interviews, articles on visual arts and music.
REVIEW presents the best of Latin American literature in English translation. It contains a review section as well as major articles on the Latin American visual and performing arts.
Payment: $100 and up.
Copyright held by the Americas Society (present); Center for Inter-American Relations (back issues).
1967; 2/yr; 5,000
$14/yr ind; $22/yr inst; $7/ea
100 pp; 8½ x 11

Ad rates: $700/page/7¾ x 9¾;
$400/½ page/5 x 7

Total Circulation Services (Hackensack, NJ); Ingram Periodicals (Nashville, TN); Inland Book Co. (East Haven, CT)

THE REVIEW OF CONTEMPORARY FICTION

John O'Brien
1817 North 79th Avenue
Elmwood Park, IL 60635

Criticism, essays, reviews, translation, interviews.

Each issue is devoted to criticism on one or two contemporary novelists.

Upcoming issues are devoted to John Barth, Alexander Theroux, and a history of Grove Press.

Gilbert Sorrentino, Robert Creeley, Paul Metcalf, Carlos Fuentes, Toby Olson.

Reporting time: 2 weeks.

Copyright held by magazine; reverts to author upon publication.

1981; 3/yr; 2,800

$15/yr ind; $22/yr inst; $8/ea; 10%–40%

200 pp; 6 x 9

Ad rates: $150/page/5 x 7½

ISSN: 0276-0045

DeBoer, Inland Book Company, Small Press Distribution

RFD

Short Mountain Collective
P.O. Box 68
Liberty, TN 37095
(615) 536-5176

Poetry, fiction, essays, reviews, interviews, photographs, graphics/artwork.

RFD focuses on rural gay men in related areas of human growth and consciousness and is an open forum for new ideas, radical views and controversial issues. The scope includes articles on alternative lifestyles, homesteading skills, collectives, gardening, cooking, contact letters, poetry, fiction, prisoner section, book reviews and graphics.

Michael Mason, Harry Hay, Bru Dye, Louise Hay, Robin Walden.

Payment: 1 copy of issue published in.

Reporting time: 1–6 months.

Copyright held by author.

1974; 4/yr; 2,700

$22/yr ind 1st class; $15/yr ind 2nd class; $17/yr inst; $4.25/ea; 40%

72 pp; 8½ x 11

Ad rates: $350/page/8½ x 11; $185/½ page/4¼ x 11 or 8½ x 5½; $98/¼ page/4¼ x 5¹/₁₂

ISSN: 0149-709X

RHINO

Enid Baron & Carole Hayes
1040 Judson Avenue
Evanston, IL 60202
(312) 328-6524; (312) 864-9628
Poetry.

RHINO is a nationally recognized
annual collection of poetry by
new and established writers,
with a yearly poetry contest
judged by recognized poets. It
can be purchased in bookstores
throughout the Chicago area,
and elsewhere in the United
States. **RHINO** has been the
recipient of grants and literary
awards from the Illinois Arts
Council over the last thirteen
years.

Simon Perchik, John Dickson,
Gary Fincke, Emilie Glen, Edward Lynskey.

Payment: one copy, upon publication.

Reporting time: 1–3 months.
Copyright held by author.
1976; 1/yr; 480
$3/ea; 40%
90+ pp; 5½ x 8⅜
No ads

RHODODENDRON

Steven Jacobsen
2958 E. Louise Ave.
Salt Lake City, UT 84109
(801) 486-9455

Poetry, fiction, reviews, graphics/
artwork.

RHODODENDRON groups
widely differing types of writing
together, in the hopes of effect-
ing a cumulative dynamism and
dialogue. Anything is possible
in **RHODODENDRON**. The
magazine itself is only a vessel
or frame.

Brian Bedard, Laurel Speer, Greg
Boyd, Dan Raphael, Richard
Kostelanetz, Steve Richmond,
Wanda Coleman.

Payment: 3 copies per contributor
upon publication.

Copyright held by Steven Jacobsen; reverts to author upon publication.

1984; 4/yr; 200+
$15/yr ind & inst; $2.50/ea; 40%
40 pp; 8½ x 5½
Ad rates: variable
Flatland Distribution (Oakland,
CA)

RIVER CITY (formerly MEMPHIS STATE REVIEW)

Sharon Bryan
English Department
Memphis State University
Memphis, TN 38152
(901) 678-8888

Poetry, fiction, essays, interviews.
The magazine sponsors the River
City Writing Awards in fiction:

1st prize $2,000; 2nd prize $500; 3rd prize $300. Write for details.
Fred Busch, Marvin Bell, Mona Van Duyn, Pattiann Rogers, Luisa Valenzuela.
Payment: varies.
Reporting time: 1 month.
Copyright reverts to author.
1980; 2/yr; 1,000
$6/yr; $4/ea
100 pp; 6 x 9
$40/page

Reporting time: submissions read only in September and October.
Copyright held by Big River Association; reverts to author upon publication.
1975; 3/yr; 1,000
$14/yr ind; $24/yr inst; $5/ea; 33%
112 pp; 5½ x 8½
Exchange ads
ISSN: 0149-8851
Ingram

RIVER STYX

Jennifer Atkinson, Quincy Troupe, Editors; Andrew Haber, Managing Editor
14 South Euclid
St. Louis, MO 63108
(314) 361-0043

Poetry, fiction, interviews, photographs, graphics/artwork.
RIVER STYX is a multicultural journal of poetry, prose and graphic arts publishing works by both established and up and coming writers and artists, significant for their originality, quality, and craftsmanship.
Sharon Olds, Grace Paley, Derek Walcott, Marilyn Hacker, Howard Nemerov.
Payment: $8/page for literature: $10/page for photographs or drawings.

ROHWEDDER: International Journal of Literature and Art

H.J. Schact, Nancy Antell, Robert Dassanowsky-Harris
P.O. Box 29490
Los Angeles, CA 90029
(213) 256-5083

Poetry, fiction, reviews, translation, interviews, photographs, graphics/artwork.
A journal of international literature and art, featuring poetry and prose in original language and English translation, black and white photography and graphics, reviews and essays on pictoral and theater arts and events in the Los Angeles area and globally. We are also interested in language oriented work, experimental forms, theoretical writings on postmodernism,

open text work and new lyric
poetry.
Sarah Kirsch, Pia Tafdrup, Peter
Schneider, Juan Felipe Herrera,
Kain Karawahn.
Payment: in copies.
Reporting time: 1 month.
Copyright held by magazine; reverts to author upon publication.
1986; 2/yr; 800–1,000
$12/4 issues ind; $16/4 issues inst;
$4/ea
50 pp; 8½ x 11
Ad rates: $300/page/8½ x 11;
$170/½ page/5½ x 8½; $90/¼
page/4¼ x 5½; $50/2¾ x 4¼;
$30/1¾ x 4¼
ISSN: 0892-6956

S

ST. ANDREWS REVIEW
Ron Bayes, Editor
St. Andrews College
Laurinburg, NC 28352
(919) 276-3652

Poetry, fiction, plays, translation,
essays, reviews, interviews.
ST. ANDREWS REVIEW publishes fiction, poetry and essays
of highest quality from both
established writers and promis-

ing new authors from all over
the U.S. and abroad.
Fred Chappell, Hiroaki Sato, Soi-
chi Furuta, Yukio Mishima,
Hugh Kenner.
Payment: one copy.
Copyright held by magazine; reverts to author upon publication.
1972; 2/yr; 300
$7/ea; 30%
100 pp; 6 x 9
Ad rates: $200/page/5 x 7;
$100/½ page/2½ x 3½; $50/¼
page/1¼ x 1¾
ISSN: 0036-2751

SALMAGUNDI
Robert and Peggy Boyers, Editors;
Thomas S.W. Lewis, Associate
Editor
Skidmore College
Saratoga Springs, NY 12866
(518) 584-5000, ext 2302

Poetry, fiction, criticism, essays,
reviews, translation, interviews.
SALMAGUNDI is an international quarterly of the humanities and social sciences
publishing essays and book reviews on literature, contemporary politics, film, dance, and
current ideas. General issues
also feature original fiction,
poetry, photographs and interviews.

George Steiner, Conor Cruise
O'Brien, Nadine Gordimer,
Christopher Lasch, Susan Son-
tag, Seamus Heaney.
Payment: none.
Reporting time: 1–5 months.
Copyright held by Skidmore; reverts to author upon publication.
1965; 4/yr; 5,600
$12/yr ind; $20/yr inst; $5/ea; ne-
gotiable
160–230 pp; 8½ x 5½
Ad rates: $150/page/4 x 7; $85/½
page/4 x 3½
B.DeBoer, Periodicals In Particular (U.K.)

SALTHOUSE
A Geopoetics Journal
DeWitt Clinton
800 W. Main
Department of English
University of Wisconsin
Whitewater, WI 53190
(414) 472-1036
Poetry, fiction, reviews.
Interest is in poetry, fiction and
reviews/criticism which is influ-
enced by a sense of anthropol-
ogy, geography or history.
Richard Shelton, Jeanne Larsen,
Judith Roche, Sybil Woods-
Smith, Lynn Shoemaker.
Payment: in copies.
Not reading MSS in 1990. Will
announce call for MSS in Poets
& Writers in late 1990 or 1991.
Reporting time: 2–3 months.
Copyright held by author.
1975; irregular; 300
$6/ea; back issue is free; 40%
96 pp; 5¼ x 8½
Ad rates: $30/page; $15/½ page
ISSN: 0737-5506

SALT LICK
James Haining
1804 East 38½ Street
Austin, TX 78722
Poetry, fiction, essays, photo-
graphs, graphics/artwork.
A thrilling publication since 1969.
Gerald Burns, Michael Lally,
Robert Trammell, John Ceeley,
Julie Siegel, Michalea Moore.
Payment: in copies.
Reporting time: 2–3 weeks.
Copyright reverts to author.
1969; 2/yr; 1,500
$5/yr; $3/ea; 40%
64 pp; 8½ x 11

**SAN FERNANDO POETRY
JOURNAL**
Richard Cloke, Editor; Shirley
Rodecker, Managing Editor;
Lori C. Smith, Pub. Editor
Kent Publications, Inc.
18301 Halstead Street
Northridge, CA 91324

(818) 349-2080

Poetry.

Seeks to fuse diverse elements of contemporaneity, ranging from evocation of scientific and technical advances—cosmology, sub-atomic inner space—cyberpunk S.F.—with a pronounced interest in poetry of social protest which illuminates the ills of our time, with special emphasis on the perils of nuclear warfare.

Stan Proper, Stratton F. Caldwell, Leigh Hunt, R. Jerry Fabian, Phyllis Gershator.

Payment: in copies, discounts on subs.

Reporting time: 2–3 weeks.

Copyright reverts to author.

1978; 4/yr; 500

$10/yr; $3/ea; 20%–30%

100 pp; 5½ x 8½

Ad rates: $50/page/4½ x 7; $25/½ page/4½ x 3½

ISSN: 0196-2884

SAN FRANCISCO REVIEW OF BOOKS

Joel Smith
1117 Geary Street
San Francisco, CA 94109
(415) 771-1252

Criticism, essays, reviews, interviews, graphics/artwork.

A literary review, focusing on one to three themes per issue, with in-depth interviews and articles relating to literature and publishing. Twenty to thirty titles reviewed, with emphasis on new books, including history and non-fiction. Also reviews of nationwide cultural events—dance, art, theatre, film. Open to diverse political opinions.

Ursula K. Le Guin, James D. Houston, M.F.K. Fisher, Jeremy Larner, Larry Bensky, Isadora Alman.

Payment: variable, in pay and copies; also, trade at local establishments.

Reporting time: 6 weeks–2 months.

Copyright held by magazine; reverts to author upon request.

1975; 4/yr; 5,500

$12/yr ind; $15/yr inst; $3.50/ea; 40%

48 pp; 8½ x 11

Ad rates: $850/page/7 x 10; $500/ ½ page/7 x 4⅞; $300/¼ page/3⅜ x 4⅞

ISSN: 0194-0724

SATORI

Gary Green, Pat Sims
P.O. Box 318
Tivoli, NY 12583
(914) 757-4443

Fiction, interviews, poetry, essays, photographs, graphics/artwork.

We provide a forum for the work and ideas of artists and writers, both established and previously unpublished, focusing on those from the mid-Hudson Valley region of New York. We are selective in our choices of work, seeking new and unique ideas in fiction, non-fiction, art, and photography. Also featured is a Q & A interview each issue with an artist or writer from the region.

Mikhail Horowitz, Dick Higgins, Cynde Gregory, Alison Knowles, Robert Mezey, A.D. Coleman.

Payment: in copies, upon publication.

Copyright held by magazine; reverts to author upon publication.

1988; 4/yr; 630

$8/yr; $2/ea; 40%; 50% if non-returnable

20 pp; 8½ x 11

Ad rates: $100/page; $75/½ page; $50/¼ page

ISSN: 0898-3011

THE SEATTLE REVIEW

Donna Gerstenberger
Padelford Hall, GN-30
University of Washington
Seattle, WA 98195
(206) 543-9865, 543-2690

Poetry, fiction, essays, interviews with writers.

THE SEATTLE REVIEW is a journal of poetry and prose published twice yearly. We try to achieve a balance in our pages between the work of nationally-known writers and that of younger writers of promise.

Rita Dove, W.P. Kinsella, Ursula Le Guin, William Stafford, Frances McCue.

Payment: varies.

Reporting time: 3–4 months; 6 months summer.

Copyright held by magazine; reverts to author upon publication.

$8/yr; $16/2 yrs; $4.50/ea

100 pp; 6 x 9

Ad rates: $90/page/5 x 7; $50/½ page/5 x 4½

ISSN: 0147-6629

SECOND COMING

A.D. Winans
P.O. Box 31249
San Francisco, CA 94131
(415) 647-3679

Poetry, fiction, criticism, essays, reviews.

One-act plays, interviews, photographs, graphics/artwork.

SECOND COMING was established in December, 1971: An international literary journal,

dedicated to publishing the best poetry and prose available today, whether it comes from the U.S. or abroad. 1990 will be a sabbatical year. Will begin again in 1991.
Bob Kaufman, Charles Bukowski, Jack Micheline, James Purdy, Lynne Savitt.
Payment: in copies.
Reporting time: 1–4 weeks.
Copyright held by magazine; reverts to author upon publication.
1971; 2/yr; 1,000
$7.50/yr ind; $9/inst; $5/ea; 40%
80–216 pp; 5½ x 8½
Ad rates: $150/page; $85/½ page
ISSN: 0048-9956

SEEMS
Karl Elder
Lakeland College
Box 359
Sheboygan, WI 53082-0359
(414) 565-3871
Poetry, fiction, essays.
Philip Dacey, William Greenway, Hugh Ogden, Mark SaFranko, Kathleen Whitten, Bayla Winters.
Payment: a copy.
Reporting time: 4–8 weeks.
Copyright held by Karl Elder; reverts to author upon publication.

1971; irreg; 350
$12/4 issues; $3/ea
40 pp; 8½ x 7
ISSN: 0095-1730

SEMIOTEXT(E)
Sylvere Lotringer, Jim Fleming
P.O. Box 568
Brooklyn, NY 11211
(718) 387-6471
Fiction, criticism, essays, translation, interview, photographs.
Contemporary radical cultural politics, "movement" literatures. Also sponsors "Foreign Agents," small book series promoting contemporary radical politics and culture, philosophy and human sciences.
Michel Foucault, Roland Barthes, Felix Guattari, Jean Baudrillard, Gilles Deleuze.
Payment: none.
Reporting time: 3 months.
Copyright reverts to author upon publication.
1974; irreg; 8,000
$12/3 issues ind; $24/3 issues inst; $5/ea; 40%
320 pp; 7 x 9
ISSN: 0093-5779

SENECA REVIEW
Deborah Tall
Hobart and William Smith Colleges
Geneva, NY 14456

(315) 781-3364

Poetry, criticism, translation, interviews.

Twice a year the **SENECA REVIEW** publishes poetry and prose about poetry, with a special interest in translation.

Seamus Heaney, Rita Dove, Gregory Orr, David St. John, Gerald Early.

Payment: 2 copies.

Reporting time: 4–10 weeks.

Copyright held by Hobart and William Smith Colleges; reverts to author upon publication.

1970; 2/yr; 600

$8/yr; $15/2 yrs; $5/ea; 40%

90 pp; 5½ x 8½

Ad rates: $75/page/5 x 8

ISSN: 0037-2145

Small Press Traffic

SEQUOIA

Annie Finch

Storke Publications Building

Stanford, CA 94305

(415) 497-9282

Poetry, fiction, criticism, interviews, photographs, art.

We are eclectic but like interesting and beautiful language. Feminist, experimental, and new-formalist work is welcome. We are not receptive to typical generic "workshop" writing.

Rita Dove, Seamus Heaney, Susan

Howe, Janet Lewis, James Merrill.

Payment: in copies.

Reporting time: 2 months.

Author retains rights.

1892; 2/yr; 500

$10/yr; $5/ea

80–105 pp; 5½ x 8

Ad rates: $100/page; $60/½ page

L & S Distributors

THE SEWANEE REVIEW

George Core

University of the South

Sewanee, TN 37375

(615) 598-1245

Poetry, fiction, criticism, essays, reviews.

America's oldest literary quarterly publishes original fiction, poetry, essays on literary and related subjects, book reviews and book notices for well-educated readers who appreciate good American and English literature.

Hayden Carruth, Louis D. Rubin, Jr., George Garrett, Donald Davie, Malcolm Cowley, L.C. Knights.

Payment: $10–$12/printed page; 60¢/line for poetry.

Reporting time: 4 weeks.

Copyright held by author.

1892; 4/yr; 3,500

$15/yr ind; $20/yr inst; $6/ea

192 pp; 6 x 9

Ad rates: $175/page/4¼ x 7;
$110/½ page/4¼ x 3⅜; $80/¼
page
ISSN: 0037-3052

SEZ

Jim Dochniak
P.O. Box 8803
Minneapolis, MN 55408
(612) 822-3488

Poetry, fiction, criticism, essays, reviews, translation, interviews, photographs, graphics/artwork, reportage and commentary on issues of current cultural interest, letters, journal-diary entries.

SEZ is Minnesota's only multicultural literary magazine and one of only a few small press magazines in the U.S. which features writing by working-class poets and artists. We tend to favor the much neglected social issue-oriented writers of the Midwest, but always feature work by writers committed to the struggles for a more humane world everywhere. New poems from Nicaragua, El Salvador, etc. Financial difficulties have made it impossible for us to accept any unsolicited materials for the year.

Thomas McGrath, Ivory Giles, Nephtali De Leon, Leonel Rugama, Meridel Le Sueur.

Payment: in copies and cash, when available.

Reporting time: 6 days–6 months.

Copyright held by Jim Dochniak; reverts to author upon publication.

1978; irreg; 2,000

$7/4 issues ind; $8.50/4 issues inst; $3.50/ea; 30%

80 pp; 8½ x 11

Ad rates: inquire

ISSN: 0190-3640

SHENANDOAH

Dabney Stuart, Editor; Lynn Williams, Managing Editor
P.O. Box 722
Lexington, VA 24450
(703) 463-8765 (9–12 noon)

Poetry, fiction, essays, translations, interviews, photographs.

Consider work from both new and established writers. Annual prizes in fiction, poetry and the essay.

Seamus Heaney, Northrop Frye, Robert Wrigley, Lisa Sandlin, Shelby Hearon.

Payment: poetry: $2/line; prose: $20/page.

Reporting time: 2–4 weeks.

Copyright held by magazine; reverts to author upon publication.

1950; 4/yr; 2,100
$11/yr; $3.50/ea; 50%
100 pp; 6 x 9
Ad rates: $200/page/4½ x 7;
  $100/½ page/4½ x 3½
ISSN: 0037-3583
Ingram, Anton Mikofsky

SHOOTING STAR REVIEW

Sandra Gould Ford
7123 Race Street
Pittsburgh, PA 15208
(412) 731-7039

Poetry, fiction, essays, reviews,
  photographs, graphics/artwork.
SHOOTING STAR REVIEW is
  an award-winning illustrated
  quarterly that uses the arts to
  explore the African-American
  experience. **SHOOTING STAR
  REVIEW** publishes an international array of free lance writers
  and artists who tell the story of
  Black people. Upcoming themes
  include: "Behind Bars: Emotional, Social, Psychological as
  well as Physical," "Marching to
  a Different Beat: Celebrating
  Those Who Dare to be Different," "Saluting African-
  American Male Writers,"
  "Mothers & Daughters," and
  "Home." Guidelines available
  with SASE. Sample copy ($3)
  is sent with next bulk mailing
unless 9 x 12 envelope w/$1
  postage included.
Kristan Hunter, Dennis Brutus,
  Reginald McKnight, Jerry
  Ward, Toi Derricote, Doris Jean
  Austin, Marita Golden.
Payment: fiction $30; essays $10
  and up; poems $8.
Copyright held by **SHOOTING
  STAR REVIEW**; reverts to
  author upon publication.
1987; 4/yr; 1,500
$10/yr ind; $15/yr inst; $2.95/ea;
  20% consignment, 50% outright
  purchase
44 pp; 8½ x 11
Ad rates: $750/page; $425/½
  page; $210/¼ page
ISSN: 0892-1407
Self-distributed to over 50 bookstores nationally

THE SHORT STORY REVIEW

Dwight Gabbard, Stephen Wood-
  hams, Beth Overson, Catherine
  Jacob, Melinda Dart, George
  Knuepfel
450 Irving St. #4
San Francisco, CA 94122
Fiction.
Founded in 1983, **THE SHORT
  STORY REVIEW** publishes
  works of fiction.
Molly Giles, Amy Tan, Richard
  Cortez Day, William Heinesen,
  Sara Vogan.

Payment: none.
Reporting time: 8–12 weeks.
Copyright held by author.
1983; 4/yr; 1,500
$10/yr; $2.50/ea; 40%
20 pp; 10 x 13
Ad rates: $432/page/10 x 13½;
$254/½ page/10 x 6⅝; $149/¼
page/4¹¹⁄₁₆ x 6⅝
ISSN: 0741-0786
L-S Distributors (San Francisco);
Armadillo (Venice, CA)

SIBYL-CHILD

Nancy Arbuthnot, Saundra Maley
709 Dahlia St. NW
Washington, DC 20012
(202) 723-5468

Established in 1974, **SIBYL-
CHILD** has just gone out of
print. Back issues of
chapbooks—fiction, poetry,
translations—available at $3.50.
Doris Mozer, David Hall, Ann
Slayton, Peter Van Egmond,
William Griffiths, Nan Fry.
5½ x 8
ISSN: 0161-715X

THE SIGNAL

Joan Silva, David Chorlton
P.O. Box 67
Emmett, ID 83617
(208) 365-5812

Poetry, fiction, criticism, essays,
reviews, translation, interviews,
photographs, graphics/artwork.
We would like to create a forum
for inter-disciplinary work,
bridging between literature, art,
music; and ecological, socio/po-
litical concerns. We encourage
submissions in the socio/scien-
tific area; examples would be
archeologic, rare travel experi-
ences/philosophic essays on almost anything, but quality of
thought and expression should
be rigorous and must have literary merit.
Carolyn Stoloff, Nikla Törnlund,
Hans Raimund, Michael Ham-
burger, Merrit Clifton, David
Fisher, Philip Curtis, Li Min
Hua, Stephen Stepanchev, Ma-
lay Roy Choudhury, Maurice
Kenny.
Payment: none.
Copyright held by **THE SIGNAL**;
reverts to author upon publication.
1987; 2/yr; 425
$10/yr; $6/ea; 40%
50+ pp; 8½ x 11
Ad rates: $100/page/8½ x 11;
$65/½ page/8½ x 5½; $35/¼
page/4¼ x 2¾

SILVERFISH REVIEW

Rodger Moody
P.O. Box 3541

Eugene, OR 97403
(503) 344-5060

Poetry, short short stories, reviews, essays, translations, interviews, photographs, annual poetry chapbook contest.

The only criterion for selection of material is quality. In future issues **SILVERFISH REVIEW** wants to showcase essays on creative process as well as translations of poetry from Europe and South America. **SILVERFISH REVIEW** also sponsors an annual poetry chapbook contest.

Dick Allen, Lauren Mesa, Floyd Skloot, Enid Shomer, Robert Ward.

Payment: 5 copies, and $5 per page (when funding permits).

Reporting time: 1–4 weeks.

Copyright held by author.

1979; irreg; 750

$9/3 issues ind; $12/3 issues inst; $3/ea plus $1 postage; 40%

48 pp; 5½ x 8½

Ad rates: $50/page/4¼ x 7½; $25/½ page/4¼ x 4

ISSN: 0164-1085

Spring Church Book Company (chapbooks only), The Faxon Co., Inc; EBSCO; Boley International

SINISTER WISDOM

Elana Dykewomon
P.O. Box 3252
Berkeley, CA 94703

Poetry, fiction, criticism, essays, reviews, interviews, plays, photographs, graphics/artwork.

A lesbian/feminist journal of art, literature and politics founded in 1976 by Harriet Desmoines and Catherine Nicholson, passed on in 1981 to Michelle Cliff and Adrienne Rich, in 1983 to Melanie Kaye/Kaye/Kantrowitz and in 1986 to the current editor.

The primary commitment of the magazine is to publish creative work by lesbians from a broad range of racial, ethnic, cultural and class perspectives.

Doris Davenport, Adrienne Rich, Sandy Boucher, Chrystos, Gloria Anzaldúa, Judith Katz, Winn Gilmore, Marilyn Frye.

Payment: 2 copies.

Reporting time: 6–9 months.

Copyright held by author.

1976; 3–4/yr; 3,000

$17/yr ind; $30/yr inst; $6/ea; 40%

144 pp; 5½ x 8½

Ad rates: $150/page/4½ x 7; $75/½ page/4½ x 3¼; $40/¼ page/2 x 3½

ISSN: 0196-1853

Inland, Bookpeople

SINK

Spencer Selby
P.O. Box 590095

San Francisco, CA 94159
(415) 752-6378
Poetry.
SINK publishes innovative poetry by writers concerned with the possibilities of language, the generation and exploration of new meanings in the world and in the work.
Clark Coolidge, Steve Benson, Rosemarie Waldrop, Rae Armantrout, Ron Silliman.
Payment: in copies, upon publication.
Copyright held by **SINK** Press; reverts to author upon publication.
1986; 1–2/yr; 200
$12/yr ind; $15/yr inst; $4/ea; 40%
70 pp; 7 x 10
No ads
ISSN: 0891-298X

SIPAPU
Noel Peattie
Route 1, Box 216
Winters, CA 95694
(916) 752-1032
Reviews, interviews, conference news.
Newsletter for librarians, editors, and collectors interested in dissent (feminist, Third World, pacifist, etc.) literature, together with small press poetry. Emphasis on peace and environmental concerns; all must have a print emphasis.
Karl Kempton, Loss P. Glazier, Mary Zeppa, John Daniel, Harry Polkinhorn.
Payment: 5¢/word.
Reporting time: 5 months.
Copyright held by editor; reverts to author upon publication.
1970; 450
$8/yr; $4/ea
36 pp; 8½ x 11
No ads
ISSN: 0037-5837
EBSCO, Faxon, Popular Subscription Service, Turner

SLOW MOTION MAGAZINE
Ona Gritz, Laura Hennessey-Desena, Anne Makeever, Zack Rogow
177 Bleecker Street, #3
New York, NY 10012
(212) 228-1359
Poetry, translation (poetry).
SLOW MOTION is a poetry magazine interested in publishing new poets with social interests. We are interested in giving new poets exposure: both local and from other parts of the country.
Ruth Stone, Harry Stessel, Jack Nestor, John Oliver Simon.
Payment: in copies.

Copyright reverts to author upon publication.
1986; 2/yr; 250
$6/yr; $3/ea; 40%
40 pp; 5½ x 8½
No ads

THE SMALL POND MAGAZINE

Napoleon St. Cyr
P.O. Box 664
Stratford, CT 06497
(203) 378-4066

Poetry, fiction, essays, reviews, graphics/artwork.

Features contemporary poetry by new and established writers, but also uses short prose pieces of many genres, plus some art work—black and white only.

Renne McQuilkin, John O'Brien, Heather Tosteson, Barbara S. Parish, H.R. Coursen.

Payment: 2 copies.

Reporting time: 10–30 days, longer in summer.

Copyright held by N. St. Cyr.
1964; 3/yr; 325
$7/yr; $2.50/ea; inquire
40 pp; 5½ x 8½
Ad rates: $40/page/4½ x 7½; $25/½ page/4½ x 3½; $15/¼ page/4½ x 2¼
ISSN: 0031-721X

SONORA REVIEW

Martha Ostheimer, Laurie Schorr
Department of English
University of Arizona
Tucson, AZ 85721
(602) 621-8077 or (602) 621-3880

Poetry, fiction, reviews, translation, interviews, criticism, essays.

We're looking for the liveliest new writing we can get our hands on, including experimental and non-conformist work. Most issues are general in nature, though recent special features have profiled "Crossing Borders: Writing from Alternative Traditions" and "Voices from the Southwestern Landscape."

Jane Miller, David Foster Wallace, Ingrid Smith, Ray A. Young Bear, Tristan Tzara.

Payment: copies, annual prizes.

Reporting time: 2–3 months, longer during summer.

Copyright reverts to author.
1980; 2/yr
$8/yr; $5/ea; 40%
120 pp; 6 x 9

SOUTH CAROLINA REVIEW

Richard J. Calhoun
English Department
Clemson University
Clemson, SC 29634-1503
(803) 656-3229

Poetry, fiction, criticism, essays, reviews, translation, interviews. Listed as one of the twenty most outstanding literary magazines in the United States by the *The New York Quarterly,* **THE SOUTH CAROLINA REVIEW** is now in its twentieth year of publication. Our primary goal is to continue to publish fiction, poetry, and criticism of the quality that has earned us several Pushcart nominations, as well as, most recently, election to *The Best American Short Stories 1982* and *Prize Stories 1982: The O. Henry Awards.*

Stephen Dixon, Roseanne Coggeshall, Joyce Carol Oates, Richard Kostelanetz, Lyn Lifshin.

Payment: in issues.

Reporting time: 6 months.

Copyright held by magazine.

1968; 2/yr; 600

$5/yr ind; $3/ea; 33⅓%

96 pp; 9 x 6

Ad rates: negotiable

ISSN: 0038-3163

SOUTH COAST POETRY JOURNAL

John J. Brugaletta

English Department

California State University Fullerton

Fullerton, CA 92634

(714) 773-2454

Poetry, graphics/artwork.

SOUTH COAST POETRY JOURNAL avoids theorizing so as to remain open to every kind of excellence in poetry, no matter what the style or school. Our standards for excellence, however, are high.

Richard Eberhart, Rita Dove, Marge Piercy, William Stafford, John Hollander, Denise Levertov, Mark Strand.

Payment: in single copies.

Copyright held by **SOUTH COAST POETRY JOURNAL**; reverts to author upon publication.

1986; 2/yr; 150

$9/yr ind; $10/yr inst; $5/ea; 40%

60 pp; 5½ x 8½

No ads

ISSN: 0887-2074

SOUTH DAKOTA REVIEW

John R. Milton

University of South Dakota

Vermillion, SD 57069

(605) 677-5220, 677-5229

Poetry, fiction, criticism, essays, occasional translation and interviews.

When the material warrants, an emphasis on the American West; writers from the West;

Western places or subjects; frequent issues with no geographical emphasis. Periodic special issues on one theme, or one place, or one writer, e.g., Ross MacDonald (Spring 1986).

Edward Loomis, Max Evans, Frederick Manfred, Lloyd Van Brunt.

Payment: in copies.

Reporting time: 2 weeks–2months, slowest in summer.

1963; 4/yr; 600

$15/yr; $25/2 yrs; $5/single copy; 40%

150–190 pp; 6 x 9

ISSN: 0038-3368

THE SOUTH FLORIDA POETRY REVIEW

S.A. Stirnemann

7190 N.W. 21 Street

Fort Lauderdale, FL 33313

(305) 742-5624

Poetry, essays, reviews, interviews.

THE SOUTH FLORIDA POETRY REVIEW, a national poetry triquarterly, publishes the works of well-known poets along with the works of fresh, new talents. We are interested in contemporary poetry of the highest literary quality, work in which there is both a sense of vision and a sense of craft.

Siv Cedering, David Kirby, Lisel Mueller, Kathleen Spivack, William Stafford.

Payment: in copies; honorarium when available.

Reporting time: 4–12 weeks.

Copyright held by magazine; reverts to author upon publication.

1983; 3/yr; 750

$7.50/yr ind; $9/yr inst; $3/ea; 20%

64 pp; 6 x 9

Ad rates: $100/page/4½ x 7½

ISSN: 0885-0720

THE SOUTHERN CALIFORNIA ANTHOLOGY

Stacie Strong, Catherine Davidson

Master of Professional Writing Program

University of Southern California

WPH 404

Los Angeles, CA 90089-4034

(213) 743-8255

Poetry, fiction, interviews, graphics/artwork (on cover).

Published through the Master of Professional Writing Program at the University of Southern California, **THE SOUTHERN CALIFORNIA ANTHOLOGY** is a literary journal of fiction, poetry, and interviews. Seventy percent of the pieces are solicited. Volume VII (published April 1989) includes works by:

Philip Appleman, Madeline De-
Frees, Li Guowen, John Hol-
lander, David Madden, James
Merrill, John Frederick Nims,
James Ragan, David Ray, Hu-
bert Selby, Jr., Henry Taylor,
John Updike, Peter Vierick,
Richard Yates.
Payment: 3 copies.
Copyright held by the University
of Southern California, Master
of Professional Writing Pro-
gram; reverts to author upon
publication.
1983; 1/yr; 1,000
$6.95/yr; 40%
144 pp; 5½ x 8½
ISBN: 0-9615108-5-4
Blackwell North America, Ballen
Booksellers, Small Press Disbri-
bution

SOUTHERN EXPOSURE
Eric Bates
P.O. Box 531
Durham, NC 27702
(919) 688-8167
Essays, reviews, interviews, pho-
tographs, graphics/artwork.
SOUTHERN EXPOSURE is a
winner of the George Polk
Award and is widely respected
as the voice of the progressive
South. Investigative journalism
and oral history are emphasized.
Very little fiction or poetry,

mostly non-fiction articles on
social issues.
Payment: up to $200.
Reporting time: 6–8 weeks.
Copyright held by magazine.
1973; 4/yr; 4,000
$16/yr ind; $20/yr inst; $5/ea;
40%
Ad rates: $400/page; $270/½ page
64 pp; 8½ x 11
ISSN: 0146-809X
Ingram

SOUTHERN HUMANITIES REVIEW
Dan R. Latimer, Thomas L.
Wright
R.T. Smith, Poetry Editor
9088 Haley Center
Auburn University
Auburn, AL 36849
(205) 826-4606
Poetry, fiction, essays, reviews.
**THE SOUTHERN HUMANI-
TIES REVIEW** publishes, fic-
tion, poetry and critical essays
on the arts, literature, philoso-
phy, religion, and history. Es-
says, articles, or stories should,
in general, range between 3,500
and 5,000 words. Poems should
not exceed two pages in length.
Denise Levertov, Louis Simpson,
Donald Hall, Peter Green, Yannis Ritsos.
Payment: copies and offprints.

Reporting time: 3 months.
Copyright held by Auburn University.
1967; 4/yr; 800
$12/yr; $4/ea
100 pp; 4½ x 7½
Ad rates: $85/page/4½ x 7½;
$50/½ page/4½ x 3¾
ISSN: 0038-4186

SOUTHERN POETRY REVIEW

Robert Grey
Department of English
University of North Carolina
Charlotte, NC 28223
(704) 547-4225

Poetry, review.

Submissions accepted from both established and previously unpublished poets. **SPR** is a natural outlet for poets writing in the South, but has no regional bias. Variety in style and content encouraged.

Susan Ludvigson, Linda Pastan, David Keller, Dave Smith, Marge Piercy.

Payment: in copies.

Reporting time: 6 weeks.

Copyright held by magazine; reverts to author upon request.

1958; 2/yr; 1,100
$6/yr; $3.50/ea; 40%
80 pp; 6 x 9

No ads
ISSN: 0038-447X

THE SOUTHERN QUARTERLY: A Journal of the Arts in the South

Peggy Whitman Prenshaw
University of Southern Mississippi
Southern Station Box 5078
Hattiesburg, MS 39406-5078
(601) 266-4370

Criticism, essays, reviews, interviews, photographs.

A non-profit scholarly journal, **THE SOUTHERN QUARTERLY** includes essays, articles, interviews and reviews on the arts—defined broadly—in the southern U.S. Alternately published general and special issues include research on music, theatre, dance, literature, film, art, architecture, popular and folk arts.

Virginia Spencer Carr, W. Kenneth Holditch, Jessie Poesch, William Ferris.

Payment: none.

Reporting time: 3–6 months.

Copyright held by University of Southern Mississippi; reverts to author upon publication.

1962; 4/yr; 750
$9/yr ind; $16/2 yrs ind; 3/ea; 15%
150 pp; 6 x 9

Ad rates: $100/page/4½ x 6¾;
$75/½ page/4½ x 3⅜
ISSN: 0038-4496

$90/½ page/4½ x 3⅝; $60/¼
page/4½ x 1⅔
ISSN: 0038-4534
B. DeBoer

THE SOUTHERN REVIEW
James Olney, David J. Smith
43 Allen Hall
Louisiana State University
Baton Rouge, LA 70803
(504) 388-5108
Fiction, poetry, criticism, reviews, interviews.
THE SOUTHERN REVIEW publishes poetry, fiction, criticism, essays, reviews and excerpts from novels in progress, with emphasis on contemporary literature in the United States and abroad, and with special interest in Southern history and culture.
Wole Soyinka, Gloria Naylor, Joyce Carol Oates, Louis Simpson, John William Corrington.
Payment: $12/printed page for prose; $20/printed page for poetry; 2 complimentary copies.
Reporting time: 2 months.
Copyright held by LSU; reverts to author upon publication.
1935: original series; 1965: new series; 4/yr; 3,100
$15/yr ind; $30/yr inst; $5/ea ind; $10/ea inst
250 pp; 6¾ x 10
Ad rates: $150/page/4½ x 7½;

THE SOUTHWEST REVIEW
Willard Spiegelman, Editor; Betsey McDougall, Managing Editor
6410 Airline Road
Southern Methodist University
Dallas, TX 75275
(214) 373-7440
Poetry, fiction, essays, interviews.
THE SOUTHWEST REVIEW is a quarterly that serves the interests of its region but is not bound by them. **SWR** has always striven to present the work of writers and scholars from the surrounding states and to offer analyses of problems and themes that are distinctly southwestern and, at the same time, publishes the works of good writers regardless of their locales.
Hortense Calisher, Gwendolyn Brooks, Tom Disch, Rosanna Warren, W.M. Spackman.
Payment: varies.
Reporting time: 1 month.
Copyright held by SMU; reverts to author upon publication.
1915; 4/yr; 1,400
$16/yr ind; $20/yr inst; $5/ea; 40%

144 pp; 6 x 9
Ad rates: $175/page/25 x 42½
picas; $115/½ page/25 x 21
picas
ISSN: 0038-4712
Homing Pigeon, Total Circulation
Services

SOU'WESTER

Audrey Parente
411 Main Trail
Ormond Beach, FL 32074
Poetry, especially longer poems,
fiction.
Payment: in copies.
Reporting time: 1 month.
Copyright held by Southern Illinois University.
1960; 3/yr; 300
$4/yr; $1.50/ea
88 pp; 6 x 9
ISSN: 0098-499X

THE SOW'S EAR

Errol Hess, Larry Richman (Poetry), Mary Calhoun (Graphics)
245 McDowell Street
Bristol, TN 37620
(615) 764-1625
Poetry, reviews, interviews,
graphics, photography.
Contemporary poetry exported
from and imported into Southern Appalachia. No nostalgia.
We publish both established and
new poets, with no restrictions
on subject matter or style. We
use B & W art to complement
poetry.
Marge Piercy, Fred Chappel, Lee
Smith, David Huddle, Josephine
Jacabosen, Jin Wayne Miller.
Payment: in copies.
Reporting time: 2–3 months.
Copyright reverts to author.
1988; 4/yr; 300
$8/4 issues; $3/ea; 40%
32 pp; 8½ x 11
Free classifieds

SPARROW POVERTY PAMPHLETS

Felix and Selma Stefanile
103 Waldron Street
West Lafayette, IN 47906
(317) 743-1991
Poetry.
The one-poet-an-issue magazine,
providing a forum for mature
poets. We are in the modernist
tradition, with its emphasis on
craft, shaped language, unity of
voice and vision.
Christopher Bursk, Geraldine C.
Little, Roger Finch, Gail White,
Gray Burr, Ger Killeen.
Payment: $30, plus royalties of
20%.
Reporting time: 6 weeks. Reading
period: April and May each
year.

Copyright reverts to author on request.

1954; 3/yr; 900

$9.00/yr; $2/ea for back copies; 35%

28–32 pp; 5½ x 8½

ISSN: 0038-6588

Small Press Distribution Inc,; Spring Church (for our chapbooks)

THE SPIRIT THAT MOVES US

Morty Sklar

P.O. Box 820

Jackson Heights, NY 11372-0820

(718) 426-8788

Poetry, fiction, photographs, artwork.

We favor work that expresses feeling. Over 95% is unsolicited. Our single author issue, *The Casting of Bells*, by Jaroslav Seifert, was followed a year later by the poet's winning the Nobel Prize for literature. In 1985, editor Morty Sklar was awarded a CCLM Editor's Grant. Query first for any theme, and time-frame.

Most recent issue (Nov. 1989) is of Swedish-language women poets (bilingual edition), translated by Lennart & Sonya Bruce.

Payment: one clothbound copy

plus 40% discount on paperbacks.

Reporting time: 1 week–1 month.

Copyright reverts to author upon publication.

1975; 2/yr; 1,500

Vol. 9/$11.20; Vol. 10/$12.60; (special issues are also published clothbound); 40%

64–336 pp; 5½ x 8½

Ads in regular issues only

ISSN: 0364-4014

Inland Book Co.; Bookslinger; Small Press Distribution; Bookpeople; The Distributors

THE SPOON RIVER QUARTERLY

Lucia Getsi, Jerry Pratt

English Department

Illinois State University

Normal-Bloomington, IL 61701

(309) 438-3667

Poetry, translation, interviews, photographs.

With the change in editors, **SRQ** is broadening content beyond midwestern-realist poetry. We want poetry that is interesting and compelling. Our standards are high—the acceptance rate is about 5%. Each of the first three issues each year contains a chapbook-length feature of new poems by an Illinois poet and an interview and critical intro-

duction to the poet's work. The
fourth issue binds the three Illinois poets into an anthology
that contains an appendix of
poem drafts.
Bruce Guernsey, Linnea Johnson,
Diana Hume George, John
Knoepfle, Phil Dacey, Richard
Jackson.
Payment: 3 contributor's copies.
Reporting time: 6 weeks.
Copyright reverts to author upon
publication.
1976; 4/yr; 500
$10/yr ind; $12/yr inst; $3/ea;
40%
64 pp; 5½ x 8½
Ad rates: $100/page/5 x 8; $50/½
page/5 x 2
ISSN: 0738-8993
Illinois Literary Publishers Association; EBSCO; Ingram

**SPWAO (Small Press Writers
and Artists Organization)
SHOWCASE**
Jeannette M. Hopper
P.O. Box 397
Marina, CA 93933
Poetry, fiction, graphics/artwork.
The **SPWAO SHOWCASE** is
just what the title says, a showcase for SPWAO members to
display their best work, whether
it be art, fiction or poetry. Only
members of SPWAO may con-
tribute at this time; however, all
writers/artists/poets with interests in science fiction, fantasy,
or related genres are eligible for
SPWAO membership.
Payment: one contributor's copy.
Reporting time: 2 weeks.
Copyright held by magazine; reverts to author upon publication.
1989; 1/yr; $6.95/ea
250 pp; 5 x 7 perfect bound

STILLETTO
Michael Annis
P.O. Box 5987–Westport Station
Kansas City, MO 64111
All types except reviews or criticism / "illustrated" / Quality a
must.
All schools, all genres, street poets to academia. Content is our
highest priority. Each writer is
given a large enough section to
clearly demonstrate the author's
ability and vision. If you feel
like you have a statement to
make for posterity, make it
here.
Antler, Wm. Burroughs, Andrei
Codrescu, Diane DiPrima, Diane Wakoski, Anne Waldman.
Payment: 20 contributor copies,
First Ed.
Reporting time: to 6 months.
Copyright reverts to author/artist.

1989; 2–3/yr
$25 1st Ed. collectors; $15 Commercial Ed; 30%
180+ pp; 5 x 11¼
1043-9501
ISSN: By publisher

STONE COUNTRY

Judith Neeld
P.O. Box 132
Meneshma, MA 02535

Poetry, criticism, essays, reviews, translations, graphics/artwork.

After sixteen years in print, **STONE COUNTRY** has ceased publication of what Library Journal called an "unusual expressive voice of our times, recommended for all." Back issues are still available, at $3.50 each.

Look for works by Martha Collins, David Hopes, Linda Pastan, Robert Pinsky and others.

STORY QUARTERLY

Anne Brashler, Diane Williams
P.O. Box 1416
Northbrook, IL 60065
(312) 433-0741

Fiction and interviews.
STORY QUARTERLY is looking for great fiction.
Reporting time: 2 months.

Copyright held by magazine; reverts to author upon publication.
1974; 2/yr; 1,500
$12/4 issues; $4/ea; 40%
110 pp; 6 x 9
ISSN: 0361-0144
B. DeBoer, Ingram Periodicals

SULFUR

Clayton Eshleman
210 Washtenaw
Ypsilanti, MI 48197
(313) 483-9787

Poetry, fiction, criticism, essays, reviews, translation, photographs, graphics/artwork.

Contemporary American poetry, translations, archival materials, book reviews, reproduction of art and photography.

Jerome Rothenberg, John Ashbery, Michael Palmer, William Carlos Williams, Aimé Césaire.
Payment: $30/contribution.
Reporting time: 1–2 weeks.
Copyright held by magazine; reverts to author upon publication.
1981; 2/yr; 1,500
$12/yr ind; $17/yr inst; $8/ea; 40%
230 pp; 6 x 9
Ad rates: $150/page/6 x 9; $85/½ page/6 x 3⅞
ISSN: 0730-305X

Inland; Small Press Distribution;
  DeBoer

SUN

Bill Zavatsky
347 West 39th Street, Apt. 7N
New York, NY 10018
(212) 594-8428
Poetry, fiction, criticism, essays,
  reviews, translation, interviews.
SUN publishes poetry, fiction,
  translation and commentary
  ranging from review to essays
  to brief "ideas."
Phillip Lopate, Ron Padgett, Ly-
  dia Davis, Harvey Shapiro,
  Hugh Seidman, Rochelle
  Owens.
Payment: none.
Reporting time: 1 week–3 months.
Copyright held by author.
1966 as SUNDIAL; 1971 as SUN;
  1/yr; 500–1,000
$6/ea
250 pp; 5½ x 8½
Ad rates: $100/page; $50/½ page;
  $25/¼ page
ISSN: 0039-5374

SUN DOG: The Southeast
Review

Craig Stroupe & Jamie Granger
406 Williams Building
Florida State University
Tallahassee, FL 32306
(904) 644-4320
Poetry, fiction, graphic art.
**SUN DOG: The Southeast
  Review** reads both fiction and
  poetry year-round. We are looking for striking images, inci-
  dents, and characters rather than
  particular styles or genres. We
  also publish the winner and
  runners-up of the World's Best
  Short Short Story Contest.
Janet Burroway, David Bottoms,
  Jesse Lee Kercheval, Leon
  Stokesbury, Rick Lott, Helen
  Norris, David Kirby.
Payment: 2 copies.
Copyright held by **SUN DOG**;
  reverts to author upon publication.
1979; 2/yr; 1,250
$4/ea; 40%
90 pp; 6 x 9

SWAMPROOT

Al Masarik, Editor; Jill Andrea,
  Managing Editor
Route 2, Box 1098
Hiwassee One
Jacksboro, TN 37757
(615) 562-7082
Poetry, essays, review, interviews,
  letters, photographs, graphics,
  artwork.
Contemporary poetry biased to-
  ward clarity, brevity, strong
  imagery; works that speak

strongly of the poet's place; works that show a need to be written.

Naomi Shihab Nye, Ted Kooser, Maurya Simon, Linda M. Hasselstrom, William Klorfkorn, Diane Glancy.

Payment: 3 copies, 1 year subsc.

Reporting time: 1 week–1 month.

Copyright reverts to author.

1987; 3/yr; 1,000

$12, $15 libararies; $5/ea; usual discount

86 pp; 6 x 9

ISSN: 1045-7682

SWIFT KICK

Robin Kay Willoughby
1711 Amherst Street
Buffalo, NY 14214
(716) 837-7778

Poetry, fiction, plays, translation, photographs, graphics/artwork.

We specialize in unusual formats, genres and styles.

Jerry McGuire, Dennis Maloney, Simon Perchik, Penny Kemp, Maurice Kenny.

Payment: in copies.

Reporting time: varies.

Copyright held by magazine; reverts to author upon publication.

1980; 4/yr; 200

$20/4 issues ind; $40/4 issues inst;

$6 + postage/sample copy (checks payable to editor); 40%

ISSN: 0277-447X

T

TAPROOT: A Journal of Older Writers

Philip W. Quigg, Enid Graf
P.O. Box 488
Stony Brook, NY 11790
(516) 632-6635

Poetry, fiction, graphics/artwork, reviews, photographs.

Publish the works of older writers; especially interested in "capturing the stories, poems and recountings of things related to and growing from the vanishing oral tradition," as well as the realities of our elders' return to the mainstream of community life.

Payment: 1 copy.

Copyright held by magazine; reverts to author upon publication.

1974; 1/yr; 1,000

$4/ea; 40%

100 pp; 8½ x 11

Ad rates: $500/page; $300/½ page; $175/¼ page

ISSN: 0887-9257

TAR RIVER POETRY

Peter Makuck
English Department
East Carolina University
Greenville, NC 27834
(919) 757-6041

Poetry, reviews.

We are looking for poetry that shows skillful use of figurative language. Narrative poems, short images poems, poems in closed and open form are welcome. We are not interested in sentimental, flat statement verse. Though we often publish the work of established poets, we are open to the work of newcomers as well.

A.R. Ammons, Brenda Galvin, Sharon Bryan, Jonathan Holden, Michael Mott, Patricia Goedicke, Leslie Norris, Mark Jarman.

Payment: none.
Reporting time: 5–7 weeks.
Copyright reverts to author.
1965; 2/yr; 1,000
$8/yr; $4/ea; 40%
62 pp; 6 x 9

THE TEXAS REVIEW

Paul Ruffin
English Department
Sam Houston State University
Huntsville, TX 77341
(409) 294-1429

Poetry, fiction, criticism, essays, reviews.

We are interested in the very best fiction and poetry available; our non-fiction may be literary, historical, or "familiar." We are interested principally in reviews of contemporary poetry and fiction.

Fred Chappell, Richard Eberhart, George Garrett, Donald Justice, William Stafford, Richard Wilbur.

Payment: in contributor's copies plus one year subscription to magazine.

Copyright held by magazine; reverts to author upon publication.

1979; 2/yr; 750–1,000
$10/yr ind/inst; $5/ea; 40%
144 pp; 6 x 9
ISSN: 0885-2685

THEATER

Joel Schechter, Editor
222 York Street
New Haven, CT 06520
(203) 432-1568

Criticism, essays, reviews, plays, translation, interviews, photographs.

Each issue contains the text of a new play or translation by a leading contemporary playwright. Also interviews with theatre artists and essays

by theatre artists and critics.
Reviews of performance groups
and productions from around
the world.
Athol Fugard, Dario Fo, Eric
Bentley, Jan Kott, Theodora
Skipitares.
Payment: $150 honorarium for
plays; various amounts for articles.
Copyright reverts to author.
1968; 3/yr; 1,200
$17/yr ind; $21/yr inst; $6/ea
90–100 pp; 9½ x 9½
Ad rates: $200/page/9½ x 9½
$100/½ page/9½ x 4¾; $60/¼
page/4¾ x 4¾

THEMA
Virginia Howard
Bothomos Enterprises
Box 74109
Merairie, LA 70033-4109
(504) 887-1263
Fiction, poetry.
Stories and poems must relate to
premise specified for each is-
sue. Themes for 1990: Teacups
in the sand; The last time I saw
Jane; The Thursday night
league; Nothing ever happened
to him but weather. Themes for
1991: The perfect imperfection;
Art, the canvas freed; and more
later.
Guida Jackson, Jewell P. Rhodes,

Paul Humphrey, Regina
deCormier-Shekerjian, Ellen
Herbert.
Payment: $25 for short story; $10
for poems.
Reporting time: dependent on
deadlines.
Copyright reverts to author.
1988; 4/yr; 200
$12/yr; $5/ea; 40%
200 pp; 5½ x 8½
ISSN: 1041-4851

THIRD WOMAN
Norma Alarcón
THIRD WOMAN Office
Chicano Studies
Dwinelle Hall 3412
University of California
Berkeley, CA 94720
(415) 642-0240
Poetry, drama, fiction, narrative,
reviews, creative and critical
essays, interviews, photographs,
graphics/artwork, contributors,
news, announcements, ads.
THIRD WOMAN is an annual
anthology featuring poetry,
drama, narrative, fiction, reviews, creative and critical essays, interviews, and graphic art
by Chicanas/Latinas and Third
World Women. We accept both
Spanish and English submissions for publication.
Sandra Cisneros, Evangelina

Vigil-Pinon, Achy Obejas, Margorie Agosin, Lucha Corpi, Cherrie Moraga, Gloria Anzaldua, Ana Castillo.
Payment: copies.
Copyright held by authors.
1981; 1/yr; 1,000
$8.95/yr ind; $15/yr inst; 40%
200 pp; 5½ x 8½
Ad rates: $100/page/4½ x 7½; $50/½ page/2 x 3½
ISSN: 0889-0722
Relampago Books, Small Press Distribution, Arte Publico Press, Yankee Book Peddler

THIRTEEN

Ken Stone
Box 392
Portlandville, NY 13834
(607) 547-4301

Poetry, fiction, reviews, translations, graphics/artwork.

THIRTEEN is a poetry magazine which specializes in 13-line poetry. We have no special themes or other requirements other than the poem be 13 lines, not including title. All poems should be titled.

Rochelle Holt, Judson Crews, ave jeanne, R. H. Yodice, Sue Saniel Elkind.
Payment: 1 copy.
Reporting time: 2 weeks.
Copyright held by author.

1982; 4/yr; 350
$5/yr; $2.50/ea; 40%
40 pp; 8½ x 11½
No ads
ISSN: 0747-9727
Direct mail by publisher

THIRTEENTH MOON

Judith E. Johnson
English Department
SUNY
Albany, NY 12222

Poetry, fiction, criticism, essays, reviews, translation, interviews, photographs, graphics/artwork.

THIRTEENTH MOON is a feminist literary magazine, placing primary emphasis on the quality of writing. It is specifically interested in work from feminist, lesbian, third-world, and working-class perspectives.

Joanna Russ, Cheryl Clarke, Nelida Pinon, Marie Ponsot.
Payment: in copies.
Reporting time: varies.
Copyright held by 13th Moon, Inc.; reverts to author upon publication.
1973; 1–2/yr; 2,500
$6.50/v ind; $13/v inst; $6.50/ea; 40%
200 pp; 6 x 9⅛
Ad rates: inquire

THE THREEPENNY REVIEW

Wendy Lesser
P.O. Box 9131
Berkeley, CA 94709
(415) 849-4545

Poetry, fiction, criticism, essays, reviews, memoirs, graphics/artwork.

THE THREEPENNY REVIEW is a quarterly journal publishing essays on literature, theater, film, television, dance, music, and the visual arts, as well as new poetry, original fiction, and socio-political articles. While based in California, it is aimed at a nation-wide audience.

John Berger, Greil Marcus, Elizabeth Hardwick, Thom Gunn, Christopher Ricks.

Payment: $50–$100.

Reporting time: 3 weeks–2 months.

Copyright held by magazine; reverts to author upon publication.

1980; 4/yr; 8,000

$10/yr; $4/ea; 30%–50%

36 pp; 11 x 17

Ad rates: $600/page/10 x 14; $350/½ page/10 x 7½; $200/¼ page/4½ x 7¼

ISSN: 0275-1410

Ingram Periodicals, Total Circulation Services, Ubiquity

THUNDER & HONEY

Akbar Imhotep
P.O. Box 11386
Atlanta, GA 30310
(404) 688-3376

Poetry, fiction, interviews, photographs, graphics/artwork.

THUNDER & HONEY is primarily devoted to poetry and fiction. Future issues will have arts-related articles and some interviews.

Charlie Braxton, Nome Poem, R.F. Smith, Askia Toure, Jeanne Towns.

Payment: 15 copies.

Copyright held by magazine; reverts to author upon publication.

1984; 4/yr; 1,500

$2.50/yr; 75¢/ea

4 pp; 8½ x 11

Ad rates: $210/page/10 x 16; $120/½ page/10 x 8; $60/¼ page/5 x 4

TIGHTROPE

Ed Rayher
323 Pelham Road
Amherst, MA 01002

Poetry, fiction, translation, graphics/artwork.

We stress excellence and accessibility to unpublished or little published authors. Our format is erratic, but we always emphasize form as well as content.

Steven Ruhl, Linda Burggraf,
Gillian Conoley, Lance Liskus.
Payment: inquire.
Copyright held by magazine; reverts to author upon publication.
1977; 2/yr; 350
$10/yr; $6/ea; 40%
40 pp; size varies

TOP STORIES
Anne Turyn
228 Seventh Avenue
New York, NY 10011
Fiction, graphics/artwork.
TOP STORIES is a prose periodical; a chapbook series which
(usually) features the work of
one author/artist per issue.
Constance DeJong, Lynne Tillman, Susan Daitch, Tama Janowitz, Richard Prince.
Payment: varies.
Reporting time: 1 year.
Copyright held by author.
1979; 3/yr; 1,500
$13.50/yr ind; $14.50/yr inst;
$3/ea single issue; $6/ea double
issue; 40%
5¼ x 8¼
No ads

**TOUCHSTONE: Literary
Journal**
William Laufer
P.O. Box 8308
Spring, TX 77387

Poetry, criticism, essays, reviews,
translation, interviews, graphics/
artwork.
We are committed to publishing
non-fiction, poetry and graphics
which commercial magazines no
longer publish. We welcome
minority viewpoints, and look
for imaginative, experimental
trends.
Lyn Lifshin, Rebecca Gonzales,
Ramona Weeks, Vassar Miller,
Arthur Smith, Thomas
Kennedy, Walter McDonald,
Archie Henderson.
Payment: as finances permit.
Reporting time: 6 weeks.
Copyright reverts to author upon
request.
1976; 1/yr; 1,000
$5/ea
48 pp; 5½ x 8, perfect bound
ISSN: 1715-1697
No ads

TRANSFER
Gary Lenhart
248 West 105 Street, Apt. 6D
New York, NY 10025
(212) 691-6590; (212) 866-7595
Poetry, fiction, criticism, essays,
translation, interviews, graphics/
artwork.
Maureen Owen, Ron Padget,

Jackson Mac Low, Kimiko
Hahn, Pat Nolan.
Payment: none.
Reporting time: varies.
Copyright held by magazine; re-
verts to author upon publica-
tion.
1987; 2/yr; 500
8/yr ind; $10/yr inst; $5/ea; 40%
144 pp; 5½ x 8½
Ad rates: inquire
ISSN: 8095-4054

TRANSLATION

Frank MacShane, Franklin D.
Reeve, William Jay Smith; Di-
ane G.H. Cook, Managing Edi-
tor
Room 412 Dodge Hall
Columbia University
New York, NY 10027
(212) 854-2305

Poetry, fiction, translation.

TRANSLATION publishes new
English translations of significant contemporary works of
prose and poetry. Prose excerpts
should not exceed 30 pages.
Each volume features the literature of a particular language or
region.
Payment: in copies.
Reporting time: maximum of 6
months.
Copyright reverts to translator/au-
thor upon publication.

1972; 2/yr; 1,500
$17/yr; $8/ea
220 pp; 6 x 9
Ad rates: $500/page
ISSN: 0093-9307

TRIQUARTERLY

Reginald Gibbons
Northwestern University
2020 Ridge
Evanston, IL 60208

Fiction, poetry, essays, reviews,
translation, interviews, photographs, graphics/artwork.

TRIQUARTERLY is especially
dedicated to short fiction, although substantial amounts of
poetry are also published regularly in every issue, including
long poems. Brief book reviews
and occasional essays round out
the contents.

Stanislaw Baranczak, Thomas Mc-
Grath, Sandra McPherson, Alan
Shapiro, Meredith Steinbach,
Michael S. Harper.
Payment: $40/printed page, prose;
$3/line, poetry.
Reporting time: 2 months.
Copyright reverts to author upon
request.
1964; 3/yr; 4,000
$18/yr ind; $26/yr inst; $4/sample;
varies
250 pp; 6 x 9¼

Ad rates: $250/page/6 x 9¼;
$150/½ page/6 x 4⅝
ISSN: 0041-3097
DeBoer, Ingram Periodicals,
Bookpeople, Illinois Literary
Publishers Assoc.

TRIVIA: A Journal of Ideas
Lise Weil
P.O. Box 606
North Amherst, MA 01059
(413) 367-2254

TRIVIA publishes writing that
puts women at the center and is
especially interested in forms
that grow out of this intention.
Essays, reviews, translations
and experimental forms that
combine rigorous thinking with
uncompromising feminist vision. Articles on language and
memory, aging, lesbian ethics,
therapy, black lesbian aesthetics, feminism's seduction by
New Age philosophy.
Gloria Anzaldva, Nicole Brossard,
Michèle Causse, Mary Daly,
Jewelle Gomez, Sarah
Hoagland, Gail Scott, Christina
Thürmer-Rohr.
Reporting time: 4–6 months.
Copyright reverts to author.
1982; 3/yr; 2,000
$14/yr ind; $20/yr inst; $6/ea
120 pp; 5½ x 8½
Ad rates: inquire

ISSN: 0736-928X
Inland, Bookpeople, Ubiquity,
Small Changes

**TUCUMCARI LITERARY
REVIEW**
Troxey Kemper
3108 W. Bellevue Ave.
Los Angeles, CA 90026
(213) 413-0789

Poetry, fiction, essays, translation,
photographs, graphics/artwork,
opinion pieces, letters.
**TUCUMCARI LITERARY
REVIEW** is old fashioned and
the preference is for types of
writing in vogue in the 1930s to
1950s. Most of the poetry is
rhyming, in "standard" forms,
not disjointed phrases and odd-
shaped lines of prose arranged
like poetry. The emphasis is on
writing that "says something."
Alice Mackenzie Swaim, Marian
Ford Park, Bettye K. Wray,
Betty M. Benoit, Patricia M.
Johnson, Leonard J. Cirino.
Payment: in copies, upon publication.
Copyright held by author.
1988; bimonthly; 170
$12/yr ind & inst; $1.50/ea; 40%
40 pp; 5½ x 8½
Ads: free ads for readers

TYUONYI

Phillip Foss
Recursos de Santa Fe
826 Camino de Monte Rey
Santa Fe, New Mexico 87501
(505) 852-2734

Poetry, fiction, essays, plays,
translation.
Multi-aesthetic/multi-ethnic litera-
ture.
Bernstein, Berssenbrugge,
Mackey, Tarn, Mack Low.
Payment: copies.
Reporting time: 1–3 months.
Copyright held by author.
1985; every 9 months; 800–1,000
$14/2; $7/ea; 40%
150 pp; 8½ x 8½

VERSE

Henry Hart
English Department
William and Mary
Williamsburg, VA 23185
(804) 253-4758

Poetry, criticism, reviews, translation, interviews.
VERSE is a literary journal, begun in Oxford, England (1984),
which publishes poetry in English and in translation. The
focus is on the international
scene, and its main purpose is
to improve the understanding of
the poetries from different countries, especially Britain and the
United States.
Seamus Heaney, James Merrill,
James Dickey, A.R. Ammons,
Galway Kinnell.
Payment: none.
Copyright held by author.
1984; 3/yr; 800
$12/yr; $4/ea; 40%
80 pp; 8¼ x 5¾
Ad rates: $150/page/6 x 4; $75/½
page/3 x 4; $40/¼ page/3 x 2
ISSN: 0268-3830

**THE VIRGINIA QUARTERLY
REVIEW**

Staige D. Blackford
One West Range
Charlottesville, VA 22903
(804) 924-3124

Poetry, fiction, essays, reviews.
One of the oldest and most distinguished literary journals in the
country; contains articles and
essays covering economics, art,
the sciences, politics, and literature. Publishes high-quality fiction and poetry by established
and newer authors. 75–100
brief, tightly-written book reviews per issue.
George Garrett, Jay Parini, Joyce

Carol Oates, Mary Lee Settle, Ann Beattie.

Payment: $10/page essays & fiction; $1/line for poetry; $50/essay reviews.

Copyright held by The Virginia Quarterly Review/The University of Virginia; reverts to author upon publication.

1925; 4/yr; 4,200

$15/yr ind; $22/yr inst; $5/ea; 50%

188 pp; 5½ x 8

Ad rates: $150/page/5½ x 8; $75/½ page/5½ x 4 or 2¾ x 8

ISSN: 0042-675X

VISIONS–International, The World Journal of Illustrated Poetry

Bradley R. Strahan, Poetry Editor; Shirley Sullivan, Associate Editor

4705 South 8th Road

Arlington, VA 22204

(703) 521-0142

Poetry, reviews, translations, graphics/artwork.

We're international in scope and content. We emphasize the interplay between artwork, poem and appearance of the magazine. We look for strong, well-crafted work that has emotional content (without sentimentality). **VISIONS** publishes issues on special themes (usually once a year). Many of these, including our specials on surrealism and Francophone poetry, are still in print. We oppose the trend to publish facile word play instead of meaningful poetry. We are always interested in translations, especially from work that has not previously appeared in English and from less translated languages such as: Frisian, Basque, Telegu, Malayan, Gaelic, Macedonian, etc.

Andrei Codrescu, Ted Hughes, Marge Piercy, Marilyn Hacker, Jame Dickey.

Payment: in copies or $5–$10 when we get a grant.

Read a sample copy ($3.50) before submitting work

Reporting time: 1–3 weeks.

Copyright held by VIAS; reverts to author upon publication.

1979; 3/yr; 750

$12/yr; $4.50/ea; 30%–40%

40 pp; 5½ x 8½

ISSN: 0194-1690

VOICES INTERNATIONAL

Clovita Rice

1115 Gillette Drive

Little Rock, AR 72207

(501) 225-0166

Poetry, essays, photographs, graphics/artwork.

VOICES INTERNATIONAL focuses on high literary quality

poetry, accepting for publication poetry with strong visual imagery and haunting impact. We encourage the beginner and have no preference in subject matter (as long as in good taste) if it presents a fresh approach and special awareness.
Bob Evans, Nome Mann, Jeanne Norris, Barbara Weekes.
Payment: in copies.
Reporting time: averages 6 weeks.
Copyright held by magazine.
1966; 4/yr; 325
$10/yr; $2.50/ea
32 pp; 6 x 9

VOLITION

Bonnie Lateiner
Lateiner/Vortex/Volition
P.O. Box 20274
Tompkins Square Station
New York, NY 10009

Poetry, short stories, excerpts from longer prose pieces.
VOLITION dramatically presents strongly contrasted current fiction, poetry and prose works. The magazine exhibits variations of American writing.
Fielding Dawson, Duncan McNaughton, Al Young, Simone O, Tama Janowitz.
Payment: in copies.
Copyright reverts to author.
1982; 1/yr; 250

$4/ea; 20%–40%
50 pp; 7 x 8
Inland, Segue, Bookslinger, Small Press Distribution

VORTEX: A Critical Review

Bryce Milligan
627 E. Guenther
San Antonio, TX 78210
(817) 477-1777

Poetry, fiction, criticism, essays, reviews, translation, interviews, photographs, graphics/artwork.
We see the "Vortex" of our review as being in Texas, a funneling down from the U.S. and Canada and a funneling up from Latin America. The idea is to promote literary discourse in this hemisphere. This also means a particular emphasis upon writing in Texas. The emphasis is on real criticism of literary matters and essays on cultural topics. AFFINITIES, a literary supplement is included in each issue and features mostly poetry and a lot of that in translation.
Carlos Fuentes, Donald Hall, Octavio Paz, John Howard Griffin, Rainer Schulte.
Payment: no, but may begin soon: $50 for longer work, $25 for reviews and poetry (upon publication).
Reporting time: 30 days or less.

Copyright held by Robert Bonazzi, Latitudes Press; reverts to author upon publication.
1986; 4/yr; 1,000
$10/4 issues ind & inst; $3/ea; 40%
40 pp; 8½ x 11
Ad rates: contact magazine or CLMP for ad rates
Small Press Distribution, Inc.; Texas Circuit

VREMYA I MY (TIME AND WE)

Victor Perelman
409 Highwood Avenue
Leonia, NJ 07605
(201) 592-6155

Russian language literature and commentary. Fiction, essays, poetry, criticism, translation, graphics/artwork, interviews, photographs.
$55/yr ind; $79/yr inst; $12/ea; 40%

Joselow, Anne Pierce, Editorial Board
P.O. Box 50132
Washington, DC 20004
(202) 638-0515
Poetry, fiction, essays, reviews, plays, interviews, photographs, graphics/artwork.
Bi-monthly tabloid-size journal of arts and literature including poetry, fiction, book and art reviews, essays on the arts, original art work. Emphasis on arts of Washington, D.C. One special issue on single topic each year.
Terence Winch, Doug Lang, Lee Fleming.
Payment: $15–20/review, $50–100/article if we have it.
Reporting time: 2 months.
Copyright held by magazine; reverts to author upon publication.
1975; 6/yr; 1,500
$12/yr; $8.50/yr inst; $20/2 yrs; $2/ea; 40%
Ad rates: $250/page/16 x 11¼; $175/½ page/8 x 11¼; $135/⅓ page/7⅜ x 8
ISSN: 0163-903X

WASHINGTON REVIEW

Clarissa Wittenberg, Editor; Mary Swift, Managing Editor; Pat Kolmer, Jeff Richards, Beth

WATERWAYS

Barbara Fisher, Richard Alan Spiegel
393 Saint Pauls Avenue

Staten Island, NY 10304

(718) 442-7429

Poetry, graphics.

We publish poets of all ages and types provided we like their work and it pertains to our monthly themes. Our page size is small to encourage portability and accessibility.

Joanne Seltzer, Robert Lima, Arthur Winfield Knight, Albert Huffstickler, Ida Fasel.

Payment: 1 copy.

Reporting time: 1 month.

Copyright held by Ten Penny Players; reverts to author upon publication.

1977; 11/yr; 100–200

$20/11 issues; $2/ea; 40%–60%

48 pp; 7 x 4¼

ISSN: 0197-4777

WEBSTER REVIEW

Nancy Schapiro

Webster University

470 East Lockwood

St. Louis, MO 63119

(314) 432-2657

Poetry, fiction, essays, translation, interviews.

WEBSTER REVIEW emphasizes translations of contemporary fiction, poetry and essays. We look for quality original work in those categories. We are particularly open at this time to non-fiction of a general literary nature.

William Stafford, Jared Carter, Barbara Lefcowitz, Charles Edward Easton, Etelvina Astrada.

Payment: in copies.

Copyright held by magazine; reverts to author upon publication.

1974; 2/yr; 1,100

$5/yr; $2.50/ea; 40%

104 pp; 5½ x 8½

ISSN: 0363-1230

WEST BRANCH

Karl Patten, Robert Taylor

Bucknell Hall

Bucknell University

Lewisburg, PA 17837

(717) 524-1853

Poetry, fiction, reviews.

A twice-yearly magazine of poetry, fiction, and reviews.

David Citino, Barbara Crooker, Harry Humes, William Kloefkorn, Helena Minton.

Payment: 2 copies and 1 year subscription.

Reporting time: 6–8 weeks.

Copyright held by magazine; reverts to author upon publication.

1977; 2/yr; 500

$7/yr; $11/2 yrs; $4/ea

88–106 pp; 5½ x 8½

No ads
ISSN: 0149-6441

WEST HILLS REVIEW

William Fahey
246 Old Walt Whitman Road
Huntington Station, NY 11746
(516) 427-5240
Poetry, essays, photographs,
   graphics/artwork.
Good lyric poetry. Prose related to
   Walt Whitman.
John Ciardi, Dave Smith, Gay
   Wilson Allen, David Ignatow,
   Edmund Pennant.
Payment: none.
Reporting time: 3 months.
Copyright held by magazine; re-
   verts to author upon publica-
   tion.
1979; 1/yr; 500
$5/yr; $5/ea; 50%
125 pp; 5 x 8

WESTERN HUMANITIES REVIEW

Larry Levis, Richard Howard,
   Barry Weller
341 OSH/ University of Utah
Salt Lake City, UT 84112
(801) 581-6070
Poetry, fiction, criticism, essays,
   reviews, non-fiction.
We print fiction, poetry, film and
   book reviews, articles on the
humanities (we prefer 2–3M
   words). Our standard is excellence; we publish work by established writers as well as new
   writers.
Mary Oliver, Charles Simic, Francine Prose, Sandra McPherson,
   Philip Levine, Joseph Brodsky.
Payment: $50/poem; $150/story-
   criticism-review.
Copyright held by WESTERN
   HUMANITIES REVIEW.
1947; 4/yr; 1,100
$18/yr ind; $24/yr inst; $5/ea;
   40%; 50% to distributors
96 pp; 6 x 9
No ads
ISSN: 0043-3845

WHETSTONE

Sandra Berris, Marsh Portnoy,
   Jean Tolle
P.O. Box 1266
Barrington, IL 60011
(708) 382-5626
Poetry, short stories, novel ex-
   cerpts, essays, photography, art.
Prefer to see 3–5 poems or up to
   25–30 pages of fiction or non-
   fiction. Feature one guest artist.
   Include SASE. Especially inter-
   ested in showcasing Illinois art-
   ists, but receptive to others.
Ellyn Bache, Robert Klein Engler,
   John Jacob, William Kloefkorn,
   Paulette Roeske, Jeanne M.
   Walker.

Payment: 2 copies.
Reporting time: 3 months.
Copyright reverts to author.
1983; 1/yr; 500
$5 + $1 post; $5/ea; no disc. Re-
sale may raise price.
96 pp; 5⅞ x 9
Will consider ads for 1990 issue.
Barrington Area Arts Council,
bookstores, some Hallmark
stores

WHITE CLOUDS REVUE

Scott Preston
P.O. Box 462
Ketchum, ID 83340
Poetry, one prose piece in 4 issues
so far.
WCR is a serially-issued journal
specifically interested in delin-
eating and suggesting trends in
inter-mountain American West
Poetics, divergent from those
foisted on hapless readers &
writers by the homogenized tyr-
anny of regional MFA
syndromes and syndicates.
Charles Potts, Ed Dorn, Rosalie
Sorrels, Bruce Embree, Peter
Boweb, Brooke Medicine Ea-
gle.
Payment: several copies.
Reporting time: 2 weeks–2
months.
Copyright reverts to author.
1987; 1½/yr; 200+

$12/4 issues; $3.50/ea; 30%
28–44 pp; 7 x 8½

WHOLE NOTES

Nancy Peters Hastings
P.O. Box 1374
Las Cruces, NM 88004
(505) 382-7446
Poetry.
WHOLE NOTES features work
by unknown or beginning writers as well as established poets.
It is intentionally kept small so
that it is affordable—and highly
readable. Writers whose work
has appeared in it are Keith
Wilson, Carol Oles, Greg
Kuzma, Ted Kooser, Bill Kloefkorn.
Payment: in copies.
Copyright: Nancy Peters Hastings.
1984; 2/yr; 400
$6/yr ind, inst; $3/ea; 40%
20 pp; 5½ x 8½
Ad rates available. Contact CLMP
for information.

THE WILLIAM AND MARY REVIEW

William Clark
Campus Center
College of William and Mary
Williamsburg, VA 23185
(804) 253-4895
Poetry, fiction, criticism, inter-

views, photographs, graphics/ artwork.

THE WILLIAM AND MARY REVIEW is an internationally-distributed literary magazine published by graduate and undergraduate students of The College of William and Mary, without faculty supervision or censorship. It is the express purpose of **THE WILLIAM AND MARY REVIEW** to publish the work of established writers as well as that of—and with an emphasis on—new, vital voices.

Amy Clampitt, Julie Agoos, Carole Glickfeld, David Ignatow, Dana Gioia.

Payment: in copies.

Copyright held by College of William and Mary, and Editor; reverts to author upon publication.

1962; 1/yr; 5,000

$4.50/yr ind; $8/yr inst; $5/ea; 40%

120 pp; 6 x 9

ISSN: 0043-5600

WILLOW SPRINGS

Gillian Conoley

P.U.B. P.O. Box 1063

Eastern Washington University

Cheney, WA 99004

(509) 458-6429

Poetry, fiction, essays, reviews, translation, graphics/artwork, interviews.

WILLOW SPRINGS is committed to the imagination and the power of language fully engaged in the act of telling. We publish high quality poetry, fiction, translation, essays, and art.

Russell Edson, Thomas Lux, Alberto Rios, Madeline DeFrees, Olga Broumas, Jane Miller, Donald Revell.

Payment: 2 copies on publication.

Reporting time: 6 weeks.

Copyright reverts to author.

1977; 2/yr; 1,000

$8/yr; $4/ea; 40%

104 pp; 6 x 9

Ad rates: $125/page/4¼ x 7; $75/½ page/4¼ x 3½; $50/¼ page/2⅛ x 3½

ISSN: 0739-1277

Pacific Pipeline, Small Changes

WIND

Quentin R. Howard

R.F.D. #1, Box 809K

Pikeville, KY 41501

(606) 631-1129

Poetry, fiction, criticism, reviews from small presses only.

Focus and emphasis are on the writers who have something special to say: nothing cold and lifeless. **WIND** is highly eclectic; any form, subject matter or approach.

Hale Chatfield, John Svehla, Philip Miller, Carolyn Osborn, Frances Sherwood.
Payment: in copies.
Reporting time: 2–4 weeks.
Copyright held by author.
1971; 2/yr; 450
$7/yr ind; $8/yr inst; $2.50/ea
82 pp; 5½ x 8¼
ISSN: 0361-2481
Hawley Cooke Booksellers

WINDFALL

Ron Ellis
Friends of Poetry
c/o Department of English
University of Wisconsin
Whitewater, WI 53190
(414) 472-1036

Poetry.

We are interested in short, intense, highly-crafted poems in any form. Longer poems occasionally considered. No xerox or dot matrix.

William Stafford, Ralph Mills, Francine Sterle, Sheila Murphy, Joanne Hart.
Payment: contributor's copies.
Reporting time: 8 weeks.
Copyright held by Friends of Poetry; reverts to author upon publication.
1979; 2/yr; 400

$5/yr; $3/ea
40 pp; 5½ x 8½
ISSN: 0893-3375

THE WINDLESS ORCHARD

Robert Novak
English Department
Indiana University
2101 East Coliseum
Fort Wayne, IN 46805
(219) 483-6845

Poetry, criticism, review, photographs, graphics/artwork.

Our muse is interested only in the beautiful, the sacred, and the erotic. Excited, organic forms, with thinking and feeling done in imagery and epigram.

Ruth Moon Kempher, Elliot Richman, Mike Martone, Michael Emery.
Payment: 2 copies.
Reporting time: 1 week on.
Copyright reverts to author.
1970; irregular; 320
$8/4 issues; $3/ea
52 pp; 5½ x 8
No ads

WITHOUT HALOS

Frank Finale, Lora Dunetz, Barbara Finale, Denise Hughes, H.G. Stacy, W. Swayhoover, W. Toensmann, Rich Youmans
P.O. Box 1342

Pt. Pleasant Beach, NJ 08742
(201) 240-5355
Poetry, graphics/artwork.
We consider all types of poetry—
mainstream, avant-garde, haiku,
light verse, etc. We judge each
poem not on a poet's name but
on the passion it displays, the
honesty of its roots and the
emotions which blossom from
each word.
Susan Clements, Geraldine C.
Little, Aisha Eshe, Harold Witt,
Emilie Glen.
Payment: 1 copy.
Reporting time: 3–4 months.
Copyright held by author.
1983; 1/yr; 1,000
$3.75/ea
58 pp; 8½ x 5½
No ads

WITNESS
Peter Stine
31000 Northwestern Highway
Suite 200
Farmington Hills, MI 48018
(313) 626-1110
Fiction, essays, poetry, interviews,
photographs, graphics/artwork.
WITNESS presents nationally
known writers, as well as new
talent, and highlights the role of
the modern writer as witness.
The magazine features a diverse
selection of writings—fiction,
poetry, essays, journalism,
interviews—and regularly de-
votes every other issue to illu-
minating a single subject of
wide concern.
Gordon Lish, Joyce Carol Oates,
Robert Coover, Lynn Sharon
Schwartz, Madison Smartt Bell.
Payment: $6/page for prose,
$10/page for poetry.
Reporting time: 2–3 months.
Copyright held by Witness; reverts
to author upon publication.
1987; 3/yr
In spring 1990 **WITNESS** will be
published tri-annually. Subscription rates: $15/3 copies per
year; $6/single copies
160 pp; 6 x 9
Ad rates: $100/page/5 x 7; $60/½
page/5 x 3½
ISSN: 0891-1371
Bernhard DeBoer, Inland Book
Company

WOMAN POET
Elaine Dallman
P.O. Box 60550
Reno, NV 89506
(702) 972-1671
Poetry, criticism, graphics/art-
work, interviews.
The West, the East, the Midwest,
the South.

Marilyn Hacker, Lisel Mueller, Judith Minty, Rosalie Moore, Mona Van Dyne, Josephine Jacobsen
$12.95/ea paperback; $19.95/ea hardcover. Resale discount varies.
Inland

WOMEN & PERFORMANCE: A JOURNAL OF FEMINIST THEORY

Editorial Board; Jill McDougall, Managing Editor
721 Broadway/Sixth Floor
New York, NY 10003
(212) 998-1625

Essays, criticism, plays, reviews, interviews, translation.
Hélène Cixous, Marianne Goldberg, Ann Gavere Kilkelly, Karen Laughlin, Phyllis Zatlin.
$12/yr ind; $25/yr inst; $7/ea; $9/ea back issues; 40%

WOMEN'S QUARTERLY REVIEW

Camille Errante
P.O. Box 708
New York, NY 10150
(212) 675-7794

Poetry, fiction, reviews, interviews, photographs, graphics, artwork.
WOMEN'S QUARTERLY

REVIEW is a feminist magazine relating to women's changing roles in society, politics, and the arts. **WQR** publishes articles, short stories, poetry, and original material.
Catherine Allport, Jana Harris, Sandra Lundy, Gale Jackson, Pat Carr.
Payment: in copies.
Reporting time: 8–10 weeks.
Copyright held by Errante-Sargenti Publications, Inc.
1984; 4/yr; 1,000
$10/yr ind; $25/yr inst; $3/ea
16–24 pp; 11 x 14
Ad rates: $280/page/10 x 13; $150/½ page/9⅝ x 6¼; $75/¼ page/4¾ x 6¼
ISSN: 0882-1135

THE WOMEN'S REVIEW OF BOOKS

Linda Gardiner
Wellesley College Center for Research on Women
Wellesley, MA 02181
(617) 431-1453

Reviews, poetry.
In-depth reviews of books by and about women, in all areas, both academic and general-interest; feminist in orientation but not committed to any one brand of feminism or any specific political position.

June Jordan, Diane Wakoski,
Gerda Lerner, Michelle Cliff,
Jane Marcus.
Payment: varies, $50 minimum.
Reporting time: 1 month–6 weeks.
Copyright held by Women's Review; reverts to author upon
publication.
1983; 11/yr; 11,500
$16/yr ind; $25/yr inst: $2/ea;
40%
28 pp; 10 x 15
Ad rates: $1,050/page/10 x 15;
$555/½ page/10 x 7½; $290/¼
page/4¾ x 7½
ISSN: 0738-1433

THE WORCESTER REVIEW

Rodger Martin
6 Chatham Street
Worcester, MA 01609
(588) 797-4770; (603) 924-7342
Poetry, fiction, criticism, essays,
graphics/artwork, photographs.
We look for quality poetry and
fiction, and also articles and
essays about poetry that have a
New England connection.
Richard Eberhart, Judith Stein-
bergh, Walter McDonald,
William Stafford, Kathleen
Spivack.
Payment: 2 copies plus honorar-
ium dependant upon grants.
Reporting time: 12–16 weeks.
Copyright held by Worcester Re-

view of the Worcester County
Poetry Assoc.; reverts to author
upon publication.
1973; 2/yr; 1,000
$10/yr; $5/ea; 40%
80 pp; 6 x 9
$195/Full page display; $100/½
page; $55/¼ page
ISSN: 8756-5277

THE WORMWOOD REVIEW

Marvin Malone
P.O. Box 8840
Stockton, CA 95208-0840
(209) 466-8231
Poetry, reviews, translation,
graphics/artwork.
Poetry and prose-poems reflecting
the temper and depth of the
present time. All types and
schools from traditional-
economic through concrete,
dada and extreme avant-garde.
Special fondness for prose poems and fables. Each issue has
a yellow paper section devoted
to one poet or topic. One chapbook per year.
Charles Bukowski, Lyn Lifshin,
Ronald Koertge, Gerald Locklin, Judson Crews.
Payment: 3–6 copies of magazine
or cash equivalent.
Copyright held by Wormwood
Review Press; reverts to author
upon request.

1959; 4/yr; 700
$8/yr ind; $9/yr inst; $4/ea; 40%
48 pp; 5½ x 8½
ISSN: 0043-9401

THE WRITERS' BAR-B-Q

Timothy Osburn; Ed. Board:
Becky Bradway, Gary Smith,
Gael Cox Carnes, Marcia Womack
924 Bryn Mawr Boulevard
Springfield, IL 62703
(217) 525-6987
Fiction, photographs, graphics/art-
work.
THE WRITERS' BAR-B-Q,
winner of grants from CCLM
and the Illinois Arts Council,
publishes literate, unpretentious
fiction. All subjects and genres
are encouraged. Anything well-
written and entertaining is carefully considered. We like stories
with a sense of humor, and a
fresh (and sometimes skewed)
view of the world. THE WRIT-
ERS' BAR-B-Q is a potluck of
styles, subject and characters.
Dan Curley, Nolan Porterfield,
Laurence Gonzales, Karen
Peterson, Sandra Kolanciewicz,
Kate Horsley, Michael C.
White.
Payment: in 3 copies, upon publication.
Copyright held by Sangamon

Writers, Inc.; reverts to author
upon publication.
1987; 2/yr; 750
$10/yr; $5/ea; 40%
92 pp; 8½ x 11
Ad rates: $75/½ page/4½ x 7½;
$50/⅓ page/2½ x 9, 3 x 7½, or
4½ x 5

WRITERS FORUM

Alex Blackburn, Editor; Craig
Lesley, Bret Lott, Fiction Edi-
tors; Victoria McLabe, Poetry
Editor
University of Colorado at Colorado Springs
Colorado Springs, CO 80933-7150
(719) 599-4023
Poetry, fiction.
We want the finest in contemporary short story and poetry, with
some focus and emphasis on the
trans-Mississippi West with its
varieties of place and experience.
Gladys Swan, Ron Carlson, Frank
Waters, Kenneth Fields, David
Ray.
Payment: none.
Reporting time: 3–6 weeks.
Copyright held by UCCS; reverts
to author upon publication.
1974; 1/yr; 1,000
$8.95/yr ind; $7.20/yr inst;
$8.95/ea
200 pp; 8½ x 5½

WRITER'S JOURNAL (formerly **The Inkling**)
Valerie Hockert
P.O. Box 9148
N. St. Paul, MN 55109
(612) 433-3626
Essays, poetry, reviews, criticism, interviews, commentaries, writing techniques.
Provides writers and poets with practical advice and guidance, motivation and authorative instruction in the craft of writing. Includes book reviews, essays, poetry, legal advice and references.
John Hall, Dennis E. Hensley, Marilyn Bailey, Betty Ulrich, Ester M. Leiper, Herman Holtz, Ken Strandberg.
Payment: variable.
Reporting time: 2–6 weeks.
Copyright held by Minnesota Ink, Inc., reverts to author upon publication.
1980; 6/yr; 21,000
$13.50/yr; $3/ea; 50%
36 pp; 8 x 10½
Ad rates: $450/page/6¾ x 9; $235/½ page/6¾ x 4½ or 3⅛ x 9
ISSN: 0891-9759
Ingram, Ubiquity, Armadillo, Homing Pigeon, ARA, Bernhard DeBoer

WYOMING, THE HUB OF THE WHEEL . . . A Journey for Universal Spokesmen
Lenore A. Senior, Managing Editor; Dawn Senior, Art and Assistant Editor
Box 9
Saratoga, WY 82331
(307) 326-5214
Poetry, fiction, graphics/artwork, essays, translation, photographs.
WYOMING, THE HUB OF THE WHEEL . . . A Journal for Universal Spokesmen attempts to reach a general audience interested in peace, humanism, the environment, society, and universal messages. Each issue is devoted to the themes of Peace, The Human Race, Positive Relationships, and the Human Spirit and all its Possibilities.
Graciany Miranda-Archilla, B.J. Buckley, Eugenio de Andrade, Virginia Love Long, Rodney E.J. Chang.
Payment: 1 copy, contributor discounts.
Reporting time: 6 weeks.
Copyright held by magazine; reverts to author upon publication.
1985; 1–2/yr; 300
$10/yr; $6/ea; 40%
100 pp; 6 x 9
No ads
ISSN: 0884-2930

XANADU: A Literary Journal

Mildred M. Jeffrey, Barbara Lucas, Pat Nesbitt, Editors; Barry Fruchter, Jeanne K. Welcher, Virginia R. Terris, Consulting Editors; Lois V. Walker, Business Manager
Box 773
Huntington, NY 11743
(516) 741-7188
Poetry, essays.
XANADU publishes contemporary poetry and literary criticism.
Karen Swenson, David Ignatow, Edmund Pennant, William Stafford.
Payment: 1 copy per contributor.
Reporting time: 3 months.
Copyright reverts to author upon publication.
1975; 1/yr; 300
$4/ea plus $1 postage/handling; 20%–40%
64–76 pp; 5½ x 8½
ISSN: 0146-0463

YARROW

Harry Humes, Editor; Arnold Newman, Associated Editor
English Department
Kutztown University
Kutztown, PA 19530
(215) 683-4353
Poetry, interviews.
A journal of poetry.
William Pitt Root, Gerald Stern, Cary Waterman, John Engels.
Payment: in copies.
Reporting time: 1 month.
1981; 2/yr; 350
$5/2 yrs; $1.50/ea
36 pp; 6 x 9

YELLOW SILK: A Journal of Erotic Arts

Lily Pond
P.O. Box 6374
Albany, CA 94706
(415) 644-4188
Fiction, poetry, essays, reviews, translations, photography, graphics/artwork, cartoons, fine arts, science fiction, humor.
YELLOW SILK publishes erotic literature and arts. "All persuasions; no brutality." Literary and artistic excellence combines with healthy eroticism in this beautiful alternative to pornography.
Kotzwinkle, Shange, Paz, Hacker, Soto.
Payment: 3 copies, 1 year sub-

scription, and varying cash pay-
ments.
Reporting time: 6–8 weeks.
Copyright reverts to author after
one year; **YS** keeps non-
exclusive reprint and anthology
rights.
1981; 4/yr; 16,000
$24/yr ind; $30/yr inst; $6/ea;
40%
52 pp; 8½ x 11
ISSN: 0736-9212
Bookpeople, Inland, Ingram,
Ubiquity

YET ANOTHER SMALL MAGAZINE

Candace Catlin Hall
Box 14353
Hartford, CT 06114
(203) 549-6723
Poetry.
YASM publishes short, imagistic
poems—special interest in lesser
known poets— started broadside
inclusion highlighting a single
poem.
Lyn Lifshin, Charles Darling, Pat
Bridges, Sister Mary Ann
Henn, Neil Grill.
Payment: in copies.
Reporting time: November; read-
ing period is Aug. 1 to Oct. 31.
Copyright reverts to author.
1981; annual; 300
$1.98/ea

8–12 pp; 11 x 17
ISSN: 0278-9442

Z

ZUKUNFT

Dr. Joseph Landis, Joseph
Mlotek, Matis Olitzki
25 East 21st Street
New York, NY 10010
Poetry, fiction, criticism, essays,
reviews.
The **ZUKUNFT** is an independent
literary publication. It serves as
a vehicle for writers from many
countries and is concerned with
problems of Jewish life throught
the world. In 1982 the **ZUK-
UNFT**, the oldest continously
published Yiddish journal in the
world, celebrated its 90th anni-
versary. It has served to stimulate literary creativity for
several generations throughout
Yiddish speaking communities.
Copyright held by Congress for
Jewish Culture; reverts to author
upon publication.
1892; 10/yr; 2,500
$20/yr ind; $1.50/ea, 20% for
agencies
44 pp; 7½ x 10½

Ad rates: $100/page; $50/½ page; $25/¼ page

ZYZZYVA

Howard Junker
41 Sutter Street, Suite 1400
San Francisco, CA 94104
(415) 255-1282

Poetry, fiction, essays, plays, translations, photographs, prints, drawings.

West Coast writers, artists, and publishers.

Francisco X. Alarcón, Dorianne Laux, Tess Gallagher, August Kleinzahler, Leonard Michaels, Adrienne Rich.

Payment: $50–$250.

Reporting time: prompt.

Copyright held by magazine; reverts to author upon publication.

1985; 4/yr; 3,500

$20/yr ind; $28/yr inst; $7/ea

144 pp; 6 x 9

Ad rates: $450/page/5 x 7¾; $275/½ page/5 x 3¹³⁄₁₆; $150/¼ page/2⁷⁄₁₆ x 3¹³⁄₁₆

ISSN: 8756-5633

Bookpeople, Ingram Periodical, Inland Book, Small Press Distribution

INDEX BY STATE

GEORGIA

CHATTAHOOCHEE REVIEW,
THE—47
COTTON BOLL/ATLANTA
REVIEW—55
GEORGIA REVIEW, THE—77
THUNDER & HONEY—188
CATALYST—44

HAWAII

BAMBOO RIDGE—25
CHAMINADE LITERARY
REVIEW—46
HAWAII REVIEW—85

IDAHO

REDNECK REVIEW OF LITERA-
TURE, THE—156
SIGNAL, THE—170
WHITE CLOUDS REVUE—198

IOWA

BLUE BUILDINGS—33
HOW(ever)—89
IOWA REVIEW, THE—96
IOWA WOMAN—96
NORTH AMERICAN REVIEW,
THE—123
POET AND CRITIC—143

ILLINOIS

ACM (Another Chicago
Magazine)—9
ALTERNATIVE FICTION &
POETRY—13
ASCENT—22
B-CITY—24
CHICAGO REVIEW—48
CLOCKWATCH REVIEW—50
F MAGAZINE—67
FARMER'S MARKET—68
FORMATIONS—73
HORNS OF PLENTY: Malcolm
Cowley and his Generation—
88
ILLINOIS WRITERS REVIEW—
92
MISSISSIPPI VALLEY REVIEW—
114
NEW AMERICAN WRITING—117
NIT & WIT—122
OTHER VOICES—129
OYEZ REVIEW—130
PIKESTAFF FORUM—141
POETRY—145
POETRY EAST—146
PRIMAVERA—150
RAMBUNCTIOUS REVIEW—155
REVIEW OF CONTEMPORARY
FICTION, THE—159
RHINO—160
SPOON RIVER QUARTERLY,
END—180
STORY QUARTERLY—182
TRIQUARTERLY—190
WHETSTONE—197
WRITERS' BAR-B-Q, THE—204

INDIANA

BLACK AMERICAN LITERA-
TURE FORUM—29
CRAZYHORSE—56
INDIANA REVIEW—93
SPARROW POVERTY
PAMPHLETS—179
WINDLESS ORCHARD, THE—
200

KANSAS

CAPRICE—43
COTTONWOOD—55
KANSAS QUARTERLY—99

KENTUCKY

AMERICAN VOICE, THE—15
WIND—199

LOUISIANA

EXQUISITE CORPSE—66

INDEX BY STATE

TEXAS REVIEW, THE—185
TOUCHSTONE—189
VORTEX—194

UTAH

QUARTERLY WEST—153
RHODODENDRON—160
WESTERN HUMANITIES
REVIEW—197

VIRGIN ISLANDS

CARIBBEAN WRITER, THE—43

VIRGINIA

BOGG—35
CALLALOO—41
HAMPDEN-SYDNEY POETRY
REVIEW, THE—83
HOLLINS CRITIC, THE—88
LYRIC, THE—108
NEW VIRGINIA REVIEW—120
PIEDMONT LITERARY
REVIEW—140
SHENANDOAH—168
VERSE—192
VIRGINIA QUARTERLY
REVIEW, THE—192
VISIONS-International—193
WILLIAM AND MARY REVIEW,
THE—198

VERMONT

ANEMONE—17

GREEN MOUNTAINS REVIEW—
81
NEW ENGLAND REVIEW AND
BREAD LOAF
QUARTERLY—118

WASHINGTON

BELLINGHAM REVIEW, THE—
26
BELLOWING ARK—26
BRUSSELS SPROUT—39
CRAB CREEK REVIEW—56
FINE MADNESS—70
METAMORFOSIS—110
SEATTLE REVIEW, THE—165
WILLOW SPRINGS—199

WISCONSIN

A/B: AUTO/BIOGRAPHY
STUDIES—23
ABRAXAS—9
CREAM CITY REVIEW—57
MODERN HAIKU—114
NORTHERN REVIEW, THE—124
SALTHOUSE—162
SEEMS—166
WINDFALL—200

WEST VIRGINIA

GRAB-A-NICKEL—78

WYOMING

WYOMING, THE HUB OF THE
WHEEL—205